EXAMPLES IN MODERN MATHEMATICS AT 'O' LEVEL

Examples in Modern Mathematics at 'O' Level

COMPILED BY B. P. O'BYRNE

SCHOFIELD AND SIMS LIMITED
HUDDERSFIELD

0 7217 2142 7

First printed 1972
Second impression 1972
Third impression 1973
Fourth impression 1973
Fifth impression 1974
Sixth impression 1976
Seventh impression 1977
Eighth impression 1978
Ninth impression 1981

Printed in Great Britain by
Fletcher & Son Ltd, Norwich

Preface

This collection of examples has been made to provide material for revision in the two years prior to O-level, as well as enrichment for courses in the lower school. It should also be of value for subsidiary courses in the Sixth Form and one- and two-year courses in Colleges of Further Education. Much of the new work introduced into Mathematics syllabuses during the past ten years suffers from a shortage of examples when compared with traditional schemes. In an attempt to overcome this, I have brought together examination questions from a wide range of sources, along with a few examples of my own, to make available as large and as comprehensive a collection as possible.

The examples have been arranged into chapters on related themes. The allocation of questions to particular chapters was not always easy to decide. For example, some questions on simultaneous equations are in matrix form and have been included in the section on matrices, while others are in the section on solution of equations. A number of problems in Mathematics as examined on new syllabuses are, of course, deliberately designed to test the pupil's capacity to relate different aspects of the subject. I hope that teachers will not be offended by the classifications I have made. The answers have been published in a separate book, since many of the questions require very little written working.

The collection contains examples in some branches of the subject also examined on traditional schemes. These have been included to make coverage reasonably complete, since modern syllabuses have not discarded everything traditionally taught in school mathematics. With permission, I have converted questions to metric units based on the SI system.

For permission to use questions set in O-level examinations, and for permission to produce metricated versions of such questions, I wish to thank the Associated Examining Board for the General Certificate of Education, the University of Cambridge Local Examinations Syndicate, the University of London School Examinations Department, the Oxford Delegacy of Local Examinations, the Oxford and Cambridge Schools Examination Board, the Scottish Certificate of Education Examination Board, and the Southern Universities Joint Board. I also thank the Controller of Her Majesty's Stationery Office for permission to reproduce questions and metricated versions of questions set by the Northern Ireland General Certificate of Education Committee.

My thanks are due to those colleagues who have been kind enough to encourage me in this work and to those who have helped by working examples. In addition, I am most grateful to my wife for all her work in the compilation of this book.

B. P. O'Byrne

The source of questions is indicated by the following symbols:

AEB	Associated Examining Board for the General Certificate of Education
C	University of Cambridge Local Examinations Syndicate
L	University of London School Examinations Syndicate
NI	Northern Ireland General Certificate of Education Committee
O	Oxford Delegacy of Local Examinations
OC (SMP)	Oxford and Cambridge Schools Examination Board
SC	Scottish Certificate of Education Examination Board
SU	Southern Universities Joint Board

Contents

Chapter One

1 The universal set $E = \{1, 2, 3, 4, 5, 6, 7, 8, 9\}$, $A = \{1, 4, 9\}$ and $B = \{2, 4, 6, 8,\}$.
List the sets $A' \cap B$, $(A' \cap B)'$ and $A \cup B'$. SC

2 If $A = \{1, 2, 3, 4\}$, $B = \{2, 4, 6, 8\}$ and $C = \{1, 3, 5, 7\}$, list the members of the set $(A \cup B) \cap C$. O

3 $A = \{q, r, s, t\}$, $B = \{q, r, s\}$ and $C = \{p, q\}$. Simplify $A \cap (B \cup C)$. SC

4 Simplify $(A \cap B) \cup (A \cap B')$. OC(SMP)

5 Simplify $A \cap (B \cup B')$. OC(SMP)

6 State which one of the four statements below is **not** equivalent to the other three:

(*a*) $A \cap B = A$; (*b*) $A \cup B = B$; (*c*) $A \subset B$; (*d*) $A \subset B'$.
OC (SMP)

7 State in each case whether the statement is true or false:

(*a*) If P is a subset of Q and R is a subset of P, then R is a subset of Q.
(*b*) If x is a variable on the universal set $E = \{1, 2, 4, 16\}$ and $A = \{x : x^2 \in E\}$, then $A' = \{1, 16\}$.
(*c*) If A, X and Y are sets, then $A \cap X = A \cap Y \Rightarrow X = Y$. SC

8 Three sets A, B and C satisfy the following conditions

$$A \subset B, \quad A \cap B \cap C \neq \phi, \quad B' \cap C \neq \phi.$$

Are the following statements true or false?

(*a*) C cannot be a subset of B.

(*b*) $x \in B$ and $x \in C$ implies that x is not a member of A.

(*c*) $A \cap C$ must be a subset of $B \cap C$.

(*d*) $A' \cap B' \cap C'$ must be the null set. AEB

9 If P, Q, R are non-empty sets, say which of the following are correct and which are incorrect:

(*a*) $P \cap (Q \cup R) = (P \cap Q) \cap (P \cap R)$.

(*b*) $P \cap P = \phi$.

(*c*) $(P \cap Q) \cup (P \cap Q') = P$.

(*d*) $P \cup P = 2P$. OC (SMP)

10 Sets are defined as follows:

The Universal set $\mathscr{E}$ = {positive integers from 1 to 34 inclusive}

P = {prime numbers} F = {multiples of 5}

T = {multiples of 3} G = {numbers greater than 8}

List the members of the following sets

(i) $P \cap G$; (ii) $F \cap T$; (iii) $T \cap G'$. SU

11 If $\mathscr{E}$ = {natural numbers}, A = {odd numbers} and B = {multiples of 5}; describe the set $B \cap A'$. OC (SMP)

12

$$\mathscr{E} = \{x: -10 \leqslant x \leqslant 10\}.$$
$$P = \{x: -10 < x < 10\}.$$
$$Q = (x: -5 < x \leqslant 3\}.$$
$$R = \{x: 3 \leqslant x < 5\}.$$

Write down expressions for (*a*) P'; (*b*) $Q \cap R$; (*c*) $Q \cup R$; (*d*) $Q \cap P'$. OC (SMP)

13 If A is the set {1, 2, 3, 4} and B is the set {1, 4, 6} and the universal set $\mathscr{E}$ is {1, 2, 3, 4, 5, 6}, determine the elements of the set C, where

$$C = (A \cup B) \cap (A \cap B)'.$$ AEB

14 By using the distributive law, simplify the expression

$$A' \cup (A \cap B')$$ SU

15 Given that A and B are two sets, not the same, and that $A \cap B = A$, say which of the following statements are true,

(i) $A \subset B$; (ii) $A' = B$; (iii) $B = \mathscr{E}$; (iv) $A \cup B = B$;
(v) $A' \cap B = \phi$. SU

16 The set of divisors of a whole number n, including n itself but not 1, is denoted by $D(n)$, so that, for instance, $D(6) = \{2, 3, 6\}$.

(i) List the elements of the sets

$$D(8),\ D(20),\ D(8) \cap D(20) \text{ and } D(8) \cup D(20).$$

(ii) State the value of r for which $D(8) \cap D(20) = D(r)$. How is r related to 8 and 20?

(iii) State the least value of l for which

$$D(8) \cup D(20) \subset D(l).$$

How is l related to 8 and 20? OC (SMP)

17 If $P = \{\text{parallelograms}\}$ and $C = \{\text{cyclic quadrilaterals}\}$ then $P \cap C$ is (*a*) {rhombuses}; (*b*) {squares}; (*c*) {rectangles}; (*d*) { }. OC (SMP)

18 Sets are defined as follows:

$A = \{\text{polygons with all sides equal}\}$
$B = \{\text{polygons with all angles equal}\}$
$C - \{\text{triangles}\}$
$D = \{\text{quadrilaterals}\}$
$E = \{\text{polygons with at least one right angle}\}$
$F = \{\text{figures with at least one pair of parallel sides}\}$

State what names are given to the most general members of each of the following sets:

(i) $A \cap D$; (ii) $D \cap F$; (iii) $B \cap D$; (iv) $A \cap E \cap D$;
(v) $C \cap (A \cup B)$. SU

19 All quadrilaterals which are members of the set $\{R\}$ have property D. Is it necessarily true that quadrilaterals which have the property D are members of $\{R\}$?

Give an example to illustrate your answer. OC (SMP)

20

$\mathscr{E}$ = {triangles}; A = {obtuse-angled triangles};
B = {right-angled triangles}; C = {isosceles triangles}.

If $D \subset C$ and $D \cap A = \phi$ and $D \cap B = \phi$ describe a possible set for D.

Complete the Venn diagram to show A, B, C and D.

OC (SMP)

21 Write down, using set symbols, expressions for the sets shown shaded in the following diagrams. AEB

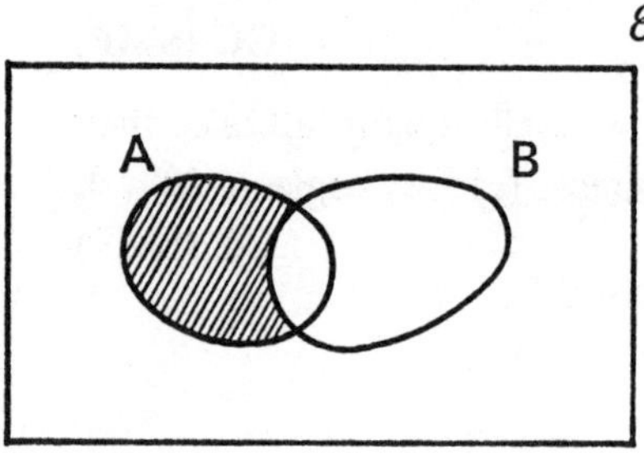

(a)

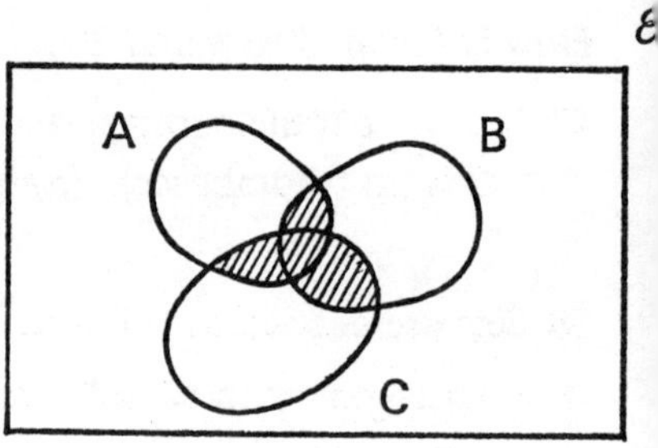

(b)

22 The Venn diagram represents subsets A and B of a universal set E. Shade on a copy of the diagram the region representing $A' \cap B$. SC

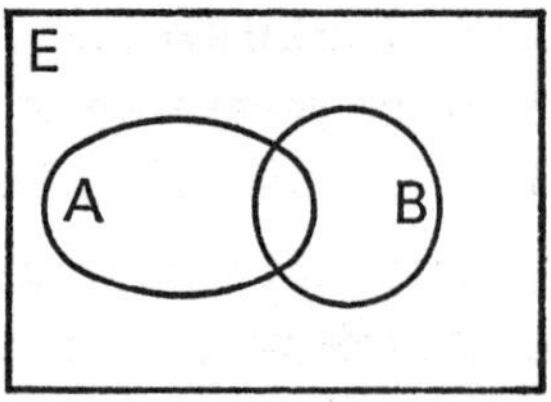

23 If $n(A \cup B) = 45$, $n(A \cap B) = 5$ and $n(B) = 22$, find the value of $n(A)$.

C

24 [A and B are sets].
If $n(A) = 9$, $n(B) = 6$ and $n(A \cap B) = 4$,
state the value of $n(A \cup B)$. OC (SMP)

25 If $n(A) = 10$ and $n(B) = 6$, what are the greatest and least values of $n(A \cup B)$?

Draw Venn diagrams to illustrate the cases in which $n(A \cup B)$ has these extreme values. OC (SMP)

26

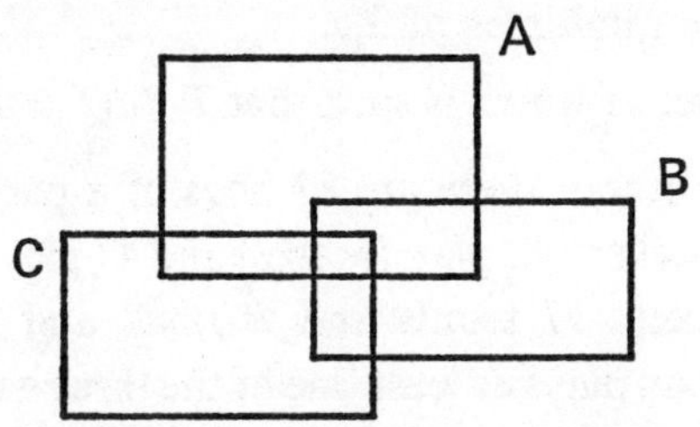

In a copy of the Venn diagram shade vertically $C \cap A$; shade horizontally $C \cap B$. OC (SMP)

27

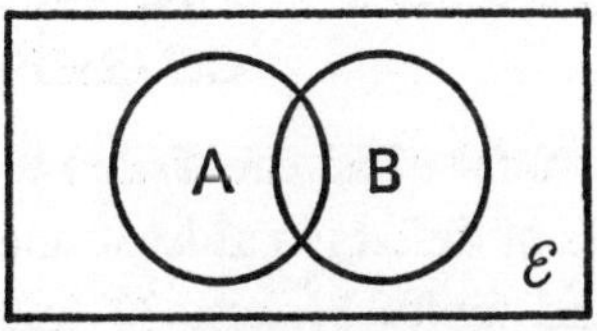

A ∪ B

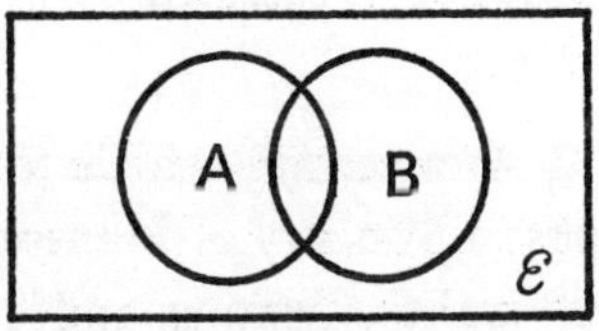

A′ ∩ B′

In a copy of one of the diagrams shown shade the set $A \cup B$ and in a copy of the other shade the set $A' \cap B'$.

What do you notice about these two sets? OC (SMP)

28 All 33 children in a certain class possess either a dog or a cat (or both). 18 have a cat and 26 have a dog. Represent these facts in a Venn diagram. What is the universal set? How many children have a dog but no cat? SU

29 Illustrate, on a Venn diagram, the relationship between the sets A, B and C given that $B \subset A$, $C \subset B'$ and $A \cap C \neq \phi$.

C

30 (i) Draw a Venn diagram to illustrate the relations between the sets:

$$\mathscr{E} = \{\text{natural numbers}\},$$
$$P = \{\text{prime numbers except 1, 2 and 3}\},$$
$$Q = \{\text{even numbers}\}$$
$$T = \{\text{multiples of 3}\}.$$

(ii) Describe a set M which is such that $T \cap Q = M$. OC (SMP)

31 In a certain school there are 87 boys of a particular year. Of these, 43 play hockey, 42 play football and 47 play tennis; 15 play tennis and hockey, 17 tennis and football and 21 hockey and football. Each boy plays at least one of the three games and x boys play all three.

Express these facts in a *large* Venn diagram, showing clearly the number in each separate region in terms either of x alone or, if you prefer, of x and other unknowns. Write down the equation(s) satisfied by the unknown(s) and hence find the value of x. OC (SMP)

32 At a certain vehicle testing station a total of 68 cars failed to pass a Ministry of Transport test because of defects in at least one of brakes, lighting and steering. 30 had faulty brakes, 30 had faulty steering and 33 had defective lights. 7 cars had both lights and steering faulty, 10 cars had faulty lights and brakes and 11 cars had poor brakes and bad steering. Draw a Venn diagram to illustrate this information. How many cars had faults of all three types? How many cars had good lights and good steering but poor brakes? SU

33 In a group of 100 children, 75 can swim and 35 can play musical instruments

$S = \{\text{swimmers}\}$, $M = \{\text{musicians}\}$ and $\mathscr{E}$ is the set of all children in the group. Draw a Venn diagram to represent S, M and $\mathscr{E}$.

If $n(S \cap M) = x$ and $n((S \cup M)') = y$, find limits between which y and x respectively lie.

Find also an equation connecting x and y.

If every child who can neither swim nor play an instrument is assisted to learn by two children who can do both, find the maximum number of learners. L

34 A sports club, of 100 playing members, fields three teams A, B and C. The table shows the number of members who played for the various teams during the season.

A	B	C	A and B	B and C	C and A
50	40	60	20	18	15

Find:

(i) how many members played for all three teams;

(ii) how many played for team C only. C

35 The local dairy is trying to economise by cutting down the frequency of unprofitable rounds. In order to discover the facts it makes a survey of its customers' requirements, which on one of the rounds yields the following facts. (A dairy product is defined as anything the roundsman sells which is not milk.)

103 customers take milk every day;

62 customers take at least one dairy product every day;

37 customers on some days take nothing at all.

(i) What is the maximum number of customers there could be on this round?

(ii) What is the minimum number of customers there could be on this round?

(iii) Of the 62 customers taking at least one dairy product every day, 37 take eggs, 17 take butter and 22 take other products. What is the minimum number of customers taking at least two of these three categories of dairy products every day? AEB

36 Sets A and B are subsets of the universal set $\mathscr{E}$ and no two of A, B, $\mathscr{E}$ are equivalent.

Illustrate in four diagrams that

$$A \subset B \Leftrightarrow B' \subset A' \Leftrightarrow A \cap B' = \phi \Leftrightarrow A' \cup B = \mathscr{E}.$$ L

37 If $\mathscr{E} = \{\text{animals}\}$, $D = \{\text{dogs}\}$ and $F = \{\text{fat animals}\}$, write a sentence equivalent to the statement $D \cap F' \neq \phi$. OC (SMP)

38 If $\mathscr{E} = \{\text{pigs}\}$, $G = \{\text{greedy pigs}\}$, $H = \{\text{healthy pigs}\}$, $F = \{\text{fat pigs}\}$, write the following statements in symbolic form:
(*a*) All healthy pigs are greedy.
(*b*) Some healthy pigs are not fat.
(*c*) All healthy pigs are greedy and fat.
(*d*) All fat pigs are either greedy or healthy, or both. L

39 Describe in words each of the two sets $A \cup B$ and $A' \cap B'$ where

$\mathscr{E}$ = the set of all rabbits;
A = the set of rabbits which have black ears;
B = the set of male rabbits. OC (SMP)

40 If A and B are any two sets, then $A \cap B = \phi$, the empty set, implies:
(*a*) $A = \phi$ or $B = \phi$,
(*b*) $A \cup B = \mathscr{E}$, the universal set,
(*c*) $(A \cap B)' = \mathscr{E}$,
(*d*) $A' \cup B' = \mathscr{E}$,
(*e*) $A' \cap B = B$. AEB

41 Are the following statements about sets A, B and C, contained in the universal set $\mathscr{E}$, true or false?
(*a*) $(A \subset B \text{ and } C \subset B) \Rightarrow A \subset C$.
(*b*) $(A \cup B = A \cap C) \Rightarrow A = B = C$.
(*c*) $(A \cup B = \mathscr{E}) \Leftrightarrow B = A'$.
(*d*) $(A \cap B = \phi) \Leftrightarrow B = A'$. AEB

42 Given any two sets A and B we define a new set $A \triangle B$ by

$$A \triangle B = (A \cap B') \cup (A' \cap B).$$

Are the following statements true or false?

(*a*) $A \triangle A = \phi$; (*b*) $A \triangle A' = \mathscr{E}$; (*c*) $A \triangle B = B \triangle A$;
(*d*) $A \triangle \phi = A$. L

43 The following statements are taken to be true:

(i) All poor men are happy.

(ii) All ambitious men are unhappy.

What can you say about the truth of these deductions?

(*a*) No unhappy man is poor.

(*b*) All happy men are unambitious.

(*c*) All poor men are unambitious.

Definitely true	Definitely false	Can be true or false
(a) (b) (c)	(a) (b) (c)	(a) (b) (c)

O

44 If all the left-handed men in Ayton are members of the town police force, which of the following statements are necessarily true and which are not necessarily true?

(*a*) All the Ayton police are left-handed.

(*b*) No Ayton man who is right-handed is a policeman.

(*c*) If a left-handed man is not a policeman he does not live in Ayton. OC (SMP)

45 The following statements are, for the purposes of this question, assumed to be true:

(i) All realists are pessimists.

(ii) Some, but not all, realists are cynics.

Comment on the truth of the following deductions:

(*a*) All cynics who are realists are also pessimists.

(*b*) Some, possibly all, cynics are pessimists.

(*c*) Some, but not all, cynics are not pessimists.

Definitely true	Definitely false	Can be true or false
(a)	(a)	(a)
(b)	(b)	(b)
(c)	(c)	(c)

O

46 In a certain district 70 per cent of the families own a TV set, and 30 per cent of the families own cars. Which of the following statements are *not necessarily* true, but *could be* true?

(*a*) All families have either a TV set or a car.
(*b*) Most car owners have a TV set.
(*c*) Fewer than half of the owners of TV sets have cars.
(*d*) If the number of car owners increased by 50 per cent of the present number there would be more car owners than TV owners.

OC (SMP)

47 When Tom is 60 or over he receives a pension provided he has retired; there are no other circumstances which entitle Tom to a pension.

Consider the following deductions:

(*a*) Tom is 60 or over $\Rightarrow$ Tom receives a pension.
(*b*) Tom is 60 or over $\Rightarrow$ Tom has retired.
(*c*) Tom has retired $\Rightarrow$ Tom is 60 or over.
(*d*) Tom receives a pension $\Rightarrow$ Tom is 60 or over.
(*e*) Tom has retired $\Rightarrow$ Tom receives a pension.

True	False
(a)	(a)
(b)	(b)
(c)	(c)
(d)	(d)
(e)	(e)

O

48 (i) Rule (1) of the constitution of a certain society states:

'All those who are neither under 21 nor are officers of the society (nor both) may vote at elections provided that they have paid their subscriptions.'

Writing A = {people under 21}, B = {officers of the society}, C = {people who have paid their subscriptions}, $\mathscr{E}$ = {people}, draw a Venn diagram and shade the part representing those who are permitted by this rule to vote.

(ii) Rule (2) states:

'All officers of the society who are under 21 may vote at elections unless they have not paid their subscriptions.'

Draw a *second* diagram and shade on it the part representing those who are permitted to vote by rule (2).

(iii) Express in your own words as briefly as possible who is allowed to vote by these two rules taken together. OC (SMP)

49 All members of a sixth-form had sat for O-level examinations in English, French, Latin, Mathematics and Physics. The sets of passes are represented by E, F, L, M and P respectively. Use symbols to represent the following results:

(*a*) All of them had passed in French or Latin or both.

(*b*) Everyone who had passed in Latin had also failed in Physics.

(*c*) No one who had passed in Mathematics had failed in English.

(*d*) Everyone who had passed in French had also passed in Mathematics.

By choosing appropriate equivalent statements in symbols, find a result connecting E and P and express the result in words.

L

50 A, B, C, D are four statements which may be either true or false. The truth of certain of these implies the truth of others, the implications being represented in the diagram. (For instance the truth of D implies that of C, but the truth of C does not imply that of D.)

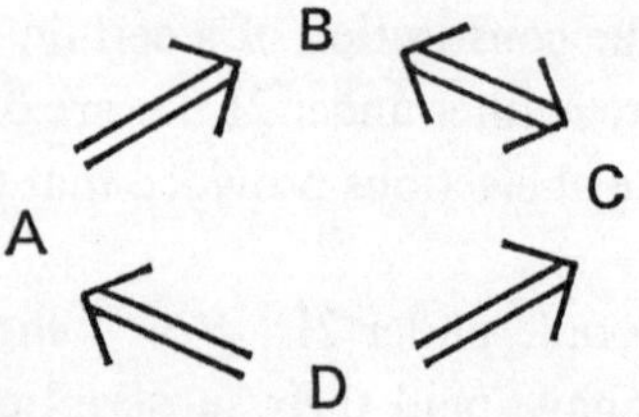

(i) If A is true which other statements *must* be true?
(ii) Which statement has the property that its truth implies the truth of all four statements A, B, C, D?
(iii) Copy the following statements and label them A, B, C, D so that all the implications of the diagram apply to them:

'The quadrilateral Q has both pairs of opposite sides equal.'
'Q is a square.'
'Q is a parallelogram.'
'Q has all four sides equal.'

OC (SMP)

51 Give a definition of a rational number. Which of the following are irrational numbers: 7, 8·35, π, 22/7, $\sqrt{2}$? SU

52 Is $(8^{\frac{1}{3}})^2$ a rational number? SC

53 For any rational numbers p and q, $p \sqcup q$ denotes $(p+q)^2$. Find the value of $5 \sqcup (3 \sqcup 2)$. L

54 A circle of radius $3\frac{1}{2}$ m has circumference 7π m. The number 7π is an element of:

(*a*) {Real numbers}; (*b*) {Rational numbers};
(*c*) {Irrational numbers}; (*d*) {Integers}. OC (SMP)

55 The set S is said to be closed under the operation $*$ if $a, b \in S \Rightarrow a * b \in S$ (e.g. the integers are closed under addition). State whether the following sets are closed or not under the operation specified:

(i) {natural numbers}	under subtraction,	
(ii) {integers}	under multiplication,	
(iii) {rationals}	under addition	
(iv) {irrationals}	under multiplication,	
(v) {prime numbers}	under addition.	SU

56 When p and q are positive numbers, $p*q$ denotes the positive number $\sqrt{(pq)}$. Find the value of $24*(4*9)$. OC (SMP)

57 If $a*b$ denotes $a + 2b$, where a and b are real numbers, calculate (i) $3 * 2$; (ii) $2 * 3$.

What do the results of (i) and (ii) show about the nature of the operation $*$? OC (SMP)

58 (i) Given that $a * b$ means a^2b, calculate $2 * 3$.
(ii) If in addition $a * b = b * a$, what can you say about a and b?
O

59 $a * b$ denotes the remainder when the product $a \times b$ is divided by 11.

(i) Evaluate $4 * 5$.
(ii) Find an integer y such that $8 * y = 1$. OC (SMP)

60 If $a * b$ denotes the average of a and b, state the value of $10 * (6 * 8) - (10 * 6) * 8$. C

61 If $a * b$ means $a + 2b$, find the values of $(2 * 3) * 4$ and $2 * (3 * 4)$. OC (SMP)

62 If x and y are numbers, $x * y$ represents the number $x + y + xy$.

(i) Solve the equation

$$x * 7 = (x * 3) + (x * 4).$$

(ii) If $x * y = 0$, express y in terms of x. State the value of x for which no value of y can be found.
(iii) Simplify $2 * (1 * x)$. OC (SMP)

63 If $x*y = x - y + xy$:

(i) Evaluate: (*a*) 5*3; (*b*) (2*1)*3; (*c*) 2*(1*3).

(ii) Give

(*a*) an example in which $x*y = y*x$;

(*b*) an example in which $x*y \neq y*x$.

(iii) Sketch a mapping diagram, including three examples, to show that $(x,y) \rightarrow x*y$ forms a mapping from the set of ordered pairs (x,y) of integers into the set of integers. NI

64 (i) It is given that $N(x)$ denotes the number of prime numbers (excluding 1) less than x.

Write down the value of $N[N(30)]$.

(ii) $p * q$ denotes the integer part of $\frac{p}{q}$:

(*a*) evaluate 200 * 13;

(*b*) find an integer y such that $200 * y = 11$. C

65 The sets A, B, C are defined as follows:

$$A = \{2, 3, 5\}; \quad B = \{3, 5, 7\}; \quad C = \{4, 5, 7, 11\}.$$

(*a*) Write down the set $A \cap B$.

(*b*) If $\pi(A)$ means the product of the elements of the set A, write down $\pi(A)$, $\pi(B)$ and $\pi(A \cap B)$, and state whether it is true or false that $\pi(A \cap B)$, is the highest factor common to $\pi(A)$ and $\pi(B)$.

(*c*) Find out whether it is true that $\pi(A \cap C)$ is the highest factor common to $\pi(A)$ and $\pi(C)$, showing your working.

(*d*) State conditions on the elements of two sets P and Q which ensure that $\pi(P \cap Q)$ is the highest factor common to $\pi(P)$ and $\pi(Q)$. OC (SMP)

66 If A and B are sets, the set

$\{x$: *either* x is in A but not in B *or* x is in B but not in $A\}$

is denoted by $A * B$.

(i) Illustrate this set on a Venn diagram.
(ii) Simplify $A * A$ and $\phi * X$, where X also is a set.
(iii) Given that $*$ is associative, prove that

$$A * (A * X) = X.$$

(iv) Use the last result to solve for X the equation $A * X = B$.

OC (SMP)

67 A, B, C are subsets of some set $\mathscr{E}$. Let $A \oplus B$ denote the set of elements belonging to A or to B but not to both A and B.
Verify, in each case by means of a pair of carefully shaded Venn diagrams or otherwise, that
(*a*) $A \oplus B = (A \cup B) \cap (A \cap B)'$
(*b*) $C \cap (A \oplus B) = (C \cap A) \oplus (C \cap B)$. L

68

*	*a*	*b*	*c*	*d*
a	*d*	*c*	*a*	*b*
b	*c*	*d*	*b*	*a*
c	*a*	*b*	*c*	*d*
d	*b*	*a*	*d*	*c*

In the table, under the operation $*$, state (*a*) the identity element; (*b*) the inverse of d.
Show that $a * (b * d) = (a * b) * d$. L

69 The diagram shows the composition table for an operation $\odot$ defined on $\{1, 2, 3\}$.

$\odot$	1	2	3
1	2	1	3
2	1	3	2
3	3	2	1

If $(2 \odot 3) \odot x = 1$, find x. SC

70 The operation $*$ on the set $S = \{2, 4, 6, 8\}$ is defined as shown in the table.

*	2	4	6	8
2	4	8	2	6
4	8	6	4	2
6	2	4	6	8
8	6	2	8	4

State whether the following statements are true or false:
(i) The set S does not have an identity element for the operation $*$.
(ii) If $p \in S$ and $p * p = 6$, then p is 4 or 6. SC

71 Call the set of rational numbers (excluding zero) *Qo*. Give an example to show that the operation of division ($\div$) is not commutative on *Qo* and another example to show that division is not associative on *Qo*. Prove that for a, b, c, members of *Qo*, one of the following statements is false.

(1) $a \div (b + c) = (a \div b) + (a \div c)$
(2) $(b + c) \div a = (b \div a) + (c \div a)$

72 State the four defining properties of the algebraic system known as a group. Copy and complete the table

Second element

	×	*i*	*a*	*b*	*c*
	i				
First	*a*				
element	*b*				
	c				

Where $i = \begin{pmatrix} 1 & 0 \\ 0 & 1 \end{pmatrix}$, $a = \begin{pmatrix} -1 & 0 \\ 0 & 1 \end{pmatrix}$,

$b = \begin{pmatrix} -1 & 0 \\ 0 & -1 \end{pmatrix}$, $c = \begin{pmatrix} 1 & 0 \\ 0 & -1 \end{pmatrix}$

and × means matrix multiplication.

State:

(1) the identity element for $\{i, a, b, c\}$ under operation ×;
(2) the inverse of each element of $\{i, a, b, c\}$ under operation ×;
(3) an example of the associative property of × on $\{i, a, b, c\}$;
(4) an example to illustrate the commutativity of × on $\{i, a, b, c\}$.

73 Operation $*$ is defined on $A = \{-2, -1, 0, 1, 2\}$ by $a * b = \dfrac{a+b}{2}$ where a and b are members of A.

State with reasons whether or not

(1) A is closed with respect to *;
(2) operation * is commutative on A;
(3) operation * is associative.

74 Consider set $M = \{1, 2, 3, 4\}$ under operation * where * is multiplication (mod 5), i.e. $a*b$ is the remainder on division of $a \times b$ by 5 for all pairs of elements a, b in M.

Construct a table showing the values of $a*b$ for all a, b in M.

Assuming that * is associative on M show that * on M satisfies the other three conditions for a group. Show that $\{1, 4\}$ forms a group under *.

75 The natural numbers (including zero) are classified into subsets 0, 1, 2, 3, 4 according to the remainder when divided by 5; e.g. 27 belongs to the subset 2. For any two elements x, y of the set of natural numbers, $x*y$ denotes $x + y + xy$. Construct a table under the operation* for the subsets 0, 1, 2, 3 only. L

76 Travellers in each of four towns W, X, Y, Z have four courses of action (a) remain (R), (b) take a bus (B), (c) take a train (T) or (d) take an aeroplane (P). Unfortunately, from any one town, only one method of transport to another exists. The following table shows the complete situation.

		To			
		W	*X*	*Y*	*Z*
	W	*R*	*B*	*T*	*P*
From	*X*	*B*	*R*	*P*	*T*
	Y	*T*	*P*	*R*	*B*
	Z	*P*	*T*	*B*	*R*

Draw a sketch of the links between the four towns and mark clearly the methods of transport (including R).

Find the single method of transport equivalent to a double journey (i) of $B * T$ (i.e. train followed by bus), (ii) of $B * B$.

Construct a table for R, B, T and P under the operation *. L

77 If a, b and c are elements of a Boolean algebra, simplify as far as possible:

(i) $a(a + b)$,

(ii) $(a + b + c(a' + b))'$,

(iii) $c(a + b)(a' + b)$,

where p' means '*not p*'.

George collects British stamps and also pictorial stamps of any country. Margaret collects only stamps issued since 1939, and she collects no British stamps except pictorial ones. Using a, b and c to denote respectively {British stamps}, {pictorial stamps} and {stamps issued since 1939}, write down expressions for the sets of stamps collected by each collector.

Hence find

(a) the kinds of stamps collected by both;

(b) the kinds of stamps collected by neither.

(Give your answers in words.) **L**

Chapter Two

1 Find a linear relation between the elements x, y of the ordered pairs (x, y) in the set $\{(x, y)\} = \{(0, 3), (1, 5), (2, 7), (3, 9), \ldots\}$. L

2 If $f(x) = 3x + 1$, find $f(f(x))$. OC (SMP)

3 If $f: x \to (4 + 3x)$, write down the values of (i) $f(-2)$ and (ii) $f(f(2))$. OC (SMP)

4 $f(x)$ is the greatest integer less than $\sqrt{x}$. Evaluate $f(f[120])$. OC (SMP)

5 A function f is defined on the set of integers by the formula $f(x) = a - 3x$. Given that $f(1) = 1$, find $f(2)$. SC

6 $S = \{p < 20: p \text{ is a prime number}\}$.
(i) List the members of S.
(ii) A relation is defined on the set S by the equation $y = x + 2$, where x and y are variables on S. List the set of ordered pairs of this relation and illustrate the relation on S by an 'arrow' diagram. SC

7 For the domain set {even numbers less than 14} and the range set {prime numbers less than 14}, plot the functions

$x \to$ smallest prime number which is larger than x,

and $x \to$ largest prime number which is a factor of x,

using either parallel scales or rectangular cartesian coordinates. L

8 Name three members of the set of ordered pairs $(x, 5x - 6)$ if x is a natural number less than 6. Find the members of this set common to the set of ordered pairs (x, x^2). L

9 The relation a R b is defined by the statement *a is older than b*. For the set of boys {Alan, Barry, Charles, David} the following statements are true:

Charles R Alan, Alan R David, Charles R Barry.

Draw a diagram to illustrate this relation and deduce whether the following statements are true, false or possibly either:

(i) Charles R David; (ii) David R Barry SU

10 Which of the properties of being reflexive, symmetric, transitive are possessed by each of the following relations defined on the given sets?

(i)	a is a factor of b	$a, b \in$ {integers}
(ii)	a is greater than b	$a, b \in$ {real numbers}
(iii)	a is a descendant of b	$a, b \in$ {all people}
(iv)	a has a common factor with b	$a, b \in$ {integers}
(v)	a has his meals with b	$a, b \in$ {men and boys}

Which of these is an equivalence relation? SU

11 The railway line from Birmingham (New Street) to London (Euston) passes through Bletchley, Hemel Hempstead, Watford, Coventry and Rugby, though not necessarily in that order.

Some trains from Coventry to Euston call at Rugby and then Bletchley while those from Rugby to Euston call at Watford. Trains from Birmingham to Watford call at Bletchley and local trains from Bletchley to London call at Hemel Hempstead. Trains from Rugby to Watford call at Hemel Hempstead.

From this information draw a graph illustrating the relation *is further from London than*, on the given set of intermediate stations. Use the transitive property of the relation to help you construct the complete graph and list the stations in their correct, order from Birmingham to Euston. SU

12 Illustrate the relation between y and x by means of a *sketch* graph in the following cases:

(i) y sq. units is the area of a circle of radius x units.
(ii) x units is the length, and y units is the breadth of a rectangle of area 36 sq. units.

(i)

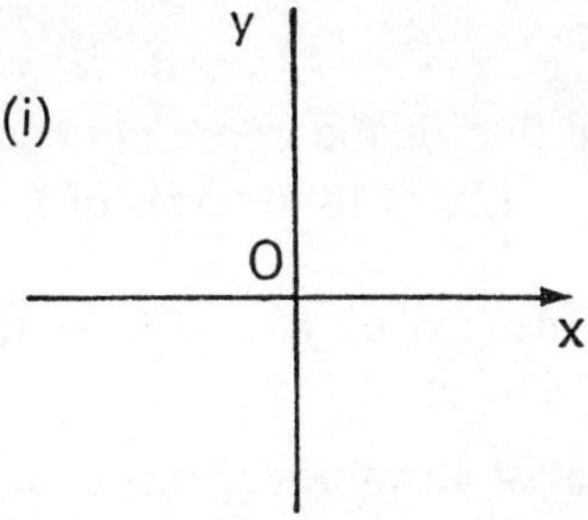

(ii)

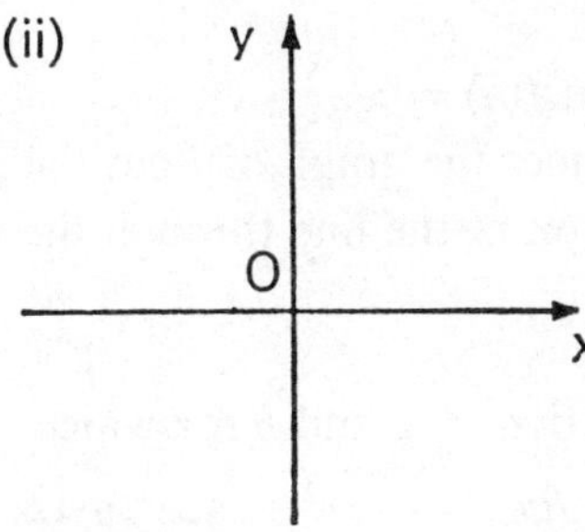

OC (SMP)

13 If x belong to the set of *integers* sketch $\{x, y : y = 1 + 2x^2\}$ and $\{x, y : y = 3^x\}$ for $-1 \leqslant x \leqslant 2$. If now x belongs to the set of *real numbers* state, with a reason, whether the curves given by the same relations will be congruent in the range $0 \leqslant x \leqslant 2$.

OC (SMP)

14 The function f maps x into y where $y = x^2 + 3$ (thus $f : x \to x^2 + 3$) and its domain is the set $\{1, 2, 3, 4, 5\}$. List all the members of the set which is the range of f. SU

15 A function $y = f(x)$ maps a number into its positive square root, thus $f : x \to +\sqrt{x}$. If the range of the function is the set $\{y : 0 \leqslant y \leqslant 3\}$ state the domain of the function. SU

16 If $S = \left\{(x, y) : 1 < x < 4, y = \dfrac{6}{2x + 1}\right\}$, find the range set of y. L

17 If $f : x \to 2x$, $g : x \to x - 3$ and $h : x \to x^2$, show that $fg : x \to 2x - 6$ and that fg and gf are not equivalent.

Express $x \to 2x^2 - 12x + 18$ in terms of f, g and h. L

18 A function f is defined by $f : x \to 3x - 1$, where x is a real number and $-2 \leqslant x \leqslant 2$.

(*a*) Represent the set of all values of $f(x)$ on a number line.
(*b*) Evaluate $f(3^{-1})$.
(*c*) Find a such that $f(a) = 3\frac{1}{2}$.
(*d*) In what point does the graph of f cut the x-axis?
(*e*) Find the equation of the line through the point (0, 5) parallel to the graph of f. SC

19 Find three functions f, g and h for which

$$fgh : x \to 3x^2 - 12x + 12.$$

Determine hgf. L

20 Is the following statement true or false?

$(-2, -2)$ is a member of the set $\{(x, y) : y = 3x + 4\}$.

SC

21 If $f : x \to x^3 - 3x^2 - x + 3$, find $f(1)$ and the values of x for which the function is zero. L

22 $f(x) = 3x + 2$ and $g(x) = 2x + 1$.
(i) Show that $f(x + y) = f(x) + f(y) - 2$.
(ii) Show that $f(g(x)) = g(f(x))$.
(iii) Solve the equation:

$$f(x) = \frac{1}{x}$$

NI

23 Given that $f: x \to 60/x$ and $g: x \to x + 10$, find the range sets of $f(x)$ and $g(x)$ when

(*a*) $x \in \{1, 2, 3, 4, 5, 6\}$,
(*b*) $x, f(x)$ and $g(x)$ are all positive integers,
(*c*) x is a positive real number.

If further, $f(x) = g(x)$, state the solution set for x in both (*a*) and (*b*) and find graphically the solution set for x in (*c*) correct to two decimal places.

If $x = \alpha$ is a solution obtained graphically, calculate $f(\alpha)$ and $g(\alpha)$ and confirm (or deny) that $f(\alpha) = g(\alpha)$. L

24 Given $f: x \to 2 \log_{10}x$ has domain $0{\cdot}1 \leqslant x \leqslant 100$, find the range of $2 \log_{10}x$. L

25 If $S = \{\sin \theta : 0° \leqslant \theta \leqslant 90°\}$ and $C = \{\cos \theta : 0° \leqslant \theta \leqslant 90°\}$, represent the mapping of $S \to C$ for the set

$$\theta = \{0°, 30°, 60°, 90°\}$$

in the following two ways:

(*a*) using two parallel scales,
(*b*) using rectangular cartesian coordinates. L

26 Copy and complete the following table:

x	0	0·2	0·4	0·6	0·8	1·0
x^2	0	0·04		0·36		1·00
$1 - x^2$	1		0·84		0·36	0
$\sqrt{(1 - x^2)}$	1	0·98		0·80		0

For the domain $0 \leqslant x \leqslant 1$, plot the graphs of $y = 0{\cdot}8$, $y = 0{\cdot}78$ and $y = \sqrt{(1 - x^2)}$.

By counting squares or otherwise, show that the area of the region $\{x \geqslant 0, y \geqslant 0, y \leqslant \sqrt{(1 - x^2)}\}$ is less than the area of the rectangle $\{0 \leqslant x \leqslant 1, 0 \leqslant y \leqslant 0{\cdot}8\}$ and greater than the area of the rectangle $\{0 \leqslant x \leqslant 1, 0 \leqslant y \leqslant 0{\cdot}78\}$. L

27 A function $f(x)$, which is always positive, has the following properties:

$$f(2) = 2,\ f(4) = 8, f(x + y) = 2f(x)f(y),$$

where x and y are any two real numbers. Find the values of $f(6)$, $f(3), f(1), f(0)$ and $f(-1)$.

Make a rough sketch of the cartesian graph of $x \to f(x)$, for both positive and negative values of x, giving the coordinates of any point or points of intersection with the axes, and indicating the shape of the curve when x is large and positive and when x is large and negative. L

28 Solve the equation:

$$\frac{2x}{3} - \frac{x}{2} = \frac{4}{5}.$$ O

29 Solve the equation:

$$\frac{2x-3}{2} + \frac{x-4}{3} = 0.$$

30 Solve the equation:

$$\frac{x+3}{5} - \frac{x+2}{2} = \frac{x+8}{4}.$$

31 Find the solution set of:

$$x(x - 3) = (x - 1)(2x - 1)$$

where x is a real number.

32 Simplify $x + 5 < 3x - 7$. OC (SMP)

33 Simplify $2(x - 1) < 3 - x$. OC (SMP)

34 State the least member of the solution set of $3x > -40$ if the universal set is the set of integers. OC (SMP)

35 If $4 - 3x \leqslant 7$, state the least value of x OC (SMP)

36 Find for what real values of x the following inequality is satisfied $5x + 2 \leqslant 12$. SU

37 For what real numbers is the inequality $3 - 2x \leqslant 7$ satisfied?

SU

38 State the smallest possible value of y if $2y - 3 \geqslant 5$.

OC (SMP)

39 If the universal set is the set of integers, write down the solution set of

$$19 < 3(x + 2) < 35.$$

C

40 Solve the inequation $\frac{3}{2}x - \frac{2}{3}(1 - 2x) < 5$, $x \in R$, and graph the solution on a number line.

SC

41 State any one solution in integers of the equation

$$3x + 2y = 17.$$

OC (SMP)

42 Sets P and Q are defined as follows:

$$P = \{(x, y): x, y \text{ real and } 3x - 2y = 7\};$$
$$Q = \{(x, y): x, y \text{ real and } x + 2y = 5\}.$$

Find $P \cap Q$.

43 Find all the elements belonging to the following set:

$$\{(x, y); x + 3y = 7\} \cap \{(x, y); x - 2y = 1\tfrac{1}{2}\}.$$

AEB

44 Sets R and S are defined as follows:

$$R = \{(x, y): x, y \text{ real and } 8x - 3y = 39\};$$
$$S = \{(x, y): x, y \text{ real and } 7x + 5y = -4\}.$$

Find $R \cap S$.

45 Solve the system of equations:

$$3x + 2y - 1 = 0;$$
$$9x - 4y + 17 = 0.$$

SC

46 A pair of simultaneous linear equations in two unknowns could have

(*a*) no; (*b*) one; (*c*) two; (*d*) more than two solutions.

(A solution is a pair of values, one for each of the two unknowns.)

AEB

47 Real numbers a and b are such that

$$3a - 2b = 4$$
$$4a + 3b = 11$$

find the values of a, b, $\frac{a}{b}$.

48 If $(5, k)$ is a solution of the equation $2x + y = 7$, find k. SC

49 Find an equation which together with $2x - 3y = 1$ has the unique solution $x = 5$, $y = 3$. AEB

50 If x and y are integers, give the solution set of ordered pairs (x, y) for which:

(*a*) $x \geqslant 0, y \geqslant 0, x + y \leqslant 2$,
(*b*) $x > 0, y > 0, x + y \leqslant 2$,
(*c*) $x > 0, y > 0, x + y < 2$. L

51 If x and y are positive integers, find the solution set of ordered pairs (x, y) satisfying $2x + 3y = 26$. If further, $x + y < 10$, find the value of $(y - x)$. L

52 Write down any pair of positive integers x and y which satisfy *both* the inequalities

$$x + 2y > 20; \quad 2x - y > 30.$$ OC (SMP)

53 Is the following statement true or false?
If $A = \{(x, y) : 2 \leqslant x < 5\}$
and $B = \{(x, y) : 3 < y \leqslant 5\}$,
then the shaded region
represents $A \cup B$.

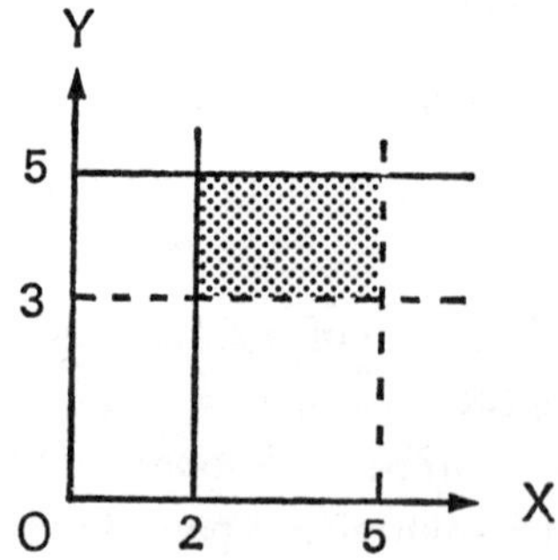

SC

54 Show in the diagram, by shading, the set A ∩ *B*, where

$$A = \{(x, y) : x > 3\} \quad \text{and} \quad B = \{(x, y) : x > y\}.$$

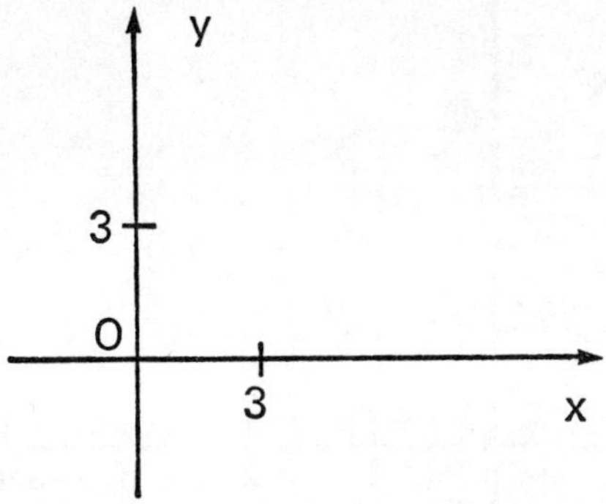

OC (SMP)

55

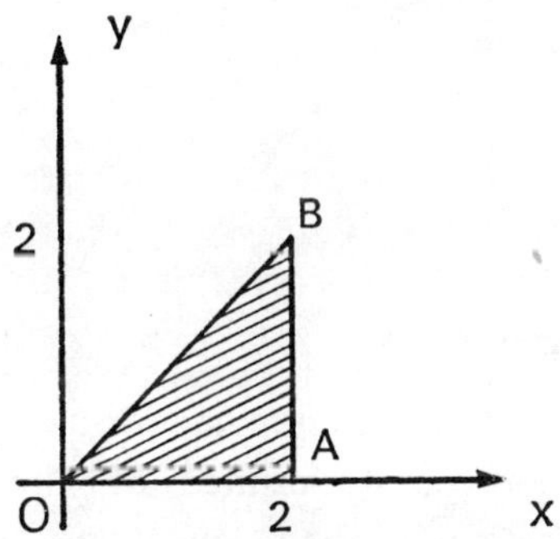

State a set of inequalities involving x and y whose solution is the shaded area together with the lines OA, OB and AB. O

56 (*a*) On a copy of the axes shown (Page 28) shade the region which represents the set, *S*, of ordered pairs (x, y) which satisfy simultaneously the following inequalities

$$x > 0, \quad x + y < 1, \quad x - y < 2.$$

(*b*) Calculate, using your diagram as a guide, but not by reading the values directly from the graph, three members of *S* for which

$$x - y = 1.$$

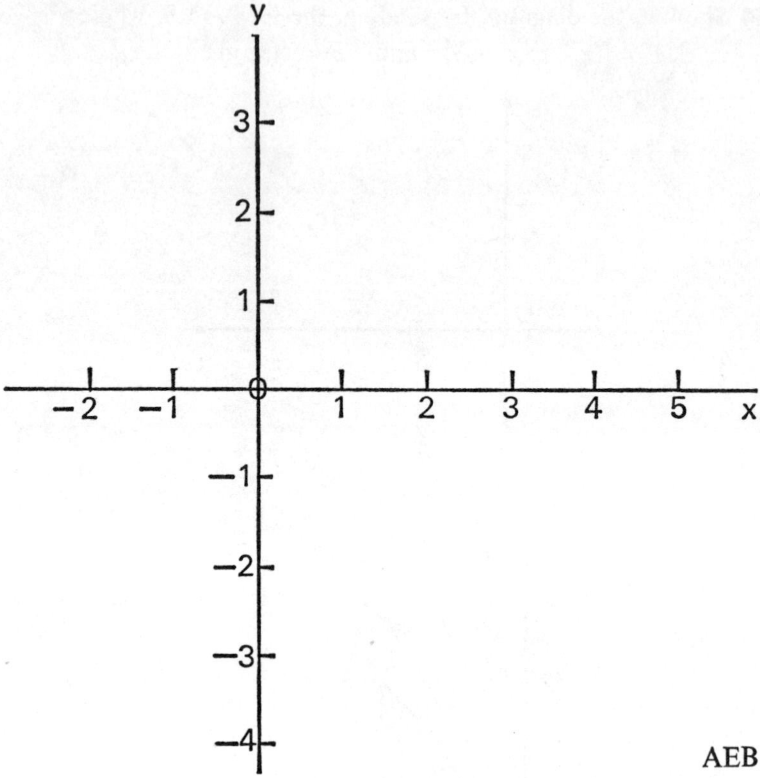

AEB

57 By drawing appropriate straight lines on a copy of the diagram, find the number of points printed on the diagram whose coordinates (x, y) satisfy all the inequalities

$$0 < x < 6; \quad 0 < y < 4; \quad x + 2y < 10.$$

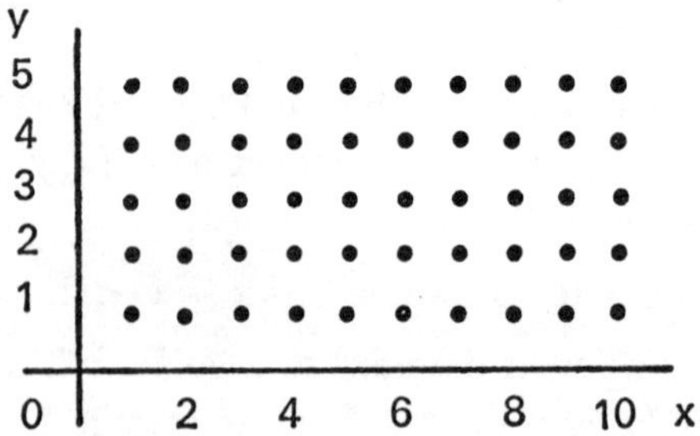

C

58 (i) On a copy of the axes shown below illustrate the set $\{(x, y); 3x + 2y = 6\}$ and indicate clearly the sets

$$\{(x, y); 3x + 2y > 6\}$$

and

$$\{(x, y); 3x + 2y < 6\}.$$

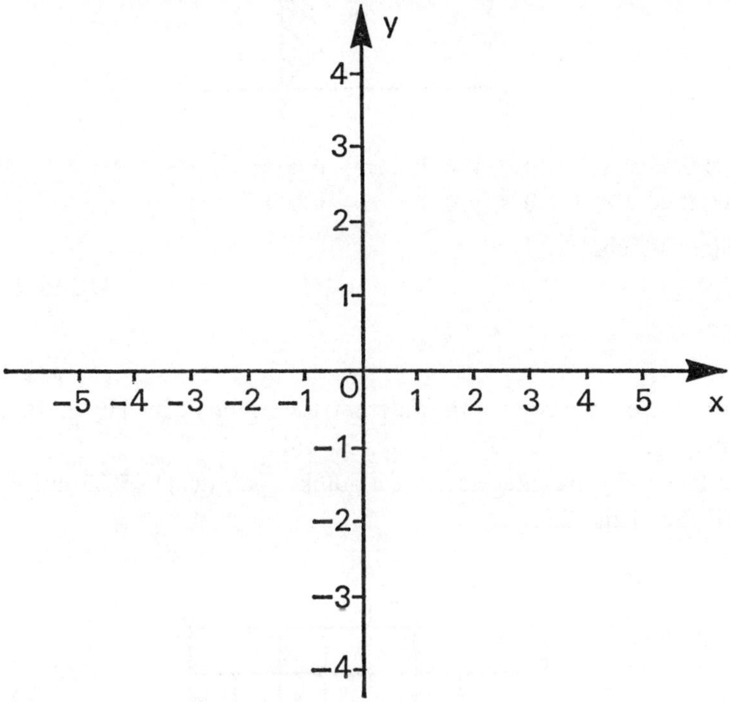

(ii) Given that $x \geqslant 0$, $y \geqslant 0$ and $3x + 2y \leqslant 6$, find the maximum value of $x + y$. AEB

59

A set of inequalities which define the shaded area shown overleaf (all the boundary is included) is one of

(*a*) $0 \leqslant x \leqslant 1, \quad 0 \leqslant y \leqslant 1, \quad x + y \leqslant 2;$
(*b*) $0 \leqslant x \leqslant 1, \quad 0 \leqslant y \leqslant 1, \quad xy \leqslant 1;$

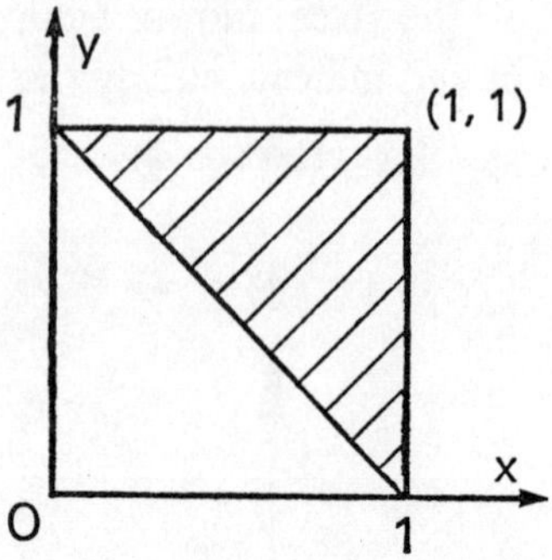

(*c*) $0 < x \leqslant 1, \quad 0 \leqslant y < 1, \quad x + y \geqslant 1;$
(*d*) $0 \leqslant x \leqslant 1, \quad 0 \leqslant y \leqslant 1, \quad x + y \geqslant 1.$

State which.

OC (SMP)

60 Shade, on a copy of the diagram, the region defined by the three inequalities $y < 2x$, $2y > x$, $x + y < 4$.

If x and y are integers, state a number pair (x, y) which satisfies all the inequalities. C

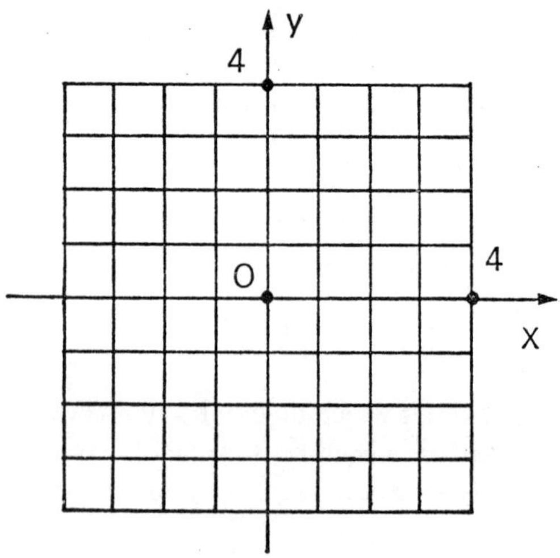

61 If $A = \{(x, y); x + y \geqslant 1$ and $B = (x, y); y \leqslant x \leqslant 1\}$, shade, in the diagram, the region defined by $A \cap B$. C

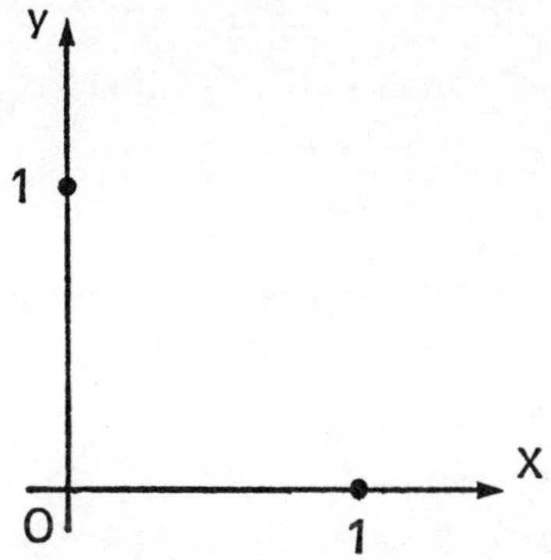

62 If:

$$\mathscr{E} = \{\text{all points of a rectangular cartesian plane}\},$$
$$A = \{(x, y) : x \geqslant 0\},$$
$$B = \{(x, y) : y \geqslant 0\},$$
$$C = \{(x, y) : x + y \geqslant 2\},$$

indicate by shading the *outside* edge of the boundaries of the regions in rough sketches, the following sets

(*a*) $A \cap B$; (*b*) $A \cup B$; (*c*) $(A \cap B \cap C)'$. L

63 If $(x - 2)(y - 4) < 0$ and $x + y > 6$, show in a sketch graph, by shading other regions, those regions of ordered pairs (x, y) which satisfy the inequalities. L

64 A triangle has vertices (0, 0), (0, 1), (1, 1). By means of linear inequalities describe the set of points **inside** the triangle. SU

65 Find the integer value of x which satisfies the equation $2x^2 - 5x - 3 = 0$. SU

66 State whether each of the following statements is true or false:

(*a*) $x = \frac{1}{2}$ satisfies the equation $\frac{x}{2} - (x - 1)^2 = 0$.

(*b*) $x(2x - 3y) = 0 \Rightarrow x = 0$ or $y = \frac{2}{3}x$. SC

67 Solve the equation $3x^2 - 6x + 2 = 0$, where x is a variable on the set of real numbers.

Give your answer correct to one decimal place. SC

68 Having written the roots of the equation $3x^2 - 4x - 2 = 0$ as $\frac{4 \pm \sqrt{p}}{6}$, give the value of p. SC

69 State whether the following equations are satisfied for (*a*) one value of x, (*b*) two values of x, or (*c*) all values of x.

(i) $(x - 3)^2 = x^2 + 6x + 5$.
(ii) $(x - 3)^2 = x^2 - 6x + 9$.
(iii) $(x - 3)^2 = 2x^2 + 9$.
(iv) $(x - 3)^2 = 36$.

Solve those equations which are of type (*a*) or (*b*). C

70 Express $(x - 2)^2$ without brackets. Hence find the solution set of each of the following equations, taking the set R of real numbers as universal set in each case.

(i) $(x - 2)^2 = x^2 - 4$.
(ii) $(x - 2)^2 = x^2 - 4x + 4$.
(iii) $(x - 2)^2 = x^2 - 4x - 4$. SC

71 Each of the following statements is either

(*a*) true for all values of x;
(*b*) true for two values of x;
(*c*) true for only one value of x;
(*d*) never true.

Distinguish which is which, and where appropriate give the solution set in the set of irrational numbers.

(i) $(3x - 2)^2 = 9x^2 - 4$.
(ii) $(3x - 2)^2 = 9x^2 - 12x - 4$.
(iii) $(3x - 2)^2 = 3x^2 + 12x + 4$.
(iv) $(3x - 2)^2 = 9x^2 - 12x + 4$. L

72 Write down and simplify a quadratic equation whose roots are 2 and $-\frac{1}{2}$. OC (SMP)

73 Find the simplest equations which have solution sets

(*a*) $\{2\}$ in the set of natural numbers;
(*b*) $\{2, -\frac{3}{4}\}$ in the set of rationals;
(*c*) $\{\pm\sqrt{2}\}$ in the set of irrationals.

Leave your answers, in factor form where possible, with integral coefficients. L

74 (In this question x belongs to the set of real numbers.) Which of the following statements are true and which false?

(*a*) $(x+1)(x-2) = 0 \Leftrightarrow x = -1$ or $x = 2$.
(*b*) $x = 3 \Rightarrow (x-3)(x+1) = 0$.
(*c*) $x(x-3) < 0 \Rightarrow 3 > x > 0$.
(*d*) $x^2 > 1 \Rightarrow x > 1$. OC (SMP)

75 Which of the following are true and which are false?

(*a*) $(x-3)(x+5) = 0 \Rightarrow x = 3$.
(*b*) $x^2 - 4x = 0 \Leftrightarrow x = 4$.
(*c*) $3x > 5y \Leftrightarrow -6x < -10y$.
(*d*) $p^2 > q^2 \Rightarrow p > q$. OC (SMP)

76 Solve each of the following equations:

(i) $(x-1)(x-9) = 0$.
(ii) $(y^2-1)(y^2-9) = 0$. NI

77 Are the following statements true or false, where x and y represent fractions?

(*a*) $x^2y + y^2x = 0 \Rightarrow x + y = 0$.
(*b*) $x^2 - y^2 = 0 \Leftrightarrow x = y$ or $x = -y$.
(*c*) $\dfrac{x}{y} > 1 \Leftrightarrow \dfrac{y}{x} < 1$.
(*d*) $x < 1$ and $y < 1 \Rightarrow xy < 1$. AEB

78 Simplify $(x+4)(x-2) > x^2 + 2$. OC (SMP)

79 If x belongs to the set of real numbers, which of the following statements are true and which are false?

(*a*) $(x - 2)(x + 3) > 0 \Rightarrow x > 2$.
(*b*) $x > 2 \Rightarrow (x - 2)(x + 3) > 0$.
(*c*) $x > 2 \Rightarrow \frac{1}{x} > \frac{1}{2}$.
(*d*) $x^2 > x \Rightarrow x > 1$. OC (SMP)

80 If the universal set is the set of positive integers, list the members of the solution set of

$$4 < \tfrac{22}{7}r^2 < 88.$$ C

81 (i) Solve the equation $p^2 + 5p - 6 = 0$. Find for what values of p the following is satisfied, $p^2 + 5p \leqslant 6$.
(ii) Find for what values of q the inequality $q(q + 1) \geqslant 0$ is satisfied. SU

82 Indicate which of the following implications are correct and which are incorrect:

(*a*) $5 - 3x < 11 \Rightarrow x < -2$;
(*b*) $(x - 3)(x + 2) > 0 \Rightarrow -2 < x < 3$;
(*c*) $x = 2 \Rightarrow x^2 - 2x = 0$;
(*d*) $(x^2 - 5x) < 0 \Rightarrow 0 < x < 5$. OC (SMP)

83 Given that $-1 \leqslant h \leqslant 1$, and that $1 \leqslant k \leqslant 2$, find the greatest and least possible values of:

(*a*) $k - 2h$; (*b*) $h^2/2k$. L

84 Which of the following statements are true and which are false? If x, y and k are any numbers and $x > y$, then

(*a*) $k + x > k + y$; (*b*) $kx < ky$;
(*c*) $\frac{x}{y} > 1$; (*d*) $x^2 > y^2$; (*e*) $(y - x)^2 < 0$. AEB

85 Which of the following statements are true and which are false? If x and y are rational numbers, $xy > 0$ implies

(*a*) $x \neq 0$; (*b*) $y > 0$;

(c) $x < 0$ and $y < 0$ *or* $x > 0$ and $y > 0$;
(d) $-xy < 0$; (e) $x + y > 0$. AEB

86 Find the solution set for the equation

$$(x - 1)(2x + 3)(x^2 - 3) = 0$$

in the set of (a) positive integers, (b) rational numbers, (c) negative irrational numbers. L

87 If $(x - 1)^2(x + 3) > 0$, which of the following are necessarily true, which necessarily false?

(a) $x > -3$; (b) $x > 1$; (c) $x > 1$ and $x < -3$.

If any statement falls into neither category write neither.

OC (SMP)

88 Which of the following statements are true and which false? The equation $x^3 - 4x^2 + 5x - 6 = 0$:

(a) has no solution between $x = 0$ and $x = 2$;
(b) has the solution $x = 3$;
(c) has one negative solution. AEB

89 (i) State the solution set of the equation

$$(2x + 5)(x^2 - 2) = 0$$

when the universal set is (a) real numbers, (b) rational numbers, (c) integers.
(ii) State the solution sets of the inequality

$$x^2 - 2 \leqslant 0$$

in the same universal sets (a), (b) and (c).
(iii) Make a table showing the sign of $(2x + 5)(x^2 - 2)$ for $x = -3, -2, -1, 0, 1, 2$ and sketch the graph of

$$y = (2x + 5)(x^2 - 2).$$

OC (SMP)

90 If $A = \{x : x - 1 < 0\}$ and $B = \{x : x^2 - 4 < 0\}$, represent A, B and $A \cap B$ on the real number line, preferably giving three separate diagrams. L

91 Using a scale of 20 mm to 1 unit for x and 10 mm to 1 unit for y draw graphs of the sets of points defined by

$$A = \{(x, y) : y = 1 + 6x - x^2, 1 \leqslant x \leqslant 6\}$$

and $$B = \{(x, y) : y = \frac{12}{x}, 1 \leqslant x \leqslant 6\}$$

where x and y are real numbers.

From the graphs:

(1) find $A \cap B$;

(2) solve the equation $1 + 6x - x^2 = 0$;

(3) solve the equation $x^3 - 6x^2 - x + 12 = 0$.

92 Using a scale of 1 unit to 10 mm for both x and y, plot accurately the graphs of the functions $y = \frac{1}{x}$ and $y = x + 1$, each with domain $-3 \leqslant x \leqslant 3$. Use your graphs to obtain both solutions to the equation $x^2 + x - 1 = 0$ to one decimal place. SU

93

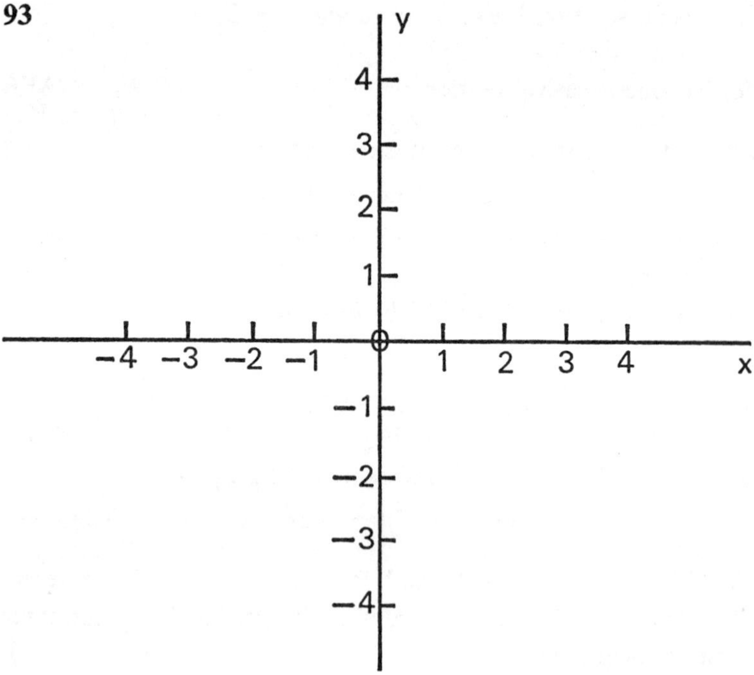

On a copy of the diagram (Page 36) draw the graph of the set of ordered pairs (x, y) such that $xy = 2$ and $\{x : \frac{1}{2} \leqslant x \leqslant 4\} \cup \{x : -\frac{1}{2} \geqslant x \geqslant -4\}$. AEB

94 On a copy of the diagram below shade the region which represents the set, S, of ordered pairs (x, y) which satisfy simultaneously the following inequalities

$$x^2 + y^2 < 1, \quad x > 0, \quad y > 0, \quad x - y > 0.$$

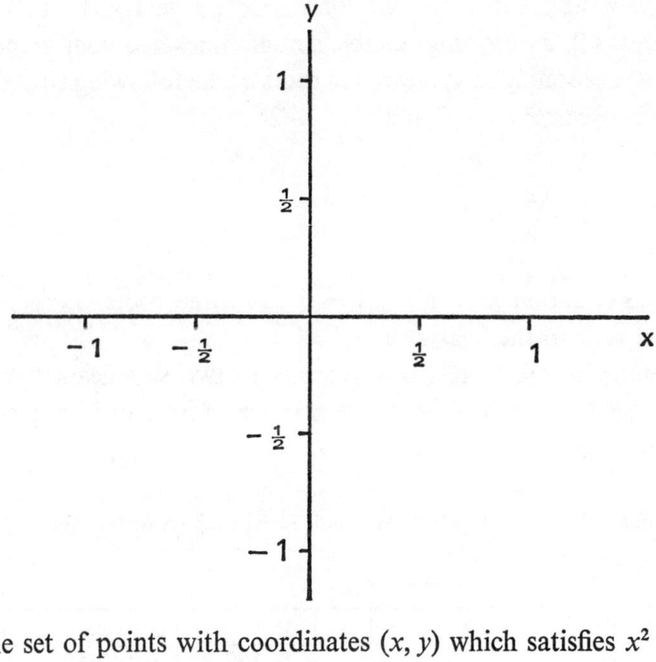

[The set of points with coordinates (x, y) which satisfies $x^2 + y^2 = 1$ is a circle, centre the origin and radius 1 unit.] AEB

95 On a copy of the given axes (Page 38), sketch the graph of $y = x^2$ for values of x from 0 to 3. Illustrate graphically the error made if the value of y when $x = 2$ is assumed to be the average of the values of y when $x = 1$ and when $x = 3$. C

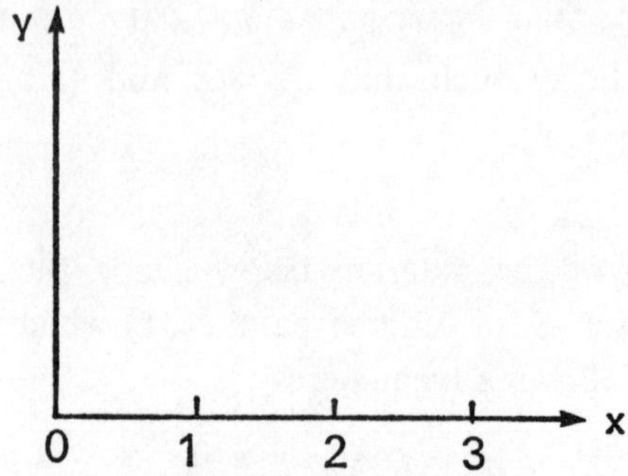

96 Draw the graph of the relation $y = x^3$ for values of x between -2 and $+2$. By drawing suitable straight lines, use your graph to find, as accurately as you can, the roots of the following equations lying between $x = -2$ and $x = +2$:

(i) $x^3 - x - 1 = 0$;

(ii) $3x^2 + 1 + \frac{4}{x} = 0$. AEB

97 The equation $x^3 - 6x - 1 = 0$ has three roots. Locate the largest root to the nearest unit.

Determine the largest root (correct to two significant figures) either by drawing an appropriate graph or graphs, or by any other suitable method. AEB

98 Given that $y = -x^3 + 3x^2 - 1$, copy and complete the following table:

x	-1	$-\frac{1}{2}$	0	$\frac{1}{2}$	1	$1\frac{1}{2}$	2	$2\frac{1}{2}$	3
y	3	$-0{\cdot}12$			1	2·37	3	2·12	

Using a scale of 10 mm to 1 unit on each axis, draw the graph of $y = -x^3 + 3x^2 - 1$ for values of x from -1 to 3.

Describe clearly any symmetrical property which the curve possesses. If the gradient of the curve at the point P is the same as the gradient when $x = \frac{1}{4}$, state the coordinates of P.

Given that

$A = \{x : -1 \leqslant x \leqslant 2\}$ and $B = \{x : -x^3 + 3x^2 \geqslant 2\}$, use your graph to find the ranges of values of x defined by $A \cap B$. C

99

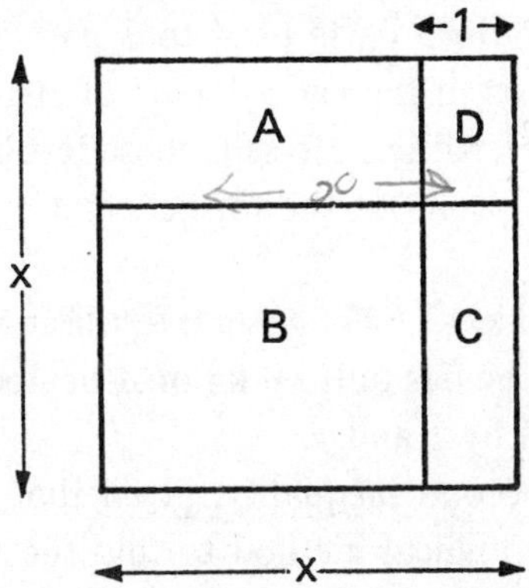

The diagram shows four rectangles A, B, C and D which together form a square of side x m.

Given that one side of D is 1 m, and that the area of $A + D$ is 4 m^2, express the other side of D in terms of x.

Given also that the area of $A + B + C$ is 11 m^2, show that $x^3 = 11x + 4$.

By drawing the graph of $y = x^3$ and an appropriate straight line, estimate the value of x. C

Chapter Three

1 A seedsman has stocks of two chemicals A and B. He can mix these in the ratio 3 parts of A to 1 part of B to produce a general fertiliser; or in the ratio 1 part of A to 3 parts of B to produce a tomato fertiliser. He sells these fertilisers in 1 kg bags, making 3p per kg profit on the former, and 6p per kg profit on the latter.

Given that he makes x kg of general fertiliser and y kg of tomato fertiliser, and that he has only 60 kg of A in stock, write down an inequality satisfied by x and y.

Write down a second inequality, given that the stock of B is 30 kg and use a graphical method to find the values of x and y to maximise his profit. Hence find his maximum profit.

OC (SMP)

2 A doctor decides that a patient should have daily at least 32 units of vitamin B_1 and at least 30 units of vitamin B_2.

These vitamins are only available in tablets each of which contains 1 unit of vitamin B_1 and 5 units of B_2 and in capsules each of which contains 4 units of B_1 and 1 unit of B_2.

Take x as the number of tablets prescribed daily along with y capsules daily.

State

(i) the restrictions on x;
(ii) the restrictions on y;
(iii) the restrictions on x and y in relation to B_1;
(iv) the restrictions on x and y in relation to B_2.

Using 5 mm squared paper and taking 5 mm to 1 unit on each axis, illustrate graphically and by dots part of the solution set of the system of inequations corresponding to the given restrictions.

Find from the graph the values of x and y for which $x + y$ is minimised. SC

3 A coach capable of seating 44 passengers is offered for hire to the secretary of a social club at a charge of £40 for a day trip. The secretary charges £1·75 per adult and £1·00 per child, provided that each adult is responsible for at least one child and not more than three children. The trip will be cancelled if the coach hire charge cannot be covered. Any profit will be used for buying extra refreshments during the day.

By graphical methods or otherwise, find

(*a*) the greatest and least possible numbers of adults;
(*b*) the greatest and least possible numbers of children;
(*c*) the greatest and least possible profit;
(*d*) the numbers of children and adults when the profit is least.

L

4 A company produces television and radio sets. It has undertaken to supply once a week at least 100 televisions and 150 radios to one of its depots. The depot has found that it cannot store more than 600 televisions and radios combined. A television set weighs 20 kg and a radio set weighs 5 kg and the depot cannot store a total weight of more than 6000 kg. The depot sends out to shops all the televisions and radios with which it is supplied each week before the next delivery. If the company sends x televisions and y radios per week, find the constraints on x and y. Shade a region to illustrate the points with coordinates (x, y) corresponding to the possible values of x and y.

If the profit is £9 on a television and £3 on a radio, how many of each should be sent to the depot to give the maximum profit?

If the profit were £3 on a television and £9 on a radio, how would the company then maximise its profit? AEB

5 A depot for famine relief has 20 sacks of rice and 35 sacks of maize. The weight, volume and number of meal rations *for each sack* are as shown:

Sack of	Weight (kg)	Volume (m^3)	No. of meals
Rice	25	0·05	800
Maize	10	0·05	160

A delivery van is to carry the largest possible total number of meals. It can carry up to 600 kg in weight and 2 m^3 in volume.

(i) If a load is made up of x sacks of rice and y sacks of maize, say why $x \leqslant 20$ and write down three other inequalities (other than $x \geqslant 0$, $y \geqslant 0$) which govern x and y.

(ii) Illustrate these inequalities on a graph (taking the side of a large square (i.e. 20 mm) to represent 10 units for x and 10 units for y) and indicate, by the use of shading, the area in which the point (x, y) must lie.

(iii) Write down an expression for the number of meals that can be provided from x sacks of rice and y sacks of maize. Using this, find from your graph the best values to take for x and y. NI

6 An employer wishes to transport 400 workers to a factory by bus, using x single-deck buses (capacity 40 persons each) and y double-deck buses (capacity 80 persons each). The transport department has a maximum of 8 drivers on duty, and the largest number of double-deck buses available is 4. Show that $x + 2y \geqslant 10$ and write down two further inequations which represent restrictions on the values of x and y. On a suitable graph indicate clearly the six possible solutions to the problem. Find the solution with minimum cost, if the expenses of running each smaller bus are £10 and those of running each larger one £15, and determine the minimum cost. SU

7 A factory employs unskilled workers who earn £12 a week and skilled workers who earn £24 a week. The weekly wage bill must not exceed £2160. The machines require a minimum of 105 operators of whom at least 40 must be skilled. Union regulations require that the number of skilled workers should be at least half the number of unskilled workers.

(i) If x is the number of unskilled and y the number of skilled workers, write down the inequalities (other than $x \geqslant 0$, $y \geqslant 0$,) which govern x and y.

(ii) Illustrate these results on a diagram, and from your diagram obtain the range within which the number of unskilled workers must lie. OC (SMP)

8 In laying out a car park it is decided, in the hope of making the best use of the available parking area (900 m^2), to have some spaces for 'small' cars, the rest for 'large' cars. For each small space 10 m^2 is allowed, for each large space 15 m^2. Every car must occupy a space of the appropriate size.

It is reliably estimated that, of the cars wishing to park at any given time, the ratio of small to large will be neither less than 2 : 3 nor greater than 2 : 1.

(i) If there are x small spaces and y large spaces, show that $2x + 3y \leqslant 180$.

(ii) Use a graphical method to find how many small spaces must be provided in order to maximise the number of cars that can be parked under the conditions stated above. OC (SMP)

9 A sports ground is to be built with a rectangular playing field x m long and y m wide. The perimeter of this field must be more than 500 m but less than 700 m and the length must be less than twice the width. Write down three inequalities (other than $x > 0$, $y > 0$ and $x > y$) satisfied by x and y.

The grandstand on each of the longer sides will be designed to seat 50 spectators for each metre of its length, while the terrace along each of the shorter sides will be able to hold 20 per metre. If a crowd of 25 000 is to be accommodated determine, using a graphical method, the range of possible values of x.

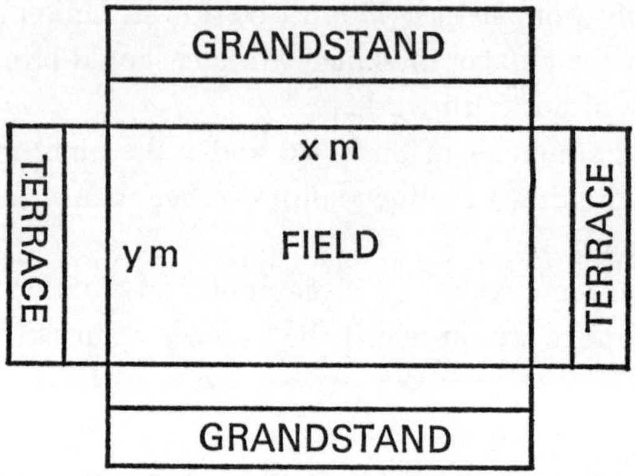

C

10 A farmer makes two types of fertiliser, X and Y, using chemicals A and B. Fertiliser X is composed of 80 per cent of chemical A and 20 per cent of chemical B. Fertiliser Y is composed of 40 per cent of A and 60 per cent of B. He requires at least 1000 kg of X and 1500 kg of Y and he has available 3000 kg of A and 2500 kg of B. If he makes x kg of X and y kg of Y, find four inequalities satisfied by x and y which express all the above conditions.

Sketch the region representing possible values of x and y and deduce that he can, in fact, make 5500 kg of fertiliser satisfying the above requirements. What are the amounts of X and Y he would make to achieve this? AEB

11 The manager of a boat-building yard decided to build only two types, a sailing boat type (X) and a motor boat type (Y). His decision about the respective numbers x and y of these types to have under construction at any one time is governed by the following facts:

(i) He has 300 square metres of floor-space. A boat of type X needs 25 m^2 of floor and a boat of type Y needs 30 m^2.

(ii) He cannot afford to have more than £1000 tied up in stores and materials for building, of which £200-worth will consist of general stores and the rest will be £80 for each X-boat and £50 for each Y-boat.
(iii) He has not sufficient skilled hands to build more than 7 X-boats.

State the inequalities (apart from $x \geqslant 0$, $y \geqslant 0$) which govern the values of x and y. Draw a diagram on graph paper to show clearly the region in which possible solutions for (x, y) are to be found. Show that one of the conditions does not affect the result and can therefore be disregarded.

If the cash profit on a boat of each type is the same and they take the same time to build, find what solution or solutions to his problem will yield the greatest total profit. O

12 A farmer wishes to make a rectangular enclosure of area 175 m^2 against an existing straight fence, using not more than 50 m of wire-netting. Suppose each of the sides at right angles to the fence measures x m and the remaining side measures y m.

(i) Write down an inequality involving x, y and 50 and draw its graph for relevant values of x and y, shading the region in which (x, y) *cannot* lie.
(ii) Write down an equation involving x, y and 175 and draw its graph on the same diagram.
(iii) State the set of values of x which give a solution to the problem.
OC (SMP)

13 The diagram (Page 46) is the plan of a running-track inside a field, l metres long and w metres wide. A and B are y metres apart and are the centres of two semicircles, radius x metres. The track is t metres wide and the spectators' enclosure on one side is d metres wide. The inside edge of the track must be 400 metres. Show that $y + \pi x = 200$.

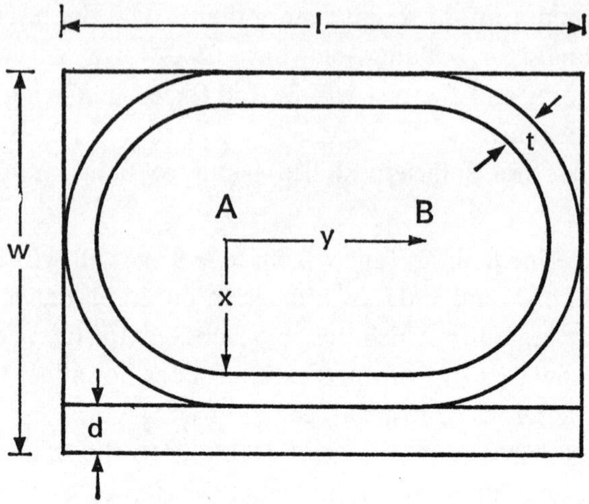

If $l = 170$, $w = 120$, $t > 8$, $d > 10$, find two inequalities for x and y other than $x > 0$, $y > 0$.

On a graph:

(*a*) show the restrictions on x and y imposed by the inequalities;
(*b*) draw the line $y + \pi x = 200$;
(*c*) indicate the line segment for which the inequalities are satisfied; state the extremes of ordered pairs (x, y) for possible running-tracks under these conditions. L

Chapter Four

1 Say for each of the following statements whether it is correct or incorrect.
$(x + 2)$ is a factor of
(*a*) $x + 3$; (*b*) $2x^2 + x + 6$; (*c*) $-2 - x$; (*d*) $x^2 + 4$;
(*e*) $x^2 + 3x + 2$. O

2 Factorise $9x^2 + 6x - 8$ where x is a real number.

3 Factorise completely: (i) $12x^2 + 22x + 6$
(ii) $9 - 24x + 12x^2$
where x is a real number.

4 (i) One factor of $x^2 + x - 2$ is $(x - 1)$. State the other factor.
(ii) State the two possible values of x for which $x^2 + x - 2 = 0$.
(iii) State the value of x for which *both* $x^2 + x - 2 = 0$ *and* $x^2 + 5x + 6 = 0$. OC (SMP)

5 Which of the following statements about the expression $x^2 + 2x - 8$ are true, and which false?
(*a*) Its value is -11 when $x = -1$.
(*b*) It may be written in the form $(x + 1)^2 - 9$.
(*c*) It is the product of $(x - 4)$ and $(x + 2)$.
(*d*) It has the value 0 when $x = 2$.
(*e*) It has the value 0 for some value of x other than $x = 2$.
OC (SMP)

6 Factorise the following expressions:
(i) $27x^2 - 12y^2$,
(ii) $3xz + 3z + x + 1$. AEB

7 Express $(x - 1)^2 + 2(x - 1)$ as a product of two factors. SC

8 Factorise completely
(i) $(x-4)^2-16$;
(ii) $2x^3+5x^2+2x$;
(iii) $3\sin^2 x+\sin x\cos x-2\cos^2 x$. AEB

9 If $9x^2+30x+k$ is a perfect square, state the value of k. L

10 Given that p and q are positive integers, find p and q such that $x^2+10x+p=(x+q)^2$. SC

11 (In this question x belongs to the set of real numbers.)
(i) The statement $(x+3)^2=x^2+6x+9$ is true for (*a*) all values of x; (*b*) only two values of x; (*c*) only one value of x; (*d*) no value of x.
(ii) The statement $(x+3)^2=x^2+4x+6$ is true for (*a*) all values of x; (*b*) only two values of x; (*c*) only one value of x; (*d*) no value of x. OC (SMP)

12 Given that $a^2+b^2=34$, and that $a+b=8$, find the value of ab. OC (SMP)

13 Given that $a+b=5$ and $ab=2$, show that $a^2+b^2=21$ and $a^2b^2=4$. Find a^4+b^4 and a^4b^4.

Given also that $b<\frac{a}{10}$, use your value of a^4+b^4 to obtain an approximation for a and hence b.

Solve $x^2-5x+2=0$ correct to two decimal places. L

14 Express kx^2-ky^2 in fully factorised form. SC

15 Factorise completely p^4-16. By taking $p=7$ find the prime factors of 2385.

16 Evaluate x^2-y^2, when $x=4\frac{3}{8}$, $y=3\frac{7}{8}$.

17 Express 21^2-18^2 as the product of factors. OC (SMP)

18 If $44^2 - 41^2 = 3p$, state the value of p. OC (SMP)

19 Evaluate $(17{\cdot}4)^2 - (7{\cdot}4)^2$ exactly. OC (SMP)

20 Which of the following statements are true and which are false?

(*a*) $\dfrac{3}{n} - \dfrac{n}{3} = \dfrac{3 - n^2}{3n}$.

(*b*) If $a + b \neq 0$, $\dfrac{2a}{a+b} + \dfrac{2b}{a+b} = 2$. SC

21 Simplify

$$\frac{m(p+q)+p+q}{p+q}.$$ C

22 The expression $\dfrac{p}{q} + \dfrac{r}{s}$ is

(*a*) equal to $\dfrac{ps+qr}{qs}$;

(*b*) equal to $\dfrac{pr}{qs}$;

(*c*) equal to $\dfrac{p+r}{q+s}$;

(*d*) not equal to any one of the answers in (*a*), (*b*) and (*c*). AEB

23 It is given that

$$\frac{1}{a} = \frac{1}{p} + \frac{1}{q}.$$

(i) Write the right-hand side as a single fraction in terms of p and q.
(ii) If $p = \frac{1}{2}$ and $q = \frac{1}{4}$, find a.
(iii) If $a > p$ state, with a reason, whether q is positive or negative.

OC (SMP)

24 Given that $p + q = 5$ and $pq = 3$, find the values of $\dfrac{1}{p} + \dfrac{1}{q}$ and $p^2 + q^2$. SU

25 Factorise $4x^2 - 1$ and $2x^2 + 5x - 3$. Hence, or otherwise, simplify

$$\frac{4x^2 - 1}{2x + 1} - \frac{2x^2 + 5x - 3}{2x - 1}, x \neq \pm\tfrac{1}{2}.$$ SC

26 Given that $d = \dfrac{k - m}{t}$, change the subject of the formula to k. SC

27 Make W the subject of the formula $t = 15W + 20$. O

28 If $K = \sqrt{\left(\dfrac{PT}{S + T}\right)}$, express T in terms of the other letters. AEB

29 Make g the subject of the formula

$$t = 2\pi\sqrt{\left(\frac{h^2 + g^2}{h^2}\right)}$$

30 Make c the subject of the formula

$$T = \frac{3}{\sqrt{c}}.$$ OC (SMP)

31 If $p = \dfrac{20a}{\sqrt{q}}$,

(i) find p when $a = 3$ and $q = 100$;
(ii) express q in terms of a and p;
(iii) find q when $a = \frac{1}{5}$ and $p = \frac{1}{3}$. NI

32 Make x the subject of the formula

$$z = \frac{1 + \lambda x}{1 - \lambda x}.$$ AEB

33 Make V the subject of the formula

$$r = \frac{R(E - V)}{V}$$

34 If $y = \frac{x^2}{2} - \frac{1}{3}$ then x is

(*a*) equal to $\pm\sqrt{\left(\frac{y+2}{3}\right)}$; (*b*) equal to $\pm\sqrt{(6y+1)}$,

(*c*) equal to $\pm\sqrt{\left(\frac{6y-2}{3}\right)}$;

(*d*) not equal to any one of the answers in (*a*), (*b*) and (*c*). AEB

35 It is given that

$$T = \frac{3W - a}{2a}.$$

Which of the following statements are true and which are false?

(*a*) The formula may also be written

$$T = \frac{3W}{2a} - \frac{1}{2}.$$

(*b*) $T = 0$ when $a = 3W$.

(*c*) $W = \frac{2aT}{3} + a$.

(*d*) If $a = W$, then $T = 1$. OC (SMP)

36 You are given that $Ps = \frac{1}{2}mv^2 - \frac{1}{2}mu^2$. Indicate which of the following deductions are correct:

(*a*) $\frac{2Ps}{m} = u^2 - v^2$;

(*b*) $s = \frac{m(v^2 - u^2)}{2P}$.

(*c*) $P = 0$ and $m \neq 0 \Rightarrow v$ is numerically equal to u;

(*d*) $-v = u \Rightarrow P = 0$ or $s = 0$. OC (SMP)

37 A, P and R are positive real numbers and n is a positive integer. If $R = \sqrt[n]{(A/P)}$, express A in terms of P, R and n.
Find the difference between A and P when $P = 10\,000$, $R = 1{\cdot}04$ and $n = 2$. L

38 Each of the following arguments is at some stage incorrect. Copy out the arguments and in each case cross out the first incorrect step, and write a correct form of that step.

(i)
$$x^2 = a^2 - a^2w^2,$$
$$a^2w^2 = a^2 - x^2,$$
$$aw = a - x,$$
$$w = \frac{a - x}{a}.$$

(ii)
$$c = ax + b,$$
$$\frac{c}{a} = x + b,$$
$$x = \frac{c}{a} - b.$$

OC (SMP)

39 Each of the following arguments is at some stage incorrect. Copy out the arguments and in each case cross out the first incorrect step and write a correct form of that step.

(i)
$$E = a(x + by),$$
$$E = ax + aby,$$
$$aby = E - ax,$$
$$b = \frac{E - ax}{ay},$$
$$b = \frac{E - x}{y}.$$

(ii)
$$\frac{aw + a^2}{L} = b,$$
$$\frac{aw}{L} = b - a^2,$$
$$w = \frac{L(b - a^2)}{a}.$$

OC (SMP)

40 Calculate V from the formula
$$V = d^2\sqrt{H},$$
given that $d = 0{\cdot}83$ and $H = 1{\cdot}50$. Answer to two decimal places.

SC

41 The strength formula for gear teeth is $W = \dfrac{SFY}{P}$.

Make S the subject of the formula and calculate S (to two significant figures) when $W = 1000$, $F = 1{\cdot}25$, $Y = 0{\cdot}336$ and $P = 8$.

42 Is the following statement true or false?

When $a = 3$, $b = -2$, then $\dfrac{a-b}{a+b} = -5$. SC

43 Given that $y = \dfrac{15}{x}$, calculate y when

(i) $x = \frac{1}{2}$;
(ii) $x = 9$, giving your answer correct to two decimal places. O

44 (i) The energy of an electron at rest is $E = mc^2$ units where $m = 7{\cdot}60 \times 10^{-28}$ and $c = 3{\cdot}00 \times 10^{10}$. Evaluate E, putting your result in standard form.

(ii) When the electron is moving with velocity v its energy is obtained by multiplying E by a factor f, where

$$f = \frac{1}{\sqrt{\left(1 - \dfrac{v^2}{c^2}\right)}}.$$

Find the numerical value of f if $v = \frac{1}{2}c$.

(iii) An *approximate* formula for f is $1 + \dfrac{v^2}{2c^2}$. What is the error, to the nearest one per cent, in using this formula for the case $v = \frac{1}{2}c$?

(iv) Using the correct formula obtain an expression for v in terms of c and f. O

45 The mass of a metal cylinder is given by $M = \pi(R^2 - r^2)ld$. Make r the subject of the formula and calculate r (to two significant figures) when $\pi = 3{\cdot}142$, $R = 4{\cdot}5$, $M = 11\,190$, $l = 50$ and $d = 8{\cdot}9$.

46 The electrical resistance R of a wire varies directly as the length L. Calculate the entry s in the table.

L	80	120
R	3·2	s

SC

47 Is the following statement true or false?

According to the table u varies as t.

t	0	4	5	10
u	0	10	12·5	25

SC

48 Some corresponding values of f and w are shown in the table:

f	100	200	300	500
w	30	15	10	6

Which one or more of the following is a possible relation between f and w?

(*a*) w is directly proportional to f;
(*b*) w is inversely proportional to f;
(*c*) $w = \frac{3}{10}f$;
(*d*) $fw = 3000$. OC (SMP)

49 The following figures are taken from the dial of a radio set:

Wavelength (w metres)	200	300	400	500	600
Frequency (f kilocycles)	1500	1000	750	600	500

State how f varies with w and write down a formula connecting them. OC (SMP)

50 If $y \propto x^2$,

(i) what happens to y when x is trebled?
(ii) Copy and complete the table of values shown:

x	2	3	
y	12		108

NI

51 If $y \propto x^2$ and $y = 12$ when $x = 2$, find y when $x = 5$.

OC (SMP)

52 Some corresponding values of x and y are shown in the table:

x	1	5	10	20
y	5	125	500	2000

Which one or more of the following could be true?
(*a*) $y \propto x^2$; (*b*) $y = 5x$; (*c*) $y = 5x^2$; (*d*) $y = 30x - 25$.
OC (SMP)

53 If $y \propto x^3$ copy and complete this table of values:

x	2	6	8	
y	0·1			12·5

If $y = ax^3$, what is the value of a? OC (SMP)

54 $x \propto (1/y^2)$ and $x = 3$ when $y = 4$. Find x when $y = 8$.
OC (SMP)

55 If $x \propto y^3$ and the value of y is increased from 3 to 4, express this as a percentage increase and calculate the percentage change in x. Name two quantities one of which varies as the cube of the other. OC (SMP)

56

x	5	4	2	1
y	4	$6\frac{1}{4}$	25	100

There is an integral value of n not greater than 3 for which the above table of values is consistent with the statement that y is inversely proportional to x^n.
(i) State the value of n.
(ii) Give the relation between x and y in a simple form.
OC (SMP)

57 It is known that y and x, which are both positive, obey one of the following laws: $y \propto x$, $y \propto x^2$, $y \propto 1/x$, $y \propto 1/x^2$. Part of a table of corresponding values of x and y is as follows:

x	2	5	10		50
y	20		500	2000	

State which of the above laws connects x and y.

Copy and complete the table, putting in the values which have been omitted. L

58 A quantity p varies directly as q and inversely as r. If $p = 8$ when $(q, r) = (5, 20)$ calculate p when $(q, r) = (10, 10)$. SU

Chapter Five

1 Which of the following points are equidistant from (0, 0) and (0, 1)?

A (1, 1), B (1, 0), C (5, $\frac{1}{2}$), D ($\frac{1}{2}$, 1). SU

2 A straight line passes through the points (0, 3) and (2, 11). Write down:

(i) its gradient;
(ii) its equation. C

3 Is the following statement true or false?
The gradient of the line $2x + y = 1$ is 2. SC

4 What is the gradient of the straight line whose equation is $5x + 2y = 7$? OC (SMP)

5

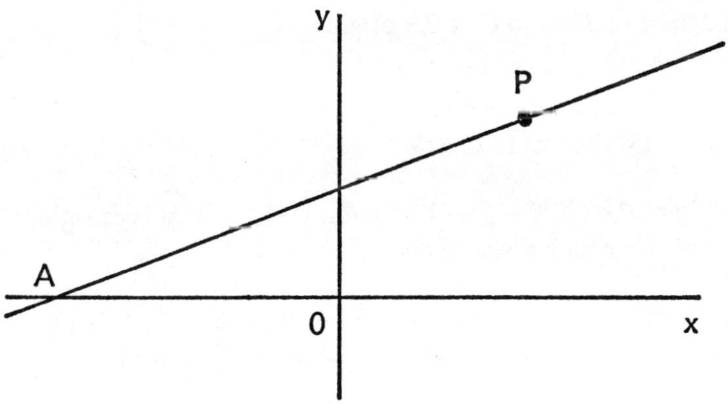

The figure shows the graph of the relation $3y = x + 4$.
State the coordinates of the point A.

The point P on the line is equidistant from the two axes. State the coordinates of P. C

6 Find the equation of the straight line joining $A\,(0, 3)$ and $B\,(3, 9)$. The line AB meets the straight line whose equation is $x + 2y = 11$ at R. Calculate the coordinates of R.

If T is the point $(13, 0)$, calculate the length of RT. C

7 Write down:

(i) the gradient of the straight line $2x + 3y = 7$;

(ii) the coordinates of the point on this line which has -1 as its y coordinate. O

8 P is the point $(3, 1)$. N is the foot of the perpendicular from P to the line $x + 2y = 10$. The equation of the line PN is

(*a*) $x + 2y = 5$; (*b*) $2x + y = 7$; (*c*) $2x - y = 5$;

(*d*) none of these. NI

9 Calculate the area of triangle PQR where P is $(3, 3)$, Q is $(4, -1)$ and R is $(-8, -4)$.

10 Point $R\,(10, 7)$ is reflected in the line $y = x$ to give point S, and point R is reflected in line $y = -x$ to give point T. M is the midpoint of RS and O is the origin.

Find: (1) the coordinates of S;

(2) the coordinates of T;

(3) the length of OM.

11 Point P is $(7, 13)$, Q is $(10, 5)$, R is $(-6, -3)$. M is the midpoint of QR. Calculate distance PM.

12 Point P is $(6, 7)$, Q is $(-1, 5)$, R is $(-4, -4)$, S is $(3, -2)$. Prove PQ is parallel to SR and QR is parallel to PS.

13 A is the point $(-4, 0)$ and B is the point $(0, 2)$. If P is the point (x, y), find expressions for AP^2 and BP^2. Hence deduce the simplest equation of the locus of points P such that $AP = BP$.

SC

14

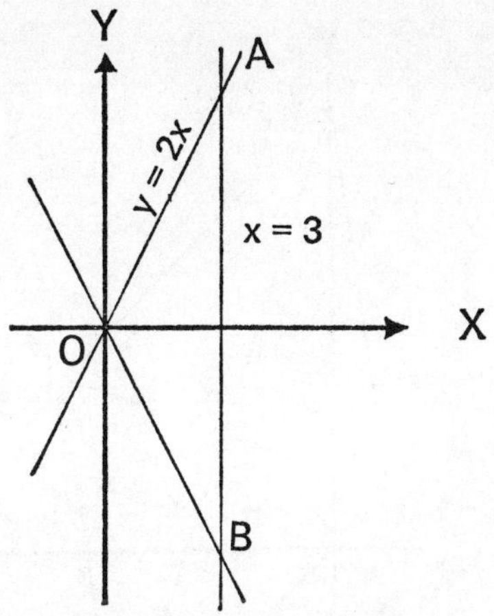

The line $y = 2x$ meets the line $x = 3$ in the point A.

(*a*) Give the coordinates of A.

(*b*) The x-axis is the axis of symmetry of triangle OAB. What special type of triangle is triangle OAB?

(*c*) State the equation of OB.

(*d*) What are the coordinates of B?

(*e*) Write down the restrictions on x for (x, y) to be a point inside triangle OAB. SC

15 An aircraft on test flight is given its position as an ordered pair (x, y) showing the distances in kilometres East and North of the control tower. At the end of the initial climb, the time is exactly noon and the aircraft is in level flight over the position A (2, 4). After cruising at constant speed relative to the ground, the point B (11, 16) is passed in 3 minutes. At what time is the aircraft due over C (29, 40)? The aircraft turns at C in the direction of a beacon sited at (93, −8) and flies for 8 minutes. At this time the aircraft is over point E, whence it flies in the direction of base (0, 0). What are the coordinates of E and what is the expected time of arrival over the control tower? SU

16 $PQRS$ is a rhombus with diagonals intersecting at T. P is the point (−1, 1), Q is the point (0, 8) and R is the point (5, 3).

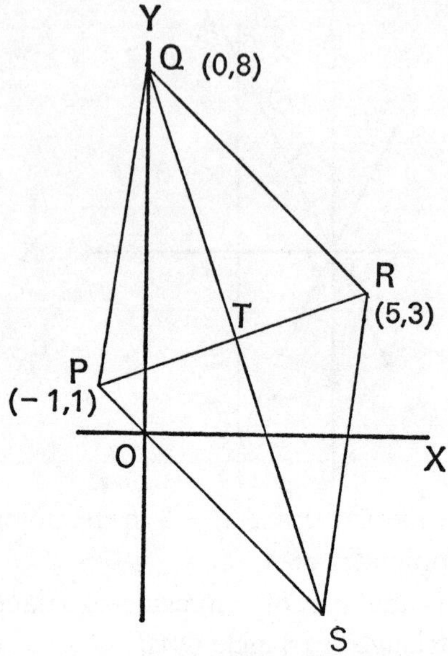

(*a*) Calculate the length of a side of the rhombus, leaving the answer in surd form.
(*b*) State the coordinates of *T*.
(*c*) If $a°$ represents the size of $\angle RQT$, express the size of $\angle QPS$ in terms of *a*.
(*d*) Give the components of the vector represented by $\overrightarrow{QR}$.
(*e*) If a tiling is made of rhombuses congruent to *PQRS*, with *PQRS* one of the tiles, determine the number *q* such that point $(17, q)$ is a tile corner on the line *PR*. SC

17 The equation of a circle is $x^2 + y^2 = 9$.
(*a*) Write down the coordinates of the centre.
(*b*) Give the area of the circle as a multiple of π.
(*c*) The circle cuts the *x*-axis in *A* and *C* and the *y*-axis in *B* and *D*. Find the area of the square *ABCD*.
(*d*) If the point $(h, 0)$ is inside the circle, give the range of values of *h*.
(*e*) Find the equation of the circle with the same centre and radius double that of the given circle. SC

18 The diagram shows a pair of coordinate axes Ox, Oy and a point A on Oy such that $OA = 1$.

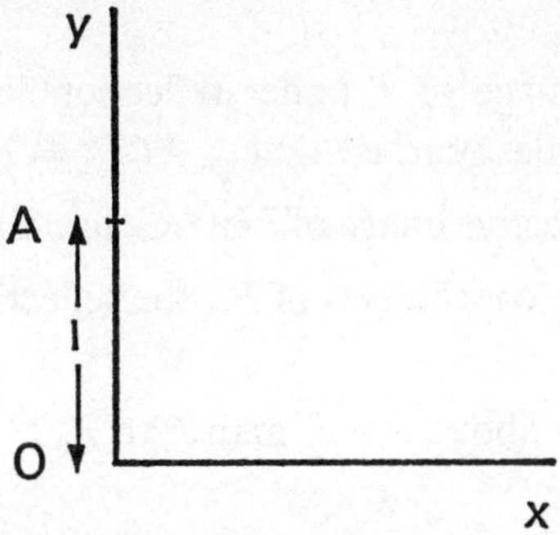

If polar coordinates are taken with O as the origin and Ox as the initial line, then

(i) the point A is correctly described in polar coordinates by

(*a*) (0, 1); (*b*) (1, 0); (*c*) (1, 90°); (*d*) (1, 0°)

(ii) the polar equation of Oy is

(*a*) $\theta = 0°$; (*b*) $\theta = 90°$; (*c*) $x = 0$; (*d*) $y = 0$

(iii) the polar equation $r = 1$ represents:

(*a*) a straight line through A parallel to Ox;

(*b*) a circle on OA as diameter;

(*c*) a circle centre O, passing through A;

(*d*) none of these. NI

19

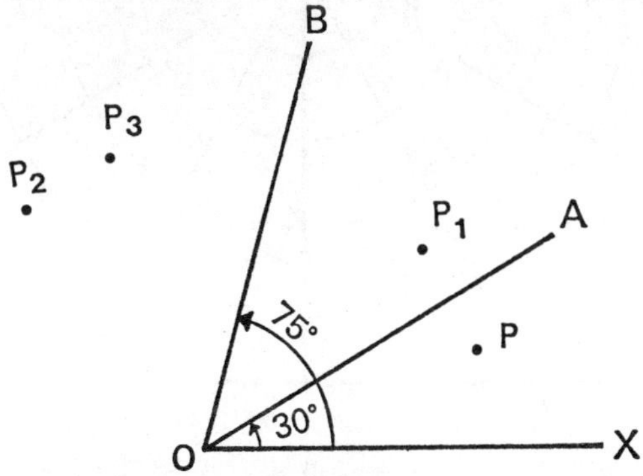

In the diagram, P is the point $(r, a°)$ in polar coordinates with respect to origin O and initial line OX. $\angle XOA = 30°$ and $\angle XOB = 75°$.

(i) If P_1 is the image of P under reflection in OA, show by a sketch with all angles marked that $\angle XOP_1 = (60 - a)°$.

(ii) If P_2 is the reflective image of P in OB, find the size of $\angle XOP_2$.

(iii) Find the polar coordinates of P_3, the reflective image of P_1 in OB.

(iv) What rotation about O will map P to P_3? SC

20

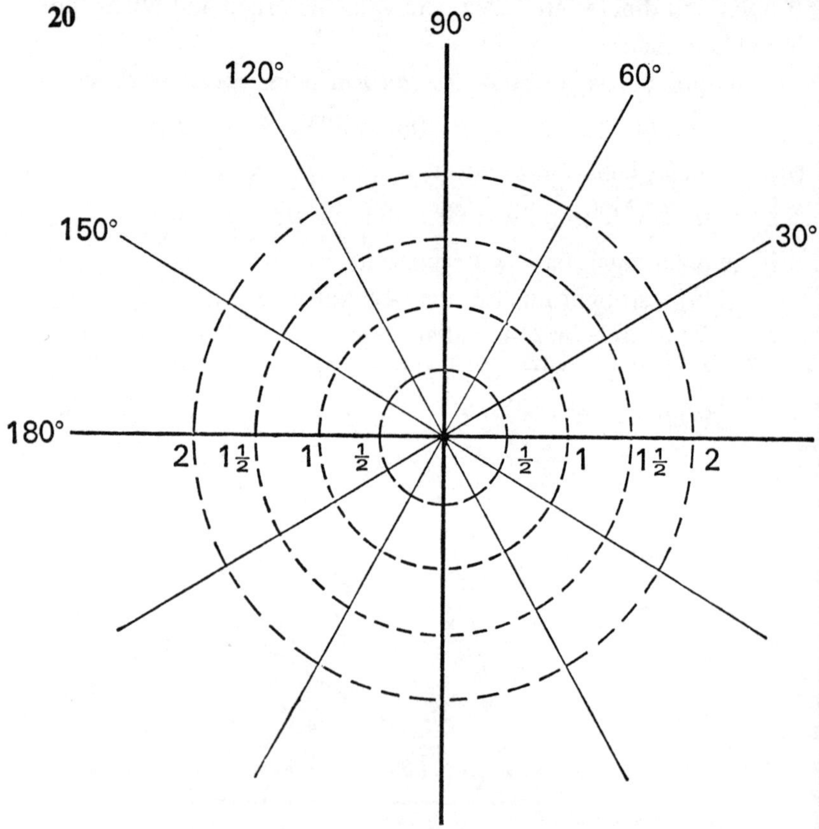

Copy the diagram and illustrate the set

$$\left\{(r, \theta°); r = \frac{20}{\theta}, 10 < \theta < 100\right\}.$$ AEB

21 Copy the diagram in question 20 and sketch the curve whose equation in polar coordinates is $r = 2 \cos \theta$. AEB

Chapter Six

1 If $f: x \to 4x^3 + 1$ and $g: x \to 6x^2$ and f' and g' are defined as derived functions, show that

$$(a)\, f'(0) = g'(0); \quad (b)\, f'(1) = g'(1).$$ L

2 (i) Find $\dfrac{dy}{dx}$ if

$$(a)\ y = 4x^2 + 5x - 3; \quad (b)\ \tfrac{1}{2}y = \tfrac{1}{2}.$$

(ii) Find the gradient of the curve $y = 7x - x^2$ at the point (2, 10).
NI

3 The rate of change of $3(x^2 - 1) + x(2x + 1)$ with respect to x at $x = 2$ is
(*a*) 18; (*b*) 16; (*c*) 20; (*d*) not equal to any of the values in (*a*), (*b*) or (*c*). AEB

4 Show that the expression $1 + 12x - x^3$ increases in value as x increases from -2 to $+2$ and after that diminishes as x increases.
AEB

5 The function $y = x^3 + 3x^2 + 2x + 4$ has

(*a*) three; (*b*) two; (*c*) one; (*d*) no

turning-points (i.e. maxima or minima). AEB

6 (*a*) The function $y = 2x^2 - 3x + 5$ has one turning-point; find it and determine whether it is a maximum or minimum.
(*b*) (i) If the radius of a circle changes from r to $r + h$, what is the average rate of change of the area of the circle with respect to the radius?
(ii) Find the instantaneous rate of change of the area when $r = 2$ units of length. AEB

7 Is it true or false that $x^2 - 3x - 7$ has a maximum value at $x = 1\frac{1}{2}$? AEB

8 A condition for $y = ax^2 + bx + c$ to have a turning-point which is a maximum is that

(*a*) $a > 0$; (*b*) $a < 0$; (*c*) $a > b$; (*d*) $c < 0$; (*e*) $b^2 > 4ac$. AEB

9 Water is flowing continuously through a pipe, the rate of discharge at time t s being w m³/s where

$$w = 3t^2 - 6t + 6.$$

(i) Find the time at which the rate of discharge of water is a minimum.
(ii) Calculate the volume of water discharged in the first 4 s.
(iii) Given that the cross-sectional area of the pipe is 1 m² and that it is full of water, write down a formula for the speed of flow of the water after t s. State the unit in which your result is expressed. NI

10 Find the derivative of y with respect to x if:

(i) $y = x^2 - 4$; (ii) $y = (x + 3)(x^2 - 2)$; (iii) $y = \int_0^x z^2 dz$. AEB

11 If $y = x^2$, calculate:

(i) the value of $\frac{dy}{dx}$ when $x = 7$;
(ii) the gradient of the chord joining the point on the curve where $x = 7$ to the point on the curve where $x = 7{\cdot}03$;
(iii) the percentage error in taking the value of this gradient for the gradient of the curve at $x = 7$;
(iv) the area enclosed between the chord and the curve. AEB

12 Find a if the gradients of the graphs of $f: x \to x^2 - x^3$ and $g: x \to x - ax^2$ are equal at $x = \frac{1}{3}$, and find another value of x for which the graphs have the same gradient.

Find the area of the region between the graphs and the ordinates for the two values of x for which their gradients are the same. L

13 (i) Sketch the graph of the curve $y = 5 + 3x - 2x^2$.
(ii) The points A and B on the curve correspond to $x = 0$ and $x = 2\frac{1}{2}$.

Find the area bounded by the chord AB and the portion of the curve above it.
(iii) Find the coordinates of the point on the curve at which the tangent is parallel to AB. AEB

14 The gradient of the graph of a function at a point (x, y) is $3x^2 + 4x$ and the graph passes through point P (1, 5).
Find:

(1) the function;
(2) the coordinates of the points L, M on the graph at which the gradient is zero;
(3) the coordinates of points S, T on the curve at which the gradient is 4.

15 In the range $0 \leqslant x \leqslant 3$, the gradient of a curve, at any point (x, y) on it, increases steadily with x. If the curve also passes through the origin illustrate its shape by means of a sketch on a copy of the diagram below. C

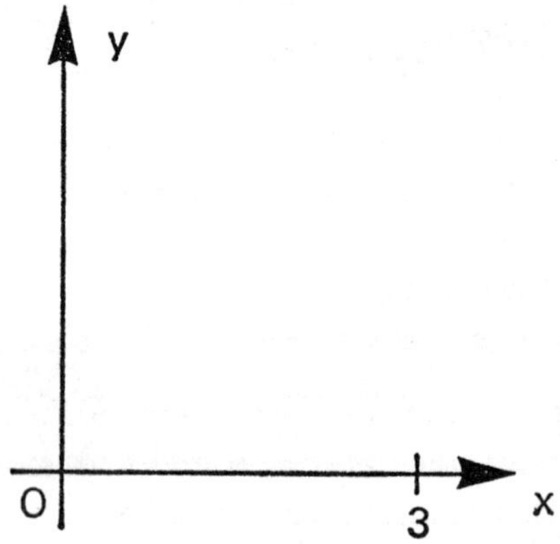

16 Find y if

$$\frac{dy}{dx} = 2x - \frac{3}{x^2}$$

and $y = 9$ when $x = 3$. AEB

17 (*a*) On a copy of the diagram below sketch the graph of $y = x^2 - 4x + 3$ between $x = 0$ and $x = 4$.

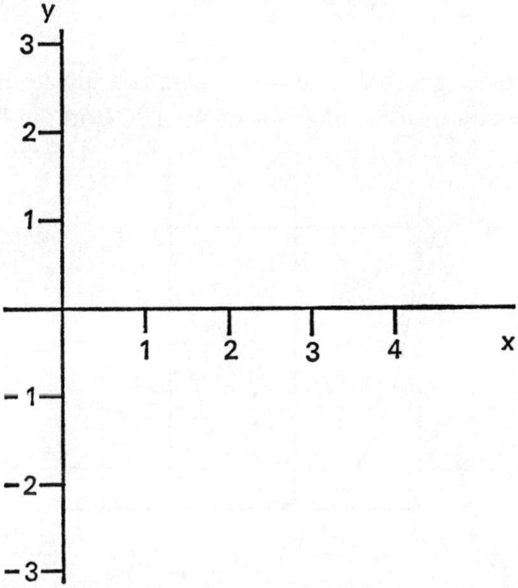

(*b*) Find the total area of the two regions bounded by this curve, the x-axis between $x = 0$ and $x = 2$, and the ordinates at $x = 0$ and $x = 2$. AEB

18 Show by a sketch the part of the graph of

$$y = 4 + 3x - x^2$$

which lies above the axis of x. Find by calculation (i) the greatest value of y and (ii) the area enclosed between the x-axis and the graph. O

19 Sketch the graph of the function $y = x^2 - x - 6$ and find the area cut off from it by the x-axis.

20 Sketch the graph of the function $y = 2 + x - x^2$ and calculate the area between the graph and the x-axis.

21 Find where the straight-line graph of the function $y = 4$ cuts the graph of function $y = 5x - x^2$ and calculate the area between them.

22 Archimedes gave the rule that a parabola divides in the ratio 1 to 2 the area of a rectangle (such as $ABCD$ in the figure) into

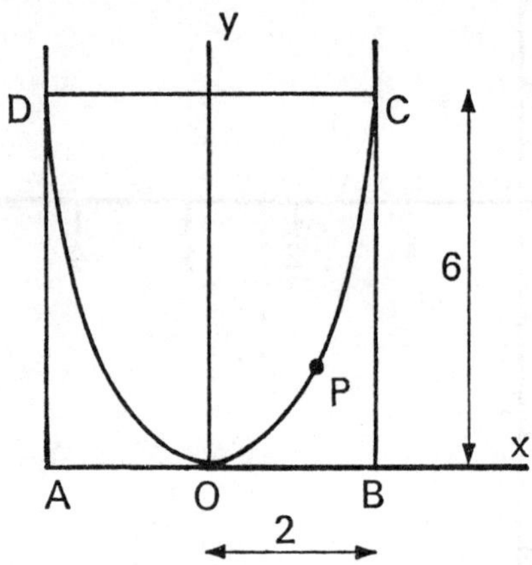

which it fits symmetrically. Taking a parabola situated as shown to have an equation $y = kx^2$ with respect to the given axes, find the value of k in this instance and verify Archimedes' rule.

Find the coordinates of the point P where the tangent to the parabola is parallel to the line OC. O

23 The diagram (Page 69) shows part of the curve $y = x^2$. P is the point (2, 4). M and N are the feet of the perpendiculars from P to the x- and y-axes as shown.

(i) the area of the region OPN is

(a) $\int_0^4 y dy$; (b) $\int_0^2 x dy$; (c) $8 - \int_0^2 x^2 dx$; (d) $8 - \int_0^4 x dy$

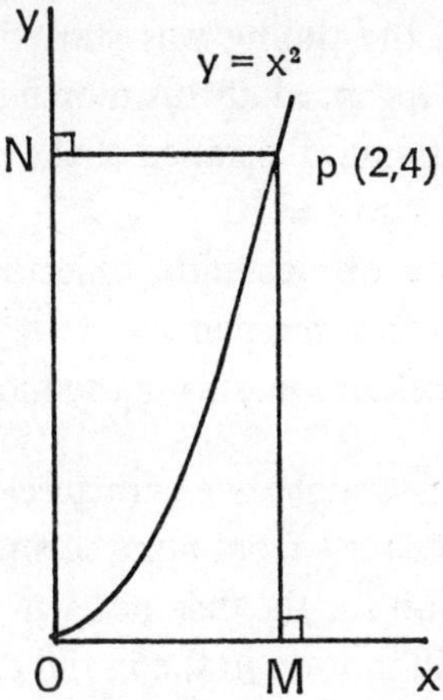

(ii) The volume swept out by rotating *OPM* about the *x*-axis is

(a) $\int_0^2 \pi x^2 dx$; (b) $\int_0^2 \pi y^2 dx$; (c) $\int_0^4 \pi y^2 dy$; (d) none of these.

NI

24 Calculate the volume of the solid of revolution formed when the area between the graph of $y = x$, the x-axis, $x = 0$ and $x = 3$ is rotated through 360° about the x-axis.

25 Find by integration the volume of the solid formed by complete rotation about the x-axis of the area between the graph of $y = \sqrt{x}$, the x-axis, $x = 0$ and $x = 4$.

26 (i) Sketch the sine curve between 0° and 360°.
(ii) Given that when x is in degrees

$$\int_a^b \sin x \, dx = \left[-\frac{180}{\pi} \cos x\right]_a^b,$$

find the total area of the regions enclosed by the sine curve and the x-axis. AEB

27 An object moved along a straight track so that its distance S metres from a fixed point P of the track, t seconds after starting timing the motion, was given by $S = 5 + 4t - t^2$.
(i) Show that when the timing was started the object was 5 m from P and calculate its speed at this moment.
(ii) Calculate the maximum distance of the object from P during the time interval $t = 0$ to $t = 5$.
(iii) Calculate the value of t when the object returned to P and the speed of the object at that moment.
(iv) Calculate the acceleration during the motion.

28 A point moves in a straight line with acceleration $(6 - 4t)\text{m/s}^2$. When $t = 0$ the point starts from point A with speed 8 m/s.
(i) Find an expression for the distance x m from A at time t s.
(ii) For how long will motion in the initial direction continue?
(iii) At what distance from A will the direction of motion be reversed?

29 The velocity v m/s of a moving body after t seconds is given by
(i) for $0 \leqslant t \leqslant 1$, $v = 3t^2 - 2t^3$;
(ii) for $t \geqslant 1$, $v = 16t^3 - 60t^2 + 72t - 27$.
Show that:

(*a*) when $t = 0$, the velocity and acceleration are both zero;
(*b*) when $t = 1$, the velocities given by (i) and (ii) are equal and the accelerations given by (i) and (ii) are equal;
(*c*) when $t = \frac{3}{2}$, $v = 0$.

Calculate the distance covered in the interval $0 \leqslant t \leqslant \frac{3}{2}$. L

30 The area under a speed–time graph represents
(*a*) acceleration; (*b*) distance; (*c*) neither of these.
AEB

31 The diagram (Page 71) shows part of a distance–time graph. Which of the following statements are true, which false?

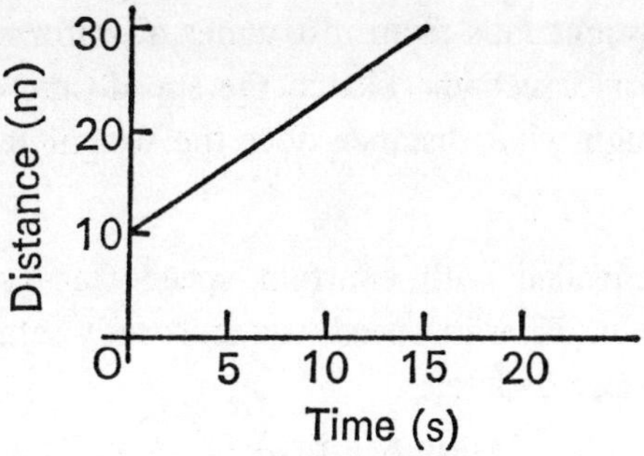

(*a*) The body starts with velocity 10 m/s.
(*b*) The body starts with velocity 2 m/s.
(*c*) The body has no acceleration.
(*d*) The distance travelled in the first 15 s is 30 m. OC (SMP)

32 An electric train accelerates uniformly from rest to 12 m/s in 10 seconds. Sketch a speed-time curve for the motion. What is the distance in metres travelled by the train during this acceleration? SU

33 A train starts from rest and accelerates at a uniform rate for 60 seconds, at the end of which time it is travelling at a speed of 30 m/s. It then travels at this constant speed. On a copy of the diagram draw the graph of speed against time, and calculate

(i) the speed after 10 s;
(ii) the distance travelled in the first 120 s. OC (SMP)

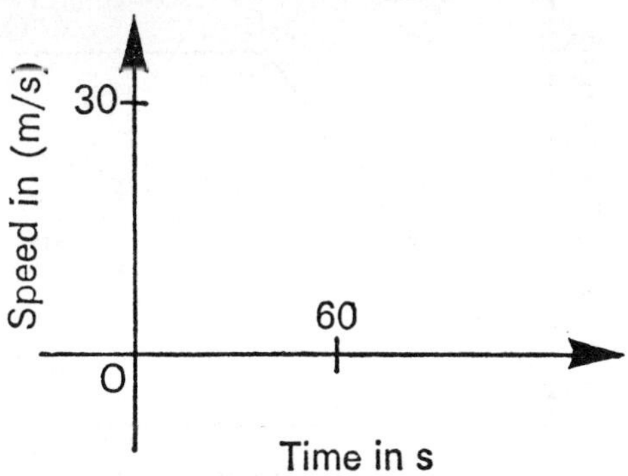

34 A heavy weight falls from rest under a uniform acceleration of 9·81 m/s^2 for 5 seconds. Sketch the speed-time curve for the motion. Through what distance does the weight fall during the motion? SU

35 A body travelled with constant speed for 6 s, covering a distance of 20 m. Then its speed was uniformly retarded and the body came to rest 3 s later.

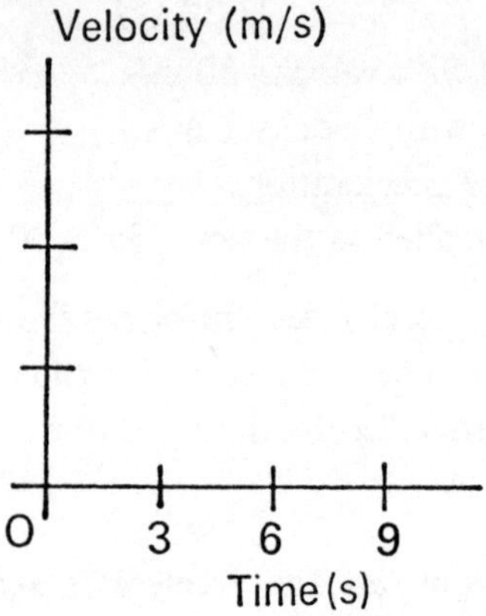

(i) Draw a graph showing the relation between velocity and time during these 9 s. (Graduate the velocity axis.)
(ii) Calculate the total distance travelled in this time.

OC (SMP)

36

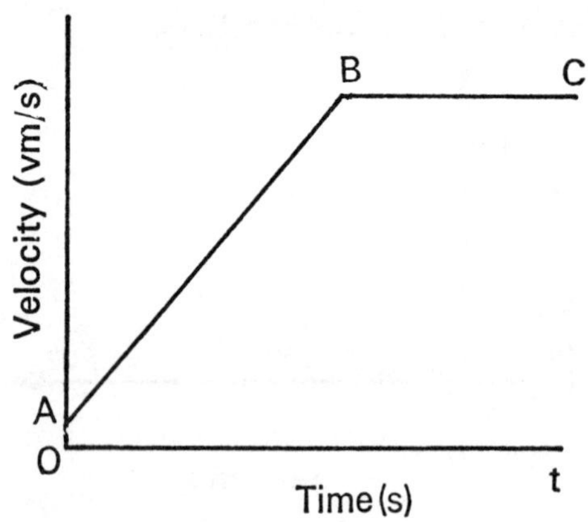

For the first 6 s of its motion the velocity of a body is given by the formula

$$v = 2 + 3t.$$

Subsequently the velocity remains constant, the velocity-time graph being the line *ABC*.

Find:

(i) the velocity corresponding to the point *B*;

(ii) the average velocity for the first 2 s;

(iii) the acceleration during the first 2 s. O

37 The graph shows the velocity *v* m/s of a car after *t* s.

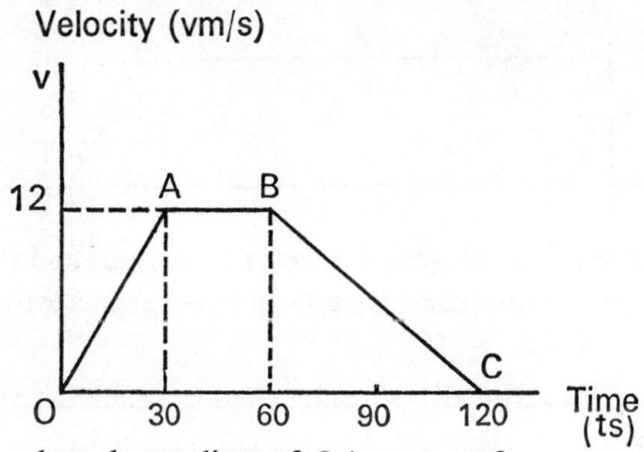

(i) What does the gradient of *OA* represent?

(ii) What is the velocity of the car when $t = 90$?

(iii) How far does the car travel between $t = 30$ and $t = 60$?

NI

38

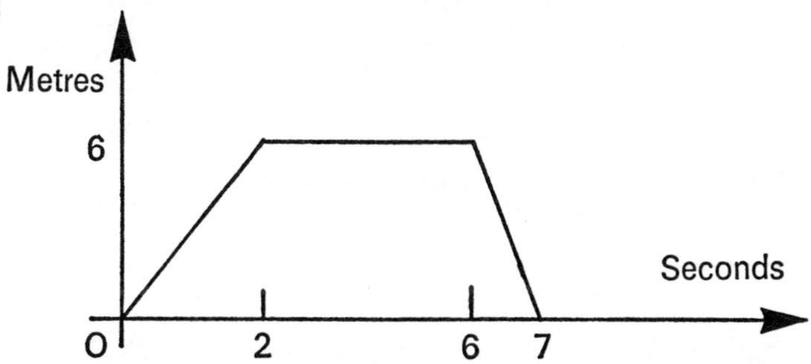

A particle moves in a straight line in such a way that its distance in metres from a fixed point is indicated by the graph.

(i) The final distance from the fixed point is

(*a*) 0 m; (*b*) 6 m; (*c*) 12 m; (*d*) 33 m.

(ii) The velocity during the last second is

(*a*) 6 m/s; (*b*) −6 m/s; (*c*) 3 m/s; (*d*) −3 m/s.

(iii) The average velocity over the first 6 seconds is

(*a*) 1 m/s; (*b*) $1\frac{1}{2}$ m/s; (*c*) 3 m/s; (*d*) 5 m/s. O

39

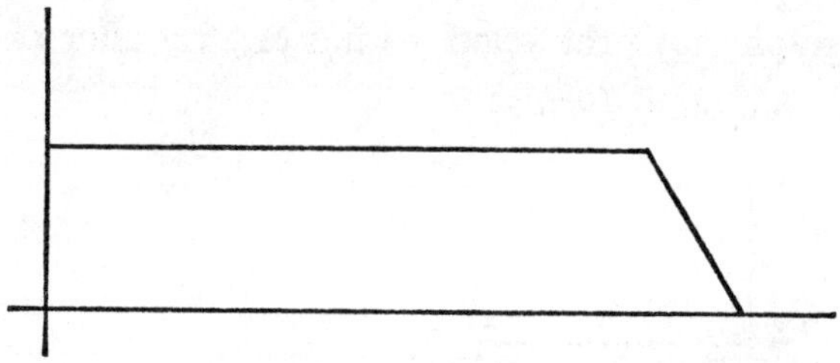

A particle travels at speed 6 m/s for 12 seconds and then slows down to rest in the next 3 seconds. The graph represents this motion.

(i) On a copy of the diagram label and graduate the axes.
(ii) Calculate the retardation in the last 3 seconds.
(iii) Calculate the total distance travelled in the 15 seconds. O

40 The diagram shows a distance–time graph drawn with uniform scales. Describe the motion in words. AEB

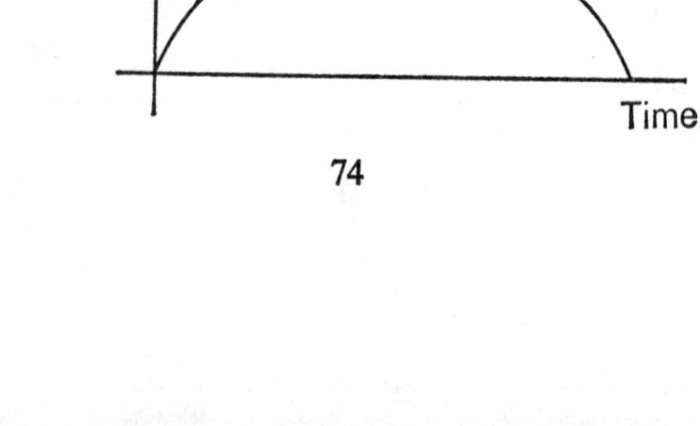

41 In an experiment, the speed of a bullet is measured electronically at intervals of $\frac{1}{10}$ s. The results are given in the following table:

Speed of bullet (m/s)	325	322	318	313	307	299	288
Time from firing (s)	0.1	0.2	0.3	0.4	0.5	0.6	0.7

(*a*) Find the average deceleration between the times 0·2 s and 0·4 s from firing.
(*b*) Estimate the distance travelled by the bullet in the interval between 0·1 s and 0·7 s. AEB

42 A tube-train starts from P and increases speed, at a steady rate, until it reaches 13 m/s. It keeps this speed for 27 s and then decreases its speed, at a steady rate, until it stops at Q. The whole journey takes 73 s.

Draw a sketch-graph showing the speed plotted against the time, marking in all the given data. Calculate the distance PQ. C

43 (i) A particle moving in a straight line has velocity v m/s at time t s, where $v = 6 \sin 15t°$. *Sketch* the velocity–time graph for values of t from 0 to 24 and briefly describe the motion, explaining in particular what is happening at times 6 s and 12 s.
(ii) Determine the distance travelled in the interval from $t = 1$ to $t = 7$. Comment briefly on your method and indicate sources of inaccuracy.

[You need not draw an accurate graph unless your method requires it.] OC (SMP)

Chapter Seven

1 The length and breadth of a rectangle are measured as 6·4 m and 3·1 m, each correct to the nearest tenth of a metre. It follows that the smallest possible value for the perimeter, correct to the nearest tenth of a metre is

(*a*) 18·6 m; (*b*) 18·8 m; (*c*) 18·9 m; (*d*) 19·0 m

OC (SMP)

2 The three sides of a triangle are measured. Their lengths, stated to the nearest 0·1 m, are 2·4 m, 2·0 m and 1·5 m. State the limits between which the perimeter must lie. OC (SMP)

3 The birth-rate per 1000 of population is calculated correct to one decimal place. For a town with exactly 43 000 inhabitants the rate was stated to be 11·2 births per 1000. The maximum number of births consistent with this statement is

(*a*) 481; (*b*) 482; (*c*) 483; (*d*) 484. OC (SMP)

4 A rectangle has its sides given as 90 mm and 30 mm, each to the nearest mm. Find:

(i) the largest possible length of the perimeter;
(ii) the smallest possible value of the area. C

5 The length and width of a rectangle are measured as 100 mm and 80 mm respectively, each measurement being given to the nearest millimetre. State extreme upper and lower limits for

(i) the perimeter of the rectangle;
(ii) the area of the rectangle. NI

6 A triangle is measured and found to have a base of 72 mm and a corresponding altitude of 54 mm, each to two significant figures.

Find an upper limit to the area of the triangle. OC (SMP)

7 If $3 - 0{\cdot}1 \leqslant a \leqslant 3 + 0{\cdot}1$ and $2 - 0{\cdot}05 \leqslant b \leqslant 2 + 0{\cdot}05$ calculate the maximum possible error in taking ab^2 to equal 12.

AEB

8 Given that the following numbers are all correct to three figures, to how many figures will the answers be accurate? Give some justification for your conclusions.

(*a*) $6{\cdot}37 + 4{\cdot}26 + 7{\cdot}31 + 8{\cdot}24$; (*b*) $1{\cdot}72 \times 2{\cdot}26$. AEB

9 (*a*) If we add two numbers which are correct to two decimal places, is it true or false that the sum is necessarily correct to two decimal places?

(*b*) If a number corrected to two decimal places equals 3·14, is it true or false that the square of the number and the square of 3·14 when corrected to two decimal places are equal? AEB

10 Express 10 300 in the form $a \times 10^n$ where $1 < a < 10$ and n is an integer. OC (SMP)

11 Express $32{\cdot}7 \times 10^{-3}$ in the form $A \times 10^n$, where

$$1 < A < 10.$$

OC (SMP)

12 Write the following numbers in standard form, i.e. $a \times 10^n$, where $1 \leqslant a < 10$ and n is an integer, and where a is to be expressed correct to three significant figures:

(i) 0·874 503; (ii) 0·097 63. AEB

13 Multiply $3{\cdot}2 \times 10^6$ by 4×10^{-3} giving the answer in the same, standard, form. OC (SMP)

14 Express $\dfrac{119 \times 10^{-3}}{7 \times 10^2}$ in the standard form $A \times 10^n$. C

15 Are the following statements true or false?

(*a*) $6{\cdot}23 \times 10^{-4} > 4{\cdot}25 \times 10^{-2}$.

(*b*) $(1{\cdot}27 \times 10^{-2}) + (2{\cdot}63 \times 10^{-4})$ is approximately equal to $1{\cdot}3 \times 10^{-2}$.

(*c*) $(7{\cdot}5 \times 10^{4}) \div (2{\cdot}5 \times 10^{6}) = 3 \times 10^{2}$.

(*d*) $0{\cdot}0037 = 3{\cdot}7 \times 10^{-3}$. AEB

16 Find the value of v, in the standard form $A \times 10^{n}$, given that $\frac{1}{2}mv^2 = 8 \times 10^9$ and $m = 10^{-3}$. C

17 Estimate to one significant figure the value of

$$\frac{108 \times 0{\cdot}009\,72.}{30\pi}$$

OC (SMP)

18 The value of

$$\frac{\pi[(7\frac{1}{2})^2 - (6\frac{1}{2})^2] \times 36}{1728}$$

lies between:

(*a*) 0·01 and 0·1; (*b*) 0·1 and 1; (*c*) 1 and 10; (*d*) 10 and 100.

OC (SMP)

19 State which of the following estimates of the value of

$$\tfrac{4}{3}\pi\frac{(18{\cdot}7)^3}{1728}$$

is the best: (*a*) 16; (*b*) 160; (*c*) 0·9; (*d*) 48. OC (SMP)

20 Find, correct to one significant figure, the value of

$$\frac{0{\cdot}31^2 \times 12{\cdot}4}{15}$$

C

21 Give an approximate value for

$\dfrac{4320 \times \sqrt{(0{\cdot}0082)}}{0{\cdot}016}$ giving one or two significant figures

OC (SMP)

22 If $\sqrt{5} = 2{\cdot}2$ and $\sqrt{50} = 7{\cdot}1$ (to two significant figures), then

(i) $\sqrt{5000}$ is approximately

(*a*) 710; (*b*) 71; (*c*) 220; (*d*) 22

(ii) $\sqrt{0{\cdot}05}$ is approximately

(*a*) 0·22; (*b*) 0·071; (*c*) $7{\cdot}1 \times 10^{-1}$; (*d*) $2{\cdot}2 \times 10^{-2}$

(iii) $\sqrt{(5 \times 10^6)}$ is approximately

(*a*) $2{\cdot}2 \times 10^6$; (*b*) 7100; (*c*) 220; (*d*) $2{\cdot}2 \times 10^3$

NI

23 State the number of significant figures in each of the following numbers: (i) 30·02; (ii) 0·700; (iii) 0·000 13. OC (SMP)

24 Re-write the number 4·997, correcting it to three significant figures. OC (SMP)

25 State the number 0·073 46 correct to three significant figures. OC (SMP)

26 (i) Express 0·266 66 . . . correct to three decimal places.
(ii) Express 0·026 66 . . . correct to two significant figures.
(iii) If $x = 0{\cdot}266\,66\ldots$, write down the value of $10x$ and from these two values obtain that of $9x$. Hence, or in any other way, express x as a rational number. OC (SMP)

27 Evaluate correct to two significant figures

$$399{\cdot}258 \div 160{\cdot}731.$$

SU

28 Evaluate

$$\sqrt{\frac{(2{\cdot}730 \times 4{\cdot}761) + (0{\cdot}732 \times 1{\cdot}798)}{15{\cdot}62}}$$

and give your answer correct to three significant figures.

AEB

29 Use your slide-rule to evaluate

$$\frac{4{\cdot}02 \times 0{\cdot}077}{65{\cdot}9}$$

OC (SMP)

30 Use a slide-rule to find the value of

$$\sqrt{(2\cdot5 \div 0\cdot76)}.$$ OC (SMP)

31 Use a slide-rule to evaluate

$$\frac{\pi(3\cdot8)^2}{144}.$$ OC (SMP)

32 Use a slide-rule to find the value of

$$\frac{2\cdot1 \times \sqrt{14\cdot7}}{0\cdot854}.$$ OC (SMP)

33 Write down from your slide-rule the square root of 40.

Say which of the following square roots can be written down without further use of your slide-rule:

(*a*) $\sqrt{(40\,000)}$; (*b*) $\sqrt{(0\cdot400)}$; (*c*) $\sqrt{(400)}$; (*d*) $\sqrt{(0\cdot004)}$.

OC (SMP)

34 The value of $\sqrt{4840}$ is (*a*) 22; (*b*) 220; (*c*) between 69 and 70; (*d*) none of these. OC (SMP)

35 Find the value of $100\{\sqrt{(0\cdot4)} - \sqrt{(0\cdot04)}\}$, giving your answer to two significant figures. C

Chapter Eight

1

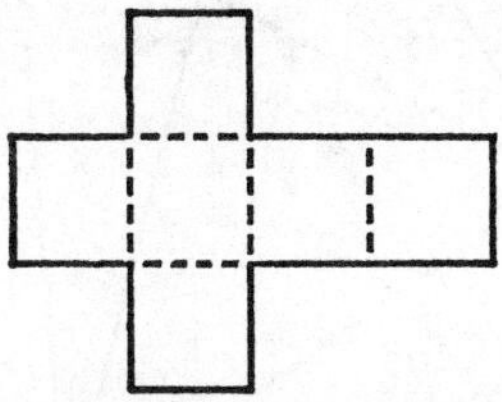

If the figure shown is cut out and folded appropriately along the dotted lines, it may be made into a cube.

Of which of the following figures may the same be said?

(a)

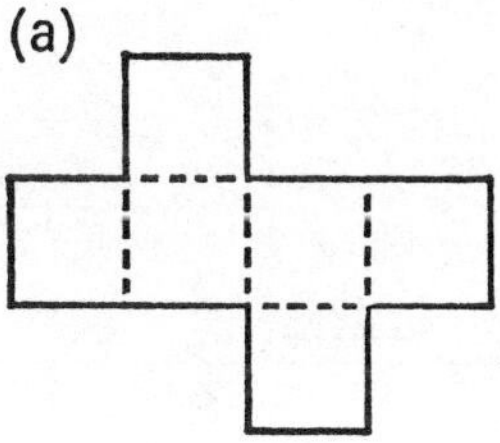

(b)

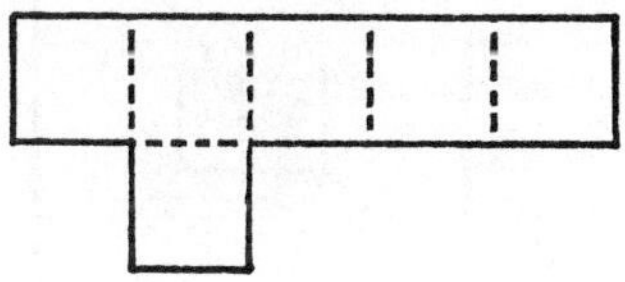

(c)

O

2 *ABCD* (on Page 82) is a regular triangular pyramid (tetrahedron) with the face *BCD* on a horizontal table.

Sketch the plan and side elevation (looking from *B* in a direction perpendicular to *CD*). O

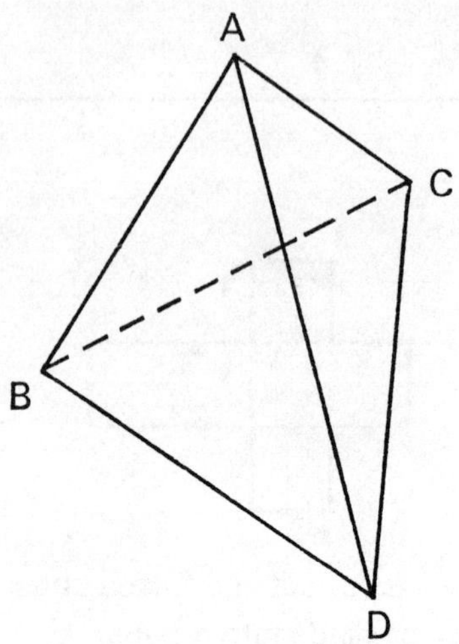

3 A plan and front elevation of an object are given. Sketch the object.

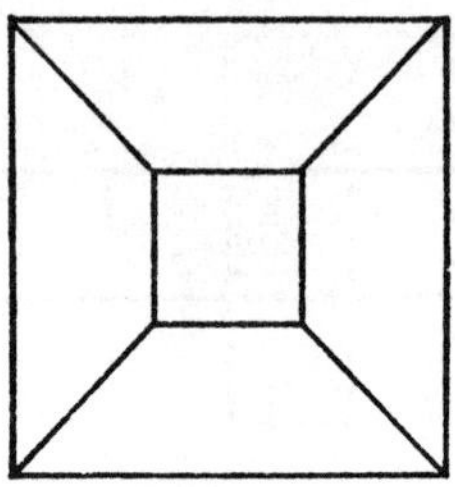

Plan

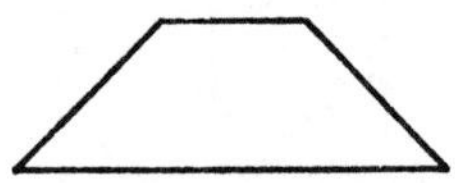

Front Elevation

4 The front and side elevations of a solid block of wood are shown.

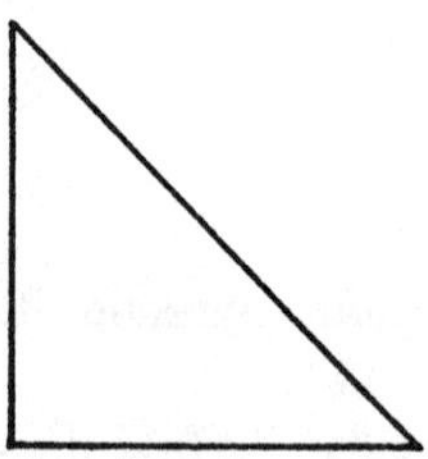

Front

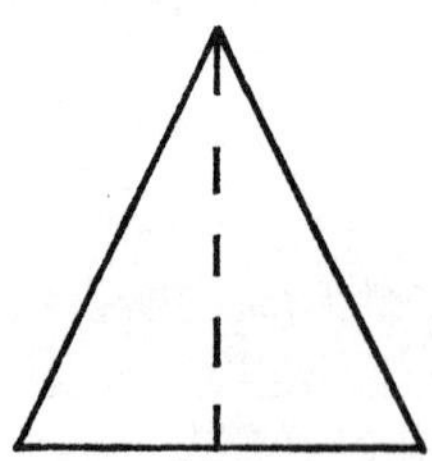

Side

The plan is

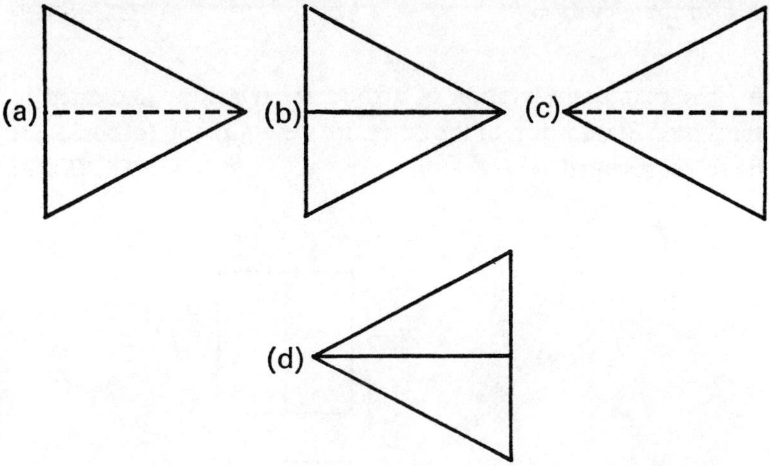

State which. OC (SMP)

5

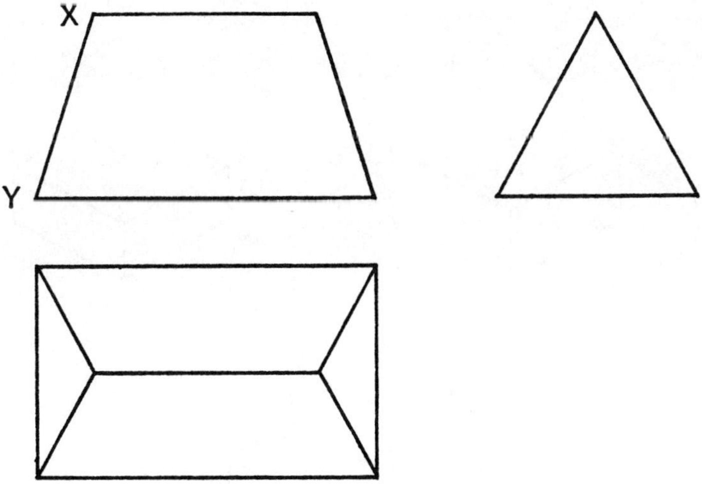

Draw a sketch (freehand if you wish) to show the shape of the solid of which two elevations and a plan are given.

Mark in your sketch a line whose true length is represented by XY in the elevation. OC (SMP)

6 The plan and elevation of a solid are related as indicated in the figure. State which of the isometric views (*a*). (*b*), (*c*) could not be so represented. OC (SMP)

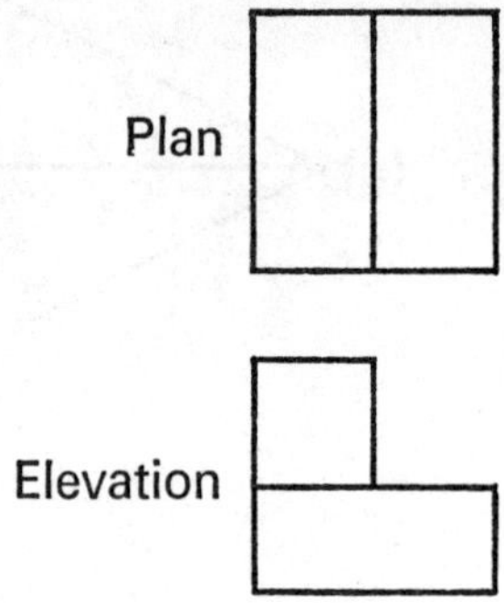

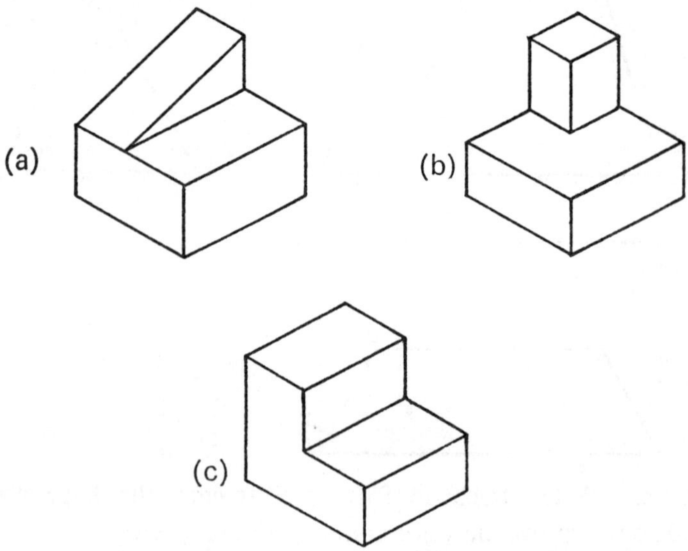

7 Three equal wooden spheres lie in contact and touch the four edges of an open rectangular box, the diameters of the spheres exceeding the width of the box.

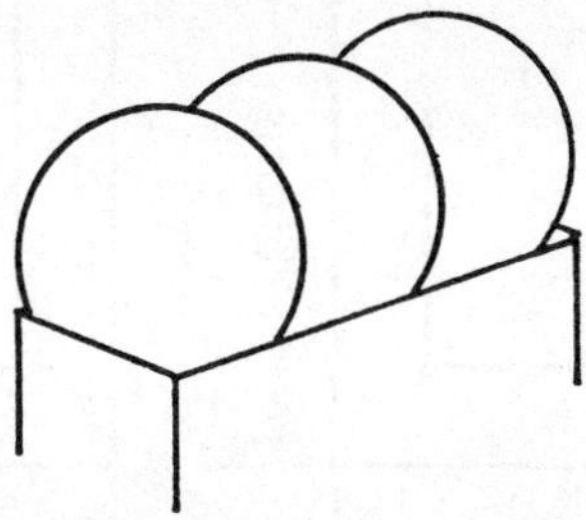

In copies of the diagrams complete a sketch of
(i) the plan;
(ii) the horizontal cross section at the level of the top of the box.

(i)

(ii)

C

8 The diagrams (Page 86) are elevations of a metal object from two perpendicular directions.

(i) On squared paper draw the plan.
(ii) On ordinary paper draw a perspective *sketch.*
(iii) Calculate the mass of the object, given that a cubic metre of the metal has a mass of 2600 kg. OC (SMP)

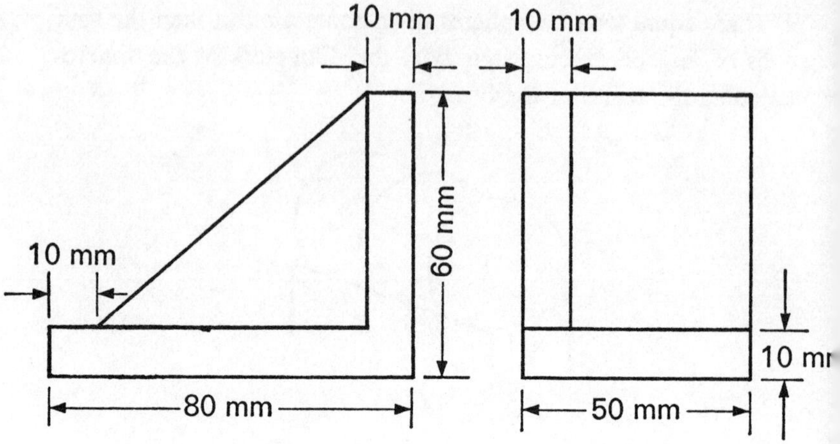

9 The diagrams below show the front and side elevations of a solid block of wood.

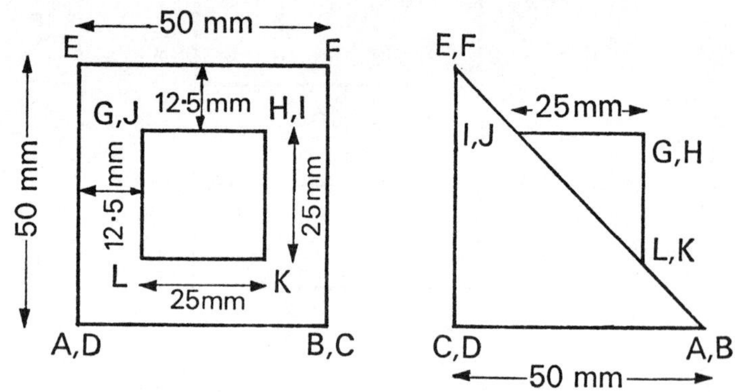

(i) Draw a neat diagram of the plan, showing all the points *A* to *L* correctly positioned.
(ii) Draw a three-dimensional sketch of the block in which *G* and *H* are visible, and letter correctly all the other visible corners.
(iii) The block is cut into two pieces along the plane *ADF*. Sketch the cross-section and letter its corners. (An accurate drawing is **not** required.) C

10 The figure, which is not to scale, shows the *end* elevation of a rectangular box with inside corners $ABCDD'\ C'\ B'\ A'$, the dashed letters referring to the distant corners in each case. The inside dimensions are 0·3 by 0·4 by 0·5 metres and the rectangular hinged lid measures 0·41 by 0·52 metres, the thickness of wood being 0·01 metres throughout the box and lid.

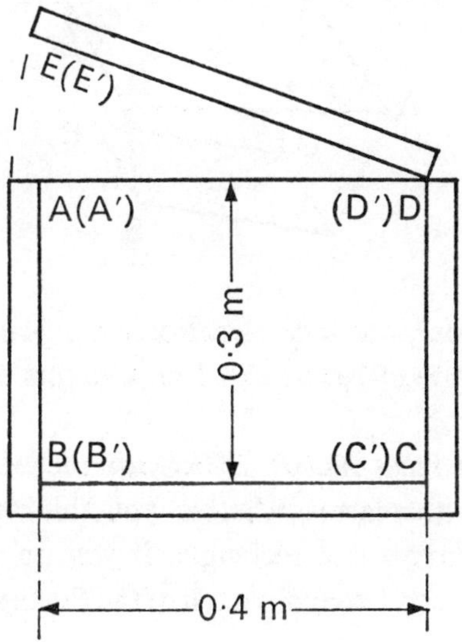

(i) After observing carefully which edges are shown as visible in the end view, state the actual dimensions of the pieces of wood used for the back and front of the box.
(ii) Draw a neat *sketch*, which need not be to any exact scale, of a front elevation of the box with the lid open as shown.
(iii) A thin rod XY 0·24 metres long is hinged at one end X to the midpoint of the inner edge AA', so that it can be used as a prop for the lid but can fold down vertically inside when not in use. When in use its end Y rests in a slight depression Z inside the lid, Z being so situated that the lid is held open as far as possible. How far is Z from the edge DD', and at what angle (to the nearest degree) is the lid held open by the prop? O

11 The diagram represents a barrow, in which the top $ABCD$ is a horizontal rectangle, $AB = 0{\cdot}6$ m, $BC = 0{\cdot}75$ m. The faces $ABQP$, $DCRS$ are inclined to the vertical at 15°, 40°, respectively. The edge PQ is 0·3 m below the top and the base $PQRS$ is at 12° to the horizontal.

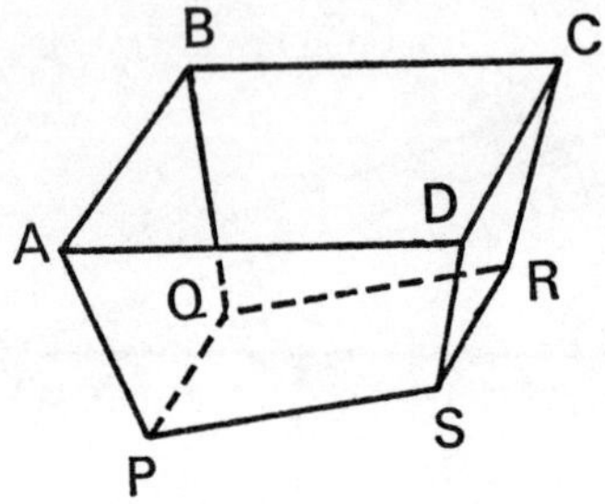

(*a*) Draw accurately the side elevation on a plane perpendicular to AB using a scale of 200 *mm* = 1 m. Use this to find the depth of S below the top.
(*b*) The two side faces $ADSP$, $BCRQ$ are inclined to the vertical at 20°. State, with reason, whether you think the bottom face $PQRS$ of the barrow is a rectangle. If you do not think it is a rectangle give a clear, lettered, sketch of the shape you do think it is.
OC (SMP)

12 When cutting a lawn, a gardener uses a mower with a cutting edge 350 mm wide. After each parallel strip cut, he cuts a return strip which overlaps the previous one by 50 mm. What width of lawn has been cut after mowing (*a*) one strip, (*b*) two strips, (*c*) three strips, (*d*) n strips?

How far, in metres, does he walk with the mower when cutting a lawn 20 m × 15·05 m lengthwise, if he walks 4 m round the mower at the end of each strip for the return journey? L

13 A lecture room is 18 m by 12 m, and one chair occupies a space, 0·5 m square. The chairs are arranged in rows, one chair's width apart, across the room, with a gap of 0·9 m on each side,

1·2 m down the middle, and 4·5 m in front of the front row. How many people can be seated if the front wall is (*a*) a shorter side, (*b*) a longer side? L

14 The density of mahogany is 512 kg/m³. Find the mass of a rectangular mahogany beam of length 2 m whose cross-section measures 0·275 m by 0·1 m. AEB

15 125 blocks, each a 25 mm cube, are placed on a table so as to form a solid cube. State the length of the edge of this cube.

The top and the four side faces of this large cube are now painted red. How many of the original 25 mm cubes have just one face painted red? C

16 A swimming bath 50 m long and 10 m wide slopes uniformly from a depth of 1 m at one end to a depth of 3 m at the other end. Calculate in kilograms the mass of water which would fill the bath (the mass of 1 m³ water is 1000 kg).

17 The diagram represents a triangle *ABC* in which $AC = 150$ mm, $BC = 200$ mm and $\angle ACB = 90°$. *D* is the foot of the perpendicular from *C* to *AB*.

Find:

(i) the area of triangle *ABC*;
(ii) the length of *AB*;
(iii) $\cos \angle BCD$.

NI

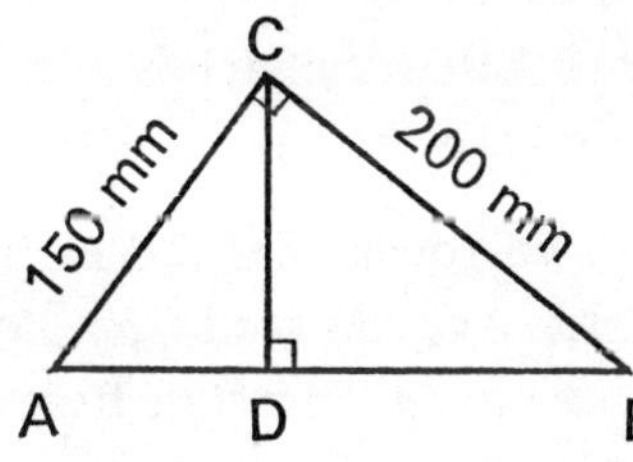

18 (i) Calculate the area of triangle *ABC*.
(ii) If *D* is the midpoint of *BC* and *E* is the midpoint of *AC*, state the area of the quadrilateral *ABDE*.

C

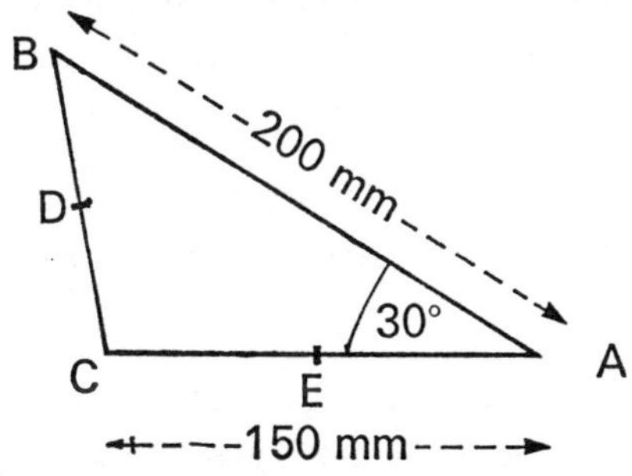

19 Find an expression for the area of an equilateral triangle inscribed in a circle of radius r mm. AEB

20 An acute-angled triangle ABC has $AC = 60$ mm, $AB = 50$ mm and an area of 900 mm^2. Calculate the length of the perpendicular from B to AC. Calculate the value of angle A. SU

21 Two sides of a triangle are known to be 70 mm and 90 mm to the nearest millimetre. The angle included between these sides is 30°. Calculate the largest and smallest possible values for the area of the triangle.

22 The following successive approximations are alleged to obtain the circumference of a circle, given the diameter:
(*a*) multiply by 3;
(*b*) add one-twentieth of the answer to (*a*);
(*c*) subtract one-three-hundredth of the answer to (*b*);
(*d*) add one-thousandth of the answer to (*c*);
(*e*) subtract one-three-thousandth of the answer to (*d*).

Use this method to find, to the nearest millimetre, the circumference of a circle of diameter 113 millimetres. L

23 If the circumference of a circle is increased from 10π mm to 12π mm, by how much is the radius increased? OC (SMP)

24 Two roads OA, OB each of length 280 metres are at right angles. Another road from A to B is a quadrant of a circle. H is a house on OA, 50 metres from A. Find whether by O or by A is the shorter route from H to a letter-box at B, and by how much. (Take $\pi = 22/7$.) SU

25 A model of a car is built to a scale of 1 in 30. If the real car's wheels have diameter 0·56 m, how many times do the wheels of the model rotate completely as it travels one metre? (Take π as 22/7.) SU

26 If the area between two concentric circles of radii 120 mm and 108 mm is $p\pi$ mm^2, give the value of p. OC (SMP)

27 A circle of wire is cut into three equal pieces, each of which is bent into a new closed circular shape. Find (*a*) the ratio of the original circumference to the total circumference of the three new circles, and (*b*) the ratio of the original area enclosed to the total areas enclosed by the three new circles. L

28

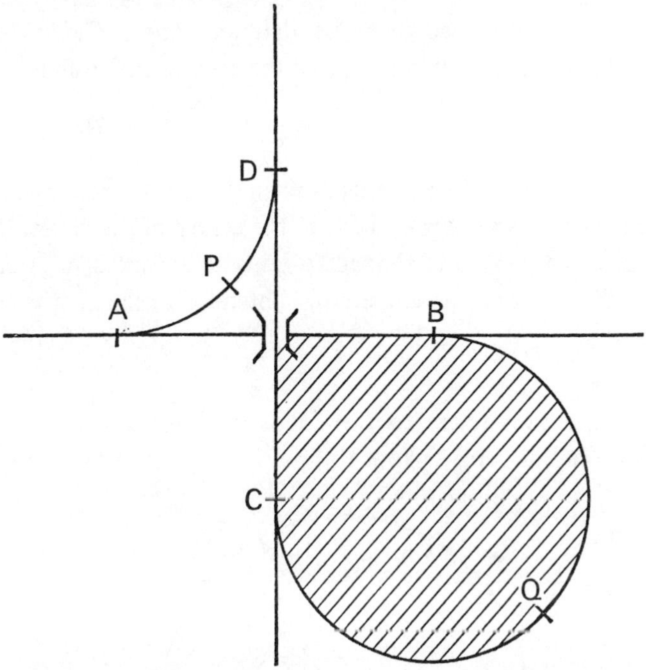

The diagram is a plan of part of the road system at the crossing of two motorways, one running east and west, the other north and south. The arcs are part of circles of radius 280 m. Vehicles travelling from *A* to *D* must go via *P*, those travelling from *D* to *A* via *C*, *Q* and *B*.

Making suitable approximations, which should be explained, calculate:

(i) the difference in length between the two routes;

(ii) the shaded area, giving your answer in m^2.

[You are advised to simplify expressions as much as possible before doing the arithmetical computations.] OC (SMP)

29 A square is inscribed in a circle. Calculate the total area of those parts of the circle outside the square as a percentage of the area of the whole circle, giving your answer correct to two significant figures. AEB

30 A circle is inscribed in an equilateral triangle. Calculate the area of the circle as a percentage of the area of the triangle. AEB

31 A piece of wire in the shape of an arc of a circle of radius 150 mm subtends an angle of 34° at the centre of the circle. If the same piece of wire is re-shaped to become an arc of a circle of radius 100 mm, find the angle now subtended at the centre of the new circle. L

32 This question refers to the following diagram of a circle centre O, radius 1 m. Take π to be 3·14 in your calculations.

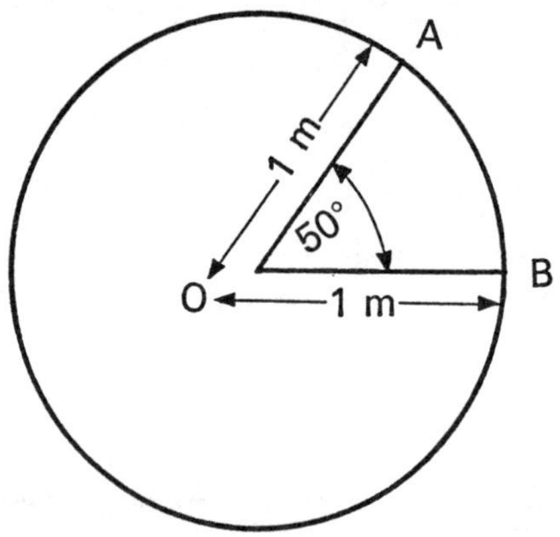

(i) Find the area of the triangle AOB.
(ii) Find the area of the sector AOB of the circle.
(iii) Express the length of the shorter arc AB as a fraction of the total circumference of the circle. AEB

33

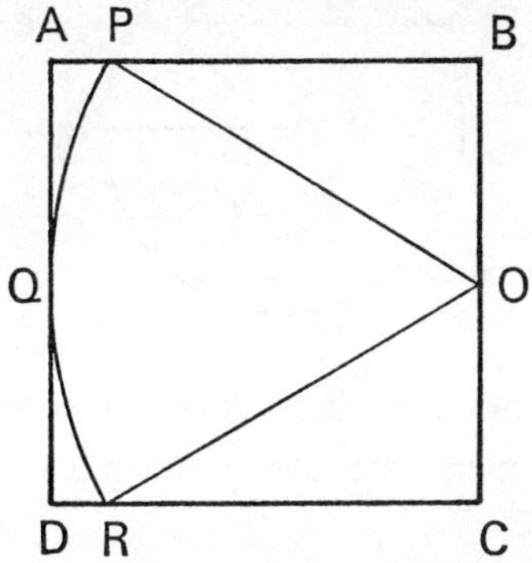

$ABCD$ is a square. O and Q are the midpoints of BC and AD. $OPQR$ is a sector of a circle. Find the percentage of the area of the square occupied by the sector. L

34 The figure shows a slice cut from a cake of radius 96 mm and uniform height. The slice is divided by the cut XY, where $XP = YQ = 12$ mm. (i) Ignoring the fact that PQ is curved, show by

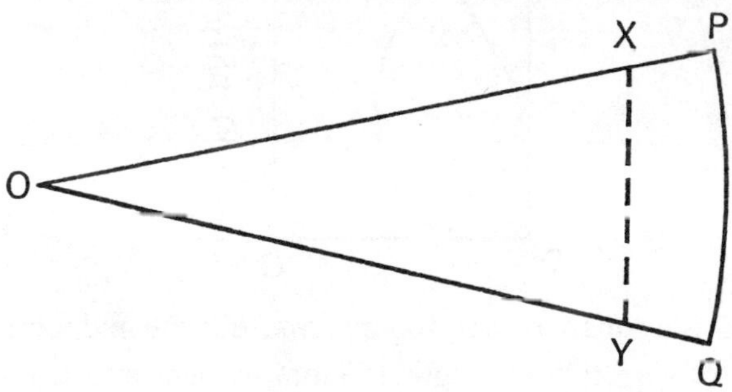

calculation that the part $XPQY$ is about a quarter of the whole slice. (ii) If $\angle POQ = 20°$, show that the ratio of the area of the triangle POQ to that of the sector POQ is

$$\frac{9 \sin 20^0}{\pi}.$$

(iii) A second cake has radius 120 mm and is uniformly three-quarters as high as the first. Calculate the angle of a slice of the second cake which is just as big as the given slice. OC (SMP)

35

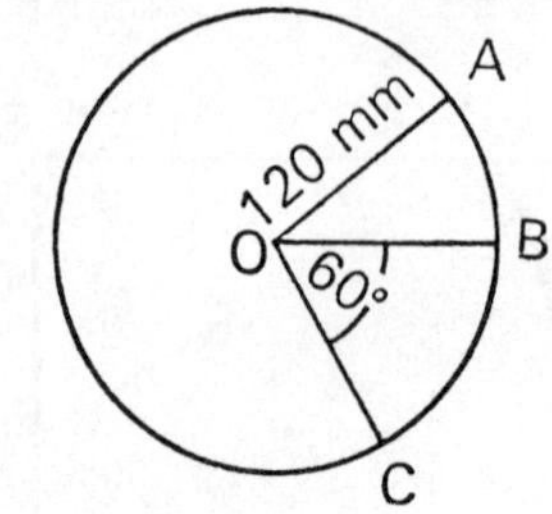

The diagram shows a circle with centre O and radius 120 mm. The distance AB, measured along the circumference, is 72 mm and $\angle BOC = 60°$.

Calculate $\angle AOB$ (*a*) in radians;

(*b*) in degrees, to the nearest degree.

Calculate also the area of the sector BOC as a multiple of π. C

36

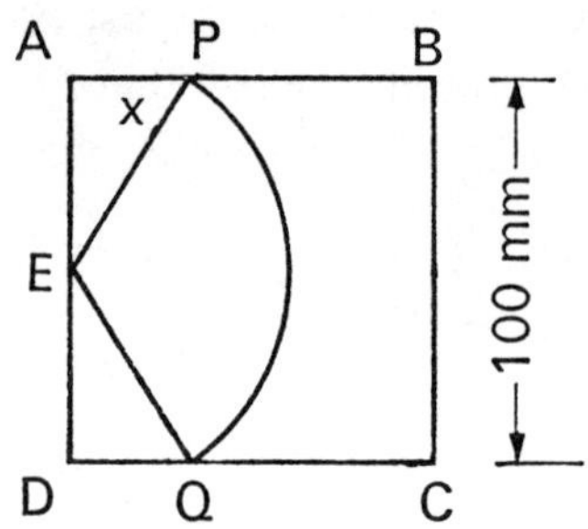

$ABCD$ is a square of side 100 mm and E is the midpoint of AD. A piece of wire PQ, of length 150 mm, is bent into the arc of a circle, centre E. If the angle x is measured in radians, show that

$$2x = 3 \sin x.$$

By drawing the curve $y = \sin x$ in the range $0 \leqslant x \leqslant \frac{1}{2}\pi$ and an appropriate straight line, estimate the value of x. C

37 A and B are two points on the circumference of a circle of radius 50 mm and centre O, such that the angle $AOB = 2\theta$ radians.

Given that the length of the *major arc AB* is four times the length of the *chord AB*, show that $4 \sin \theta + \theta - \pi = 0$.

Evaluate, as a decimal, the expression $4 \sin \theta + \theta - \pi$ when $\theta = \frac{1}{6}\pi$, $\frac{1}{4}\pi$ and $\frac{1}{3}\pi$. Hence estimate the value of θ which satisfies the equation $4 \sin \theta + \theta - \pi = 0$. C

38 The radius of a cylindrical can is 40 mm and its height is 130 mm. Calculate (to two significant figures)
(i) the volume of the can;
(ii) the area of the curved surface of the can.
(The value of π may be taken as 3·14.) NI

39 A cylindrical container has a volume of 1 m^3. If the diameter of the base is 0·8 m calculate the height to the nearest tenth of a metre. (Take $\pi = 22/7$.) SU

40 A metal sleeve has the shape of a hollow cylinder with internal diameter 12 mm and external diameter 18 mm and height 48 mm. Calculate the volume of metal in the sleeve.

The metal costs £1·25 per kilogram and 1 m^3 of the metal has a mass of 2800 kg. How many sleeves can be made with £1 worth of metal, neglecting wastage?

(Take π to be 3·14.) AEB

41 The volume V of a cylinder is given by the formula $\pi r^2 h$. If the radius of the cylinder were doubled and the height were halved, express the new volume in terms of V. C

42 [In this question take π as 3·14.]

The paper for printing the *Daily Clarion* comes to the press wound tightly on a cylindrical roller of 0·225 m diameter and 1·2 m long, to make in all a cylindrical roll of 1·025 m diameter and 1·2 m long. The paper is 0·1 mm thick.

(i) Show that the length of paper on the roll is slightly more than 7800 m.

(ii) If a copy of the *Clarion* consists of 6 sheets, each 1·2 m by 0·9 m, calculate how many complete hundreds of copies can be printed from one roll.
(iii) Given that 1 cubic metre of paper has a mass of 720 kg, calculate to two significant figures the mass (in kg) of paper in a roll. O

43

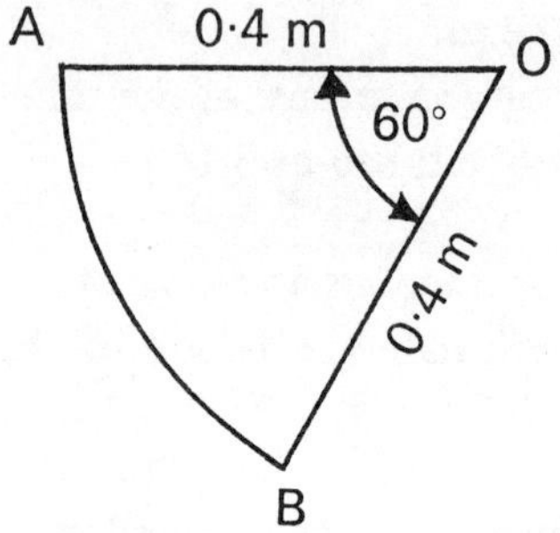

The sector of a circle shown is folded over to form a circular cone so that the arc *AB* becomes the circumference of the base.

State the radius of the base circle. OC (SMP)

44 A wooden cone has a circular base of radius 50 mm, and its vertical height is 120 mm. Calculate the slant height of the cone.

The cone stands with its axis vertical on a table. A thin hoop of radius 30 mm is placed on the cone so that it lies horizontally, touching the curved surface of the cone all round. Calculate (i) how far the centre of the hoop is below the vertex, (ii) what fraction of the volume of the cone lies above the level of the hoop, (iii) what fraction of the curved surface of the cone lies above the level of the hoop. O

45 A cone is cut by a plane parallel to its base and the slice between this plane and the base is removed. A cylinder is treated in the same way. State, in each case, whether the remaining solid is or is not similar to the original solid. If the answer in either case is 'No', give a brief justification. OC (SMP)

46 (i) A cylinder and a cone have base radius r and height $2r$ and a sphere has radius r. Show that the volumes and curved surface areas of the cylinder, sphere and cone are in the ratios $3:2:1$ and $4:4:\sqrt{5}$ respectively.
(ii) A child's toy rocket has a conical nose cap, a cylindrical body and a hemispherical base. The rocket is 130 mm long, the cap, body and base all have a base diameter of 60 mm and the body is 60 mm long. Find the volume and surface area of the toy rocket. L

47 Show that the ratio of the volume of 5 spherical balls of diameter 4 mm to the volume of 12 spherical balls of diameter 3 mm is 80 : 81. L

48 Two makes of golf-ball differ slightly in size: the diameter of one is 42 mm and that of the other 40·5 mm. Calculate the difference in their volumes as a percentage of the volume of the smaller ball. (The volume of a sphere is $\frac{4}{3}\pi r^3$.) AEB

49 The vertices of a cube lie on a sphere of radius 3 m. Calculate the length of an edge of the cube. Hence calculate the volume of the cube as a percentage of the volume of the sphere. (Volume of sphere $= \frac{4}{3}\pi r^3$. Take π to be 3·14.) AEB

50 The surface area A of a sphere is given by $A = 4\pi r^2$, where r is the radius. A manufacturer has an order for 50 000 hollow metal spheres of radius 150 mm. The spheres are made of thin copper sheet. The manufacturing process can usually be controlled to an accuracy of 0·25 mm in the radius and this is acceptable to the customer. But some few spheres are larger or smaller than this and have to be rejected: it is found that the number of spheres rejected never exceeds 2 per cent of the total production.
(i) Calculate the area of the amount of copper sheet the manufacturer would need if he could make 50 000 perfect spheres of radius 150 mm exactly. Let this area be A_1. (Assume that there is no wastage.)

(ii) Calculate the area of the amount of copper sheet the manufacturer would need to make 50 000 acceptable spheres if he encounters the worst possible conditions. Let this area be A_2. (Again, assume that there is no wastage other than that due to rejection because of unsatisfactory radius. Assume also that the average surface area of the rejected spheres is the same as that of a sphere of radius 150 mm.)
(iii) If we define the process wastage as $A_2 - A_1$, express this process wastage as a percentage of A_1.
(Take π to be 3·142.) AEB

51 A farmer has a silo which consists of a cylindrical drum 14 m high and diameter 4 m surmounted by a hemispherical cap of the same diameter. How many cubic metres of silage can be stored if this amounts to 90 per cent of the total volume of the silo? SU

52 A square pyramid of identical solid iron spheres is such that each sphere touches its neighbours. Given that the bottom layer contains 36 spheres, show that there are 91 spheres in the pyramid.

If each sphere has a radius of 0·1 m, and 1 m^3 of iron has a mass of 7700 kg, calculate the mass of the pyramid. (Volume of sphere $= \frac{4}{3}\pi r^3$; take π to be $\frac{22}{7}$.)

If all the spheres are melted down and made into one large sphere of radius R metres, show that $R^3 = 0{\cdot}091$. C

53 A solid cylinder whose height is equal to its diameter just fits inside a hollow sphere whose thickness may be neglected.

Show that the cylinder occupies a fraction $\dfrac{3\sqrt{2}}{8}$ of the volume inside the sphere. Find also the ratio of the *total* surface area of the cylinder to that of the sphere.

$$\left[\begin{array}{l}\text{volume of sphere} = \dfrac{4}{3}\pi r^3 \\ \text{Area of surface of sphere} = 4\pi r^2\end{array}\right]$$ L

54

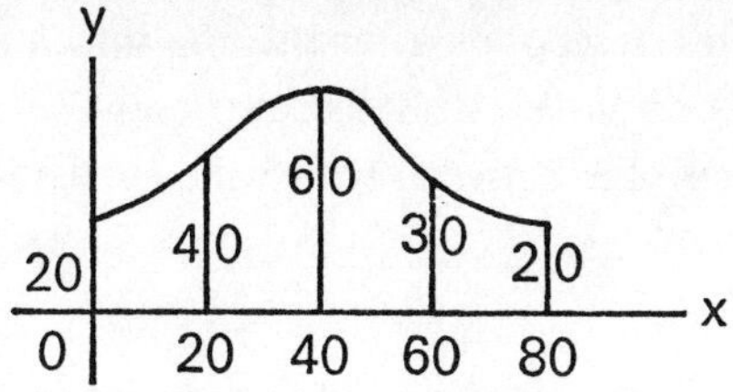

(i) If the unit on each axis is 1 mm, estimate, by the trapezium rule, or otherwise, the area under the graph.
(ii) If 10 mm on the x-axis represents 1 s and 1 mm on the y-axis represents 1 m/s, state what your estimate of the area means, giving the units. OC (SMP)

55 Using the trapezium rule, or otherwise, estimate the number of

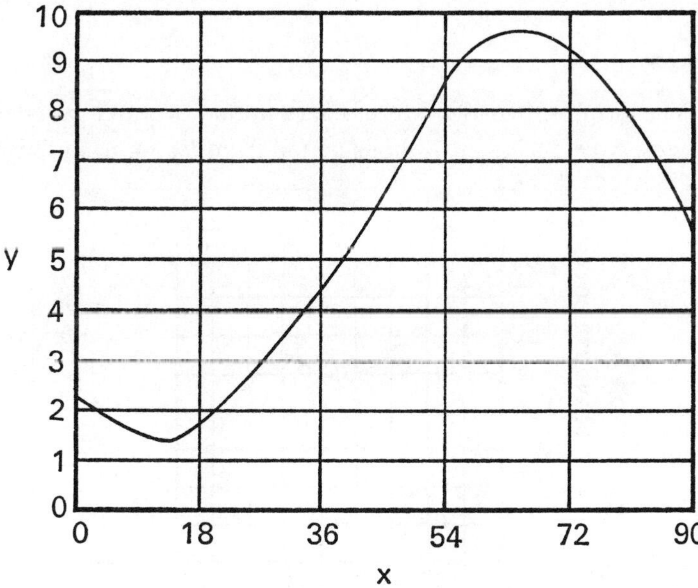

units of area in the figure bounded by the curve, the x-axis, the line $x = 0$, and the line $x = 90$.

If, on the above graph, y represents the speed in metres per second of a cyclist x seconds after turning into a road, what does the area, which you have estimated, represent?

State the values of x between which the cyclist is gaining speed.

C

56 A car travels along a road and at various intervals the following readings were taken from a specially constructed speedometer:

Speed (m/s)	0	7·3	17·3	23·3	25	18·3	8	3·3	2·7
Time (s)	0	5	10	15	20	25	30	35	40

(i) Sketch a speed–time graph representing the data and, from your graph, estimate the acceleration of the car at 15 s.
(ii) Use the trapezoidal rule to estimate the distance travelled in the first 40 s.

AEB

57 The graph shows the rate of consumption of water measured at a reservoir during an 18-hour period from 6 a.m. to midnight.

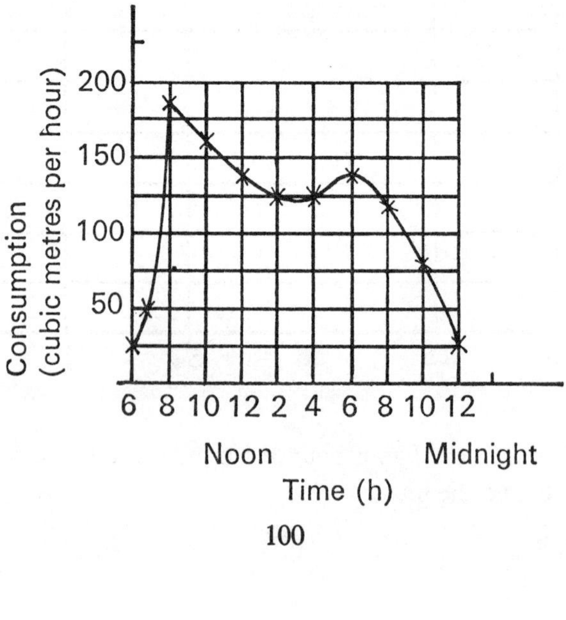

(*a*) *Estimate* the average rate of consumption of water between 8 a.m. and 2 p.m.
(*b*) *Estimate* the total amount of water used during these 6 hours.
(*c*) The reservoir is being replenished at a steady rate of 125 m^3 per hour. State between what times the level is rising.
(*d*) Suggest reasons for the general shape of this graph. Do not write more than five lines.
(*e*) By using the trapezoidal rule, or otherwise, calculate the total consumption during the 18 hours. OC (SMP)

58 A river is 30 m wide and the depth of water varies as shown in the table.

Distance from left bank (m)	0	5	10	15	20	25	30
Depth (m)	2	$2\frac{1}{4}$	$4\frac{1}{2}$	6	$5\frac{1}{2}$	$4\frac{1}{2}$	0

Show this information on a graph and use this to estimate:
(i) the depth at a position $2\frac{1}{2}$ m from the right bank;
(ii) the area of the cross-section of the river. (Make your method clear.)

Use the result of (ii) to write down an expression for the volume of water flowing per hour, given that the average speed of the stream is 1 m/s. Use your slide-rule to evaluate this. OC (SMP)

59 Estimate the area enclosed between the graph (Page 102), the x-axis and the lines $x = 4$ and $x = 7$, explaining your method. State whether your method gives an over- or an under-estimate of the true area.

Write down an equation which fits the curve.

If y represents the speed of a particle in m/s at time x s:

(i) state in general terms what the particle is doing in the time interval shown;
(ii) state the physical significance of the area that you found in the first part of this question, expressing it in the appropriate physical units. OC (SMP)

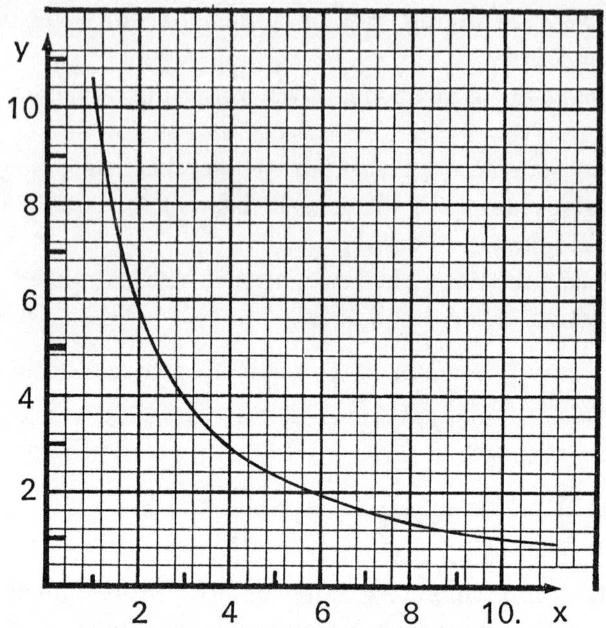

60 The figure shows the end wall of a building. With the axes shown and 1 m as the unit, the roof-line is given by $y = a + bx^2$, where a and b are constants.

(i) State the value of a and prove that $b = -0{\cdot}06$.

(ii) Calculate the values of y for $x = 2, 4, 6, 8$ and use these values to estimate the area of the wall. OC (SMP)

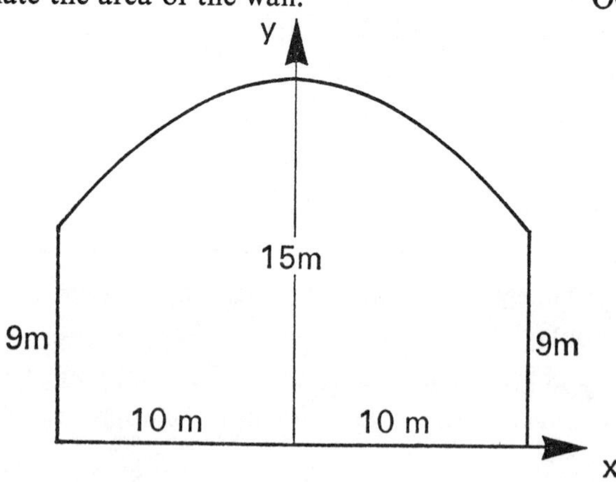

Chapter Nine

1 Nine pegs are arranged on a board in the way shown below:

Triangles are formed by placing elastic bands around three (or more) pegs. Using some suitable notation or diagrams list five of the different shapes and sizes of the triangles that may be formed. Determine the number of triangles congruent to each of those which you have listed. SU

2 The interior angles of a quadrilateral are $6x°$, $7x°$, $8x°$, $9x°$. Calculate x. Name the kind of quadrilateral when the angles $6x°$ and $9x°$ are (i) opposite, (ii) adjacent. SU

3 If A = {all quadrilaterals with at least one angle a right angle},
B = {all quadrilaterals with at least one pair of adjacent sides equal},
C = {all parallelograms},
identify the sets $A \cap C$, $B \cap C$, $A \cap B \cap C$. L

4 In the diagram shown the angle BHC is equal to (*a*) A; (*b*) $2A$; (*c*) $180° - A$; (*d*) $360° - A$. OC (SMP)

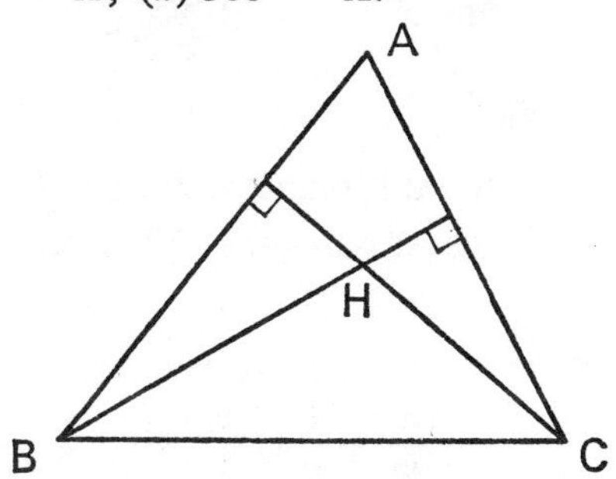

5 A regular polygon has angles of 150°. How many sides has it? OC (SMP)

6 A regular polygon has each angle equal to $x°$ where x is an integer such that $140 < x < 150$. How many sides has the polygon? OC (SMP)

7 The statement, 'Each external angle of a given regular polygon is 25°', cannot be true. Explain why. OC (SMP)

8 A floor is to be tiled with regular polygons each with the same side. By considering the angles involved show that this is possible with triangles and squares, but not with pentagons. SU

9 A floor is to be tiled with regular octagonal or square tiles each with the same side. By considering the angles involved show that this is possible with squares or with a combination of squares and octagons, but not with octagons alone. Give a rough sketch of the tiling which uses both shapes. SU

10 (i) Find the size in right angles of an interior angle of a regular polygon with n sides.

(ii)

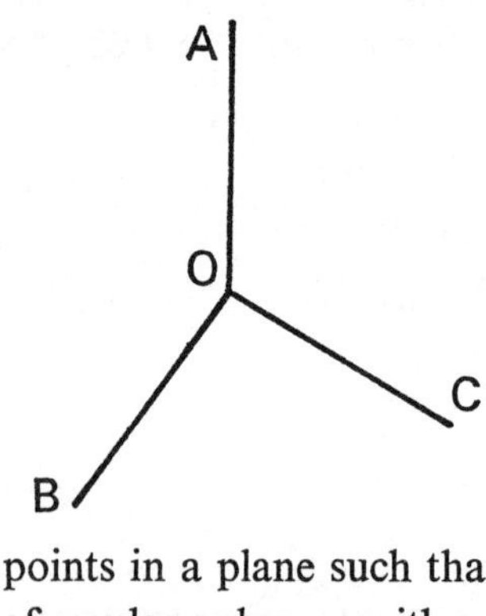

O, A, B, C, are points in a plane such that AOB, BOC, COA, are interior angles of regular polygons with m sides, n sides, and 6 sides respectively.

Show that

$$\frac{1}{m}+\frac{1}{n}=\frac{1}{3}.$$

(iii) Explain why m and n must both be greater than 3 but cannot both be greater than 6. If m is less than or equal to n show that there are only two possible pairs of values of m, n; sketch the corresponding figures, and mark in the sizes of the angles.

OC (SMP)

11 In the isosceles triangle QX and RX are the angle bisectors.
(i) Calculate $\angle QXR$ if $\angle P = 40°$.

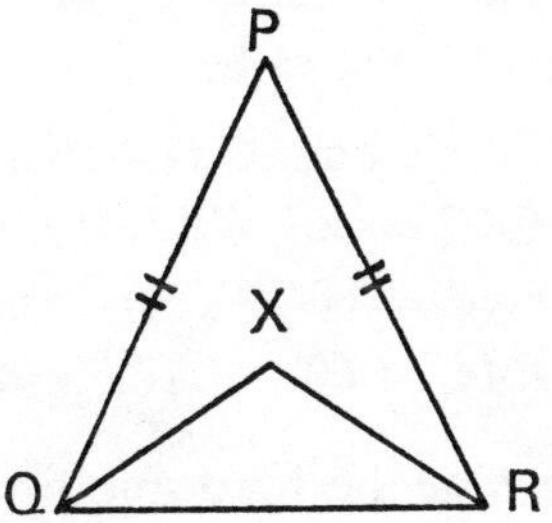

(ii) Express $\angle XQR$ in terms of x if $\angle P = x°$. OC (SMP)

12 From the following diagrams, which are not drawn to scale,

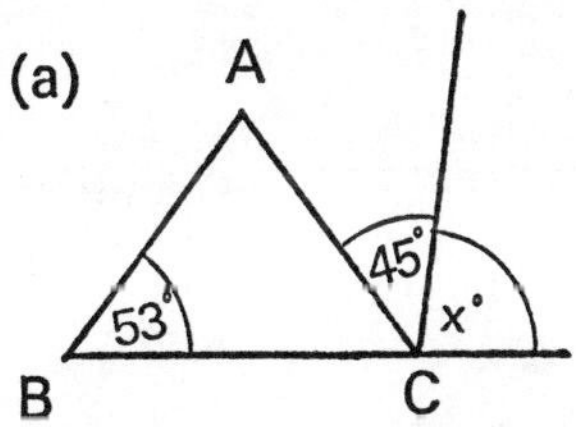

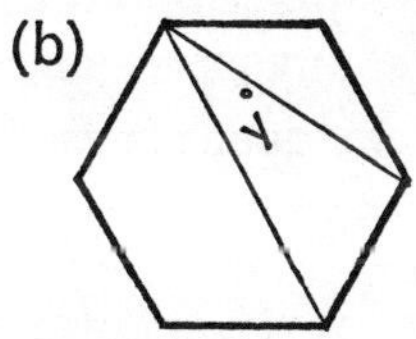

calculate x and y. In the first diagram $AB = AC$. In the second diagram, the hexagon is regular.

AEB

13 Given that angle $ABC = 40°$, $AB = 100$ mm, $AC = 80$ mm, the number of possible triangles which can be drawn with these measurements is

(*a*) none; (*b*) one; (*c*) two; (*d*) three

AEB

14 Is it true or false that the following conditions imply that the triangle ABC is congruent to the triangle DEF?

(*a*) angle A = angle D, $AB = DE$, $AC = DF$;
(*b*) angle A = angle D, angle B = angle E, angle C = angle F;
(*c*) angle A = angle D, angle B = angle E, $AB = DE$;
(*d*) angle A = angle D, $AB = DE$, $BC = EF$. AEB

15 A triangle ABC is to be drawn with each of the following sets of information. Which of the sets (*a*), (*b*), (*c*), (*d*) will enable a unique triangle to be drawn. [Unique is used in the sense that any triangle drawn with the information must be congruent to every other triangle drawn with the same information.]

(*a*) $AB = 30$ mm, $BC = 50$ mm, $CA = 10$ mm.
(*b*) $AB = 30$ mm, $\angle BAC = 60°$, $CA = 10$ mm.
(*c*) $AB = 30$ mm, $\angle BAC = 60°$, $CB = 25$ mm.
(*d*) $AB = 30$ mm, $\angle BAC = 60°$, $\angle ACB = 80°$. O

16 Is it true or false that the following figures are cyclic, i.e. a circle can be drawn passing through their vertices?

(*a*) any triangle;
(*b*) any quadrilateral;
(*c*) any square;
(*d*) any parallelogram;
(*e*) a quadrilateral with internal angles 43°, 106°, 137°, 74°, in that order. AEB

17 Is the following statement true or false?
O is the centre of the circle, $\angle AOB = 45°$ and $\angle BOC = 90°$ $\Rightarrow$ the length of chord BC is twice that of chord AB. SC

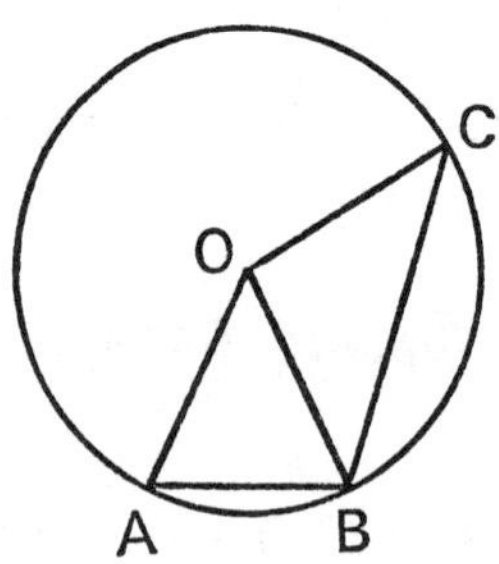

18 The centre of the inscribed circle of a triangle is the point of intersection of

(*a*) the perpendicular bisectors of the sides of the triangle;
(*b*) the internal bisectors of the angles of the triangle;
(*c*) the lines drawn from the vertices to the midpoints of the opposite sides;
(*d*) the perpendiculars from the vertices to the opposite sides.

AEB

19 A, B and C are three points on a circle whose centre is O and whose radius is 100 mm. The angle AOB is 60°. C is so placed that AC cuts OB between O and B. Calculate:

(*a*) the size of the angle ACB;
(*b*) the range of possible values of the length of AC;
(*c*) the range of possible values of the length of the arc ABC. L

20 In the figure, O is the centre of the circle.
Calculate the angles

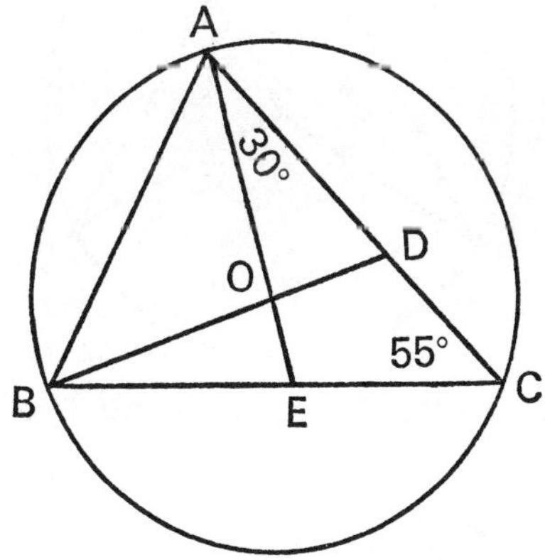

(i) DOE; (ii) DBE; (iii) ABD.

AEB

21

O is the centre of the circle and *BOC* is a diameter. Write down the value of the angle *AOC*. O

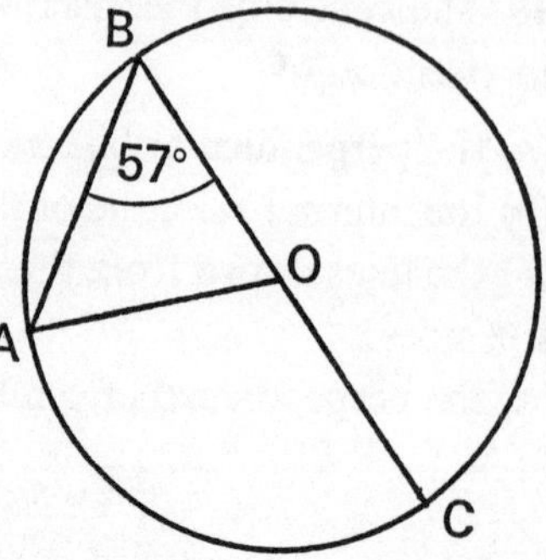

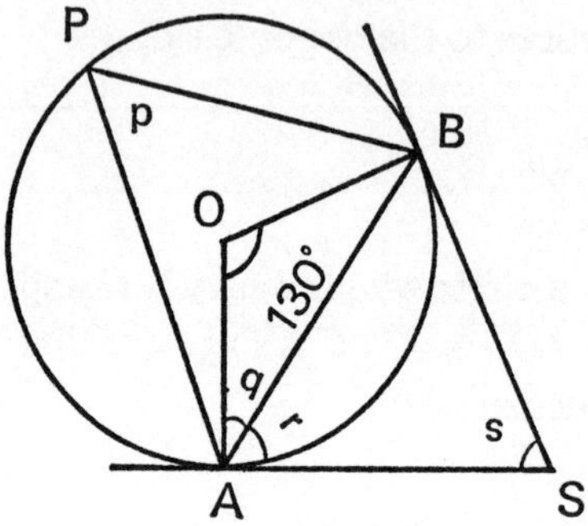

22 In the diagram *SA* and *SB* are tangents to a circle with centre *O* and $\angle AOB = 130°$. Calculate the angles marked *p*, *q*, *r* and *s*. NI

23

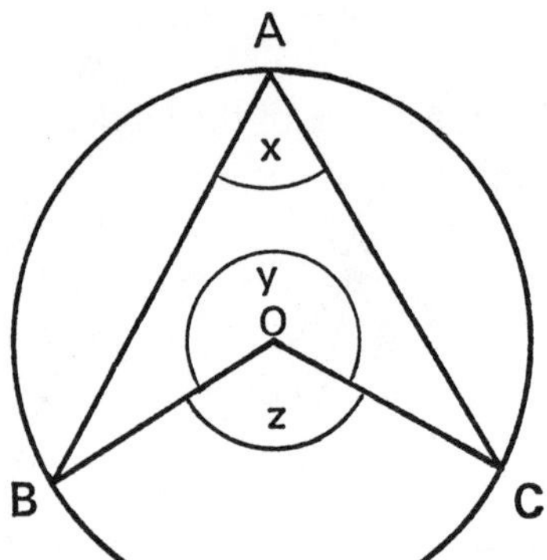

O is the centre of the circle; *A*, *B* and *C* are points on the circumference.

(i) If $x = 60°$, calculate *y*.

(ii) State the general equation relating *x* and *y*.

(iii) If the length of the minor arc $BC = 2OB$, calculate *z* in radians. O

24

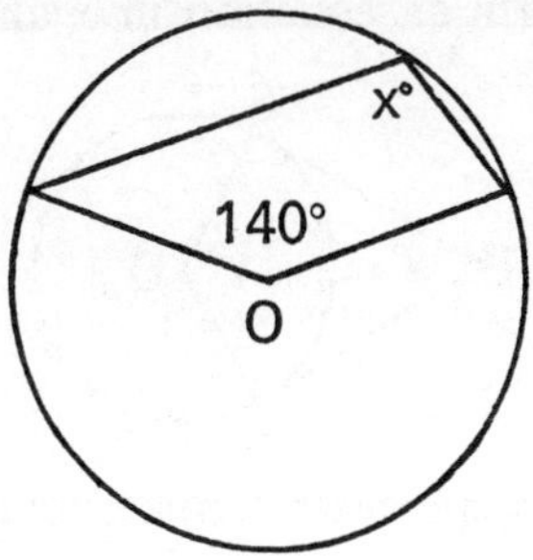

O is the centre of the circle. Find *x*. OC (SMP)

25 In the diagram *O* is the centre of the circumscribed circle of the triangle *ABC*. *AO* is produced to meet the circle at *D*.

Angle $BOC = 110°$ and angle $AOB = 130°$. Calculate: (i) angle *BAC*; (ii) angle *BDC*; (iii) angle *ADC*. SU

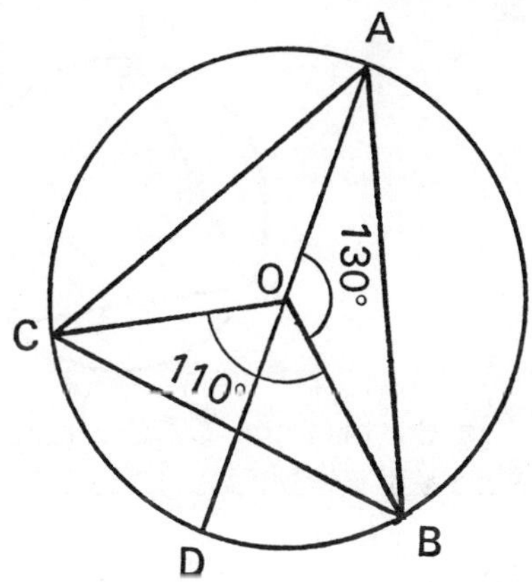

26

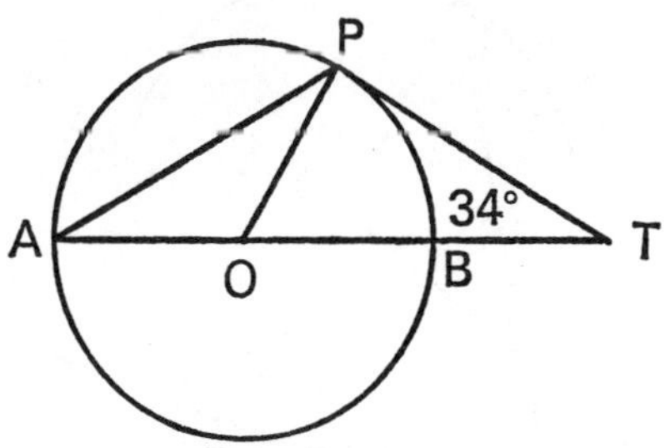

AOB is a diameter of a circle centre *O*. A tangent at a point *P* on the circle meets *AB* produced at *T*.

If angle $PTA = 34°$, calculate the size of (i) angle *TOP*; (ii) angle *OAP*. SC

27 (i) TA and TB are tangents to a circle centre O. If $\angle ATB = x°$ and $\angle AOB = y°$, form an equation in x and y.

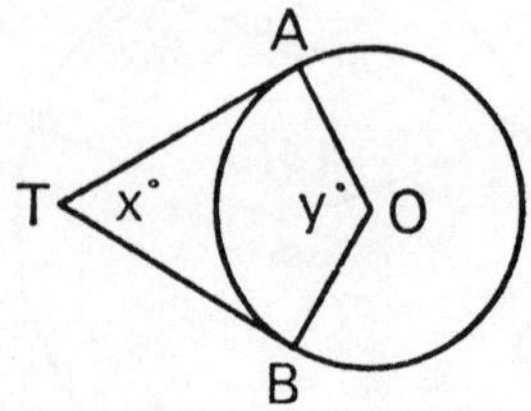

(ii) If in (i), $y < 130$, write down a corresponding inequation in x.

SC

28

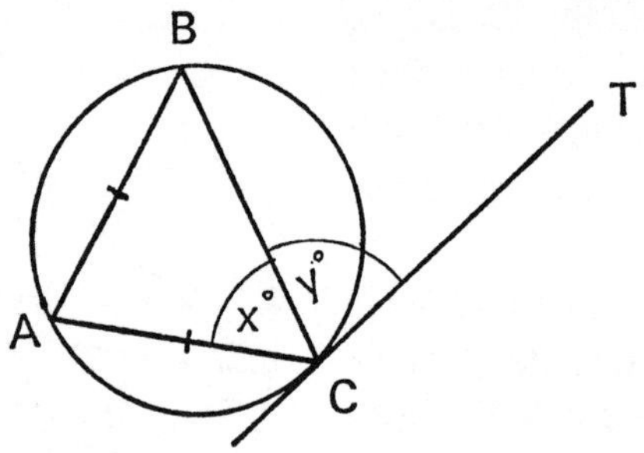

In the diagram, CT is a tangent to the circle and $AB = AC$. Find x if $y = 90°$.

OC (SMP)

29

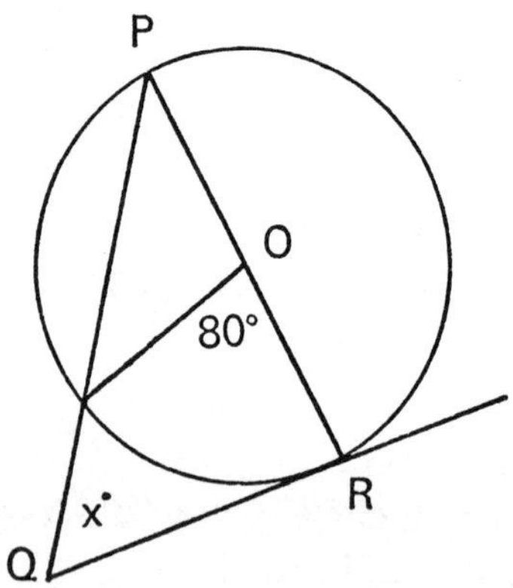

O is the centre of the circle and QR is the tangent at R. State the value of x.

C

30 FAE is a tangent to the circle. O is its centre.

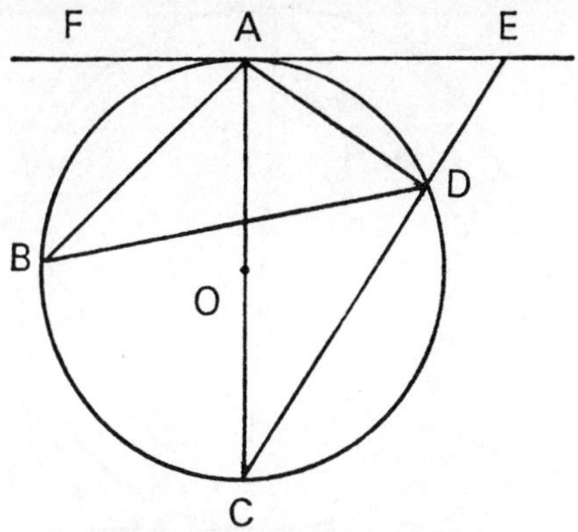

(i) Name an angle equal to $\angle ACE$.
(ii) Name two angles equal to $90° - \angle ACE$.
(iii) Using only points already labelled, name a pair of similar triangles, giving the vertices in corresponding order. OC (SMP)

31 In the following diagrams, which are not drawn to scale, calculate x, y and z. O is the centre of the circle in the first figure. TP and TP' are tangents to the circle in the second figure and $P'Q'$ is parallel to PQ.

(a)

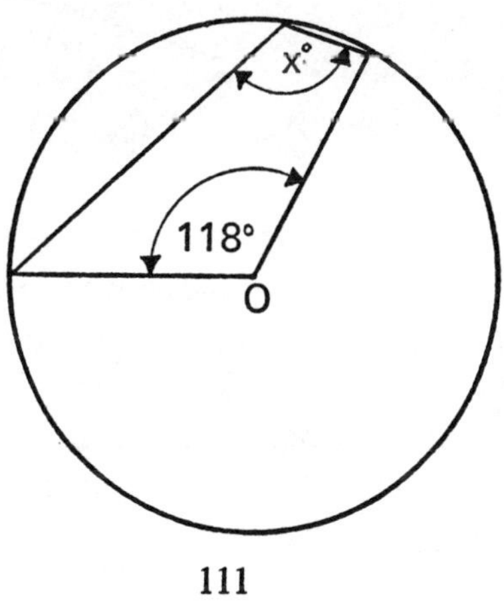

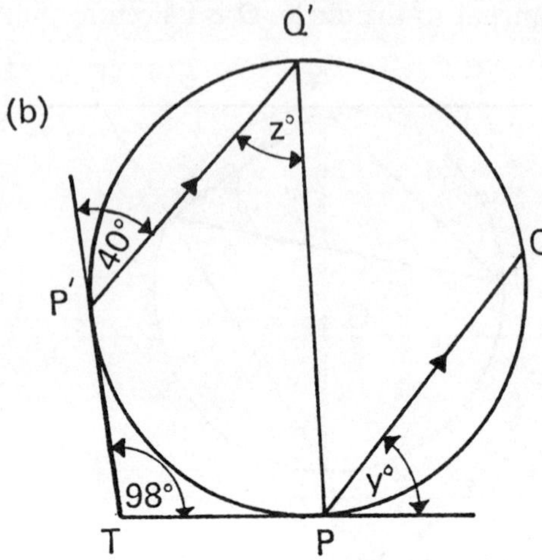

AEB

32 In the figure, *SAT* is a tangent to the circle at the point *A* and *AB* is a chord.

Which of the following are true?

Angle *SAB* is

(*a*) equal to angle *ADC*;
(*b*) equal to angle *BCA*;
(*c*) equal to angle *DAT*;
(*d*) equal to angle *BAC*;
(*e*) not equal to any one of the angles in (*a*), (*b*), (*c*) and (*d*).

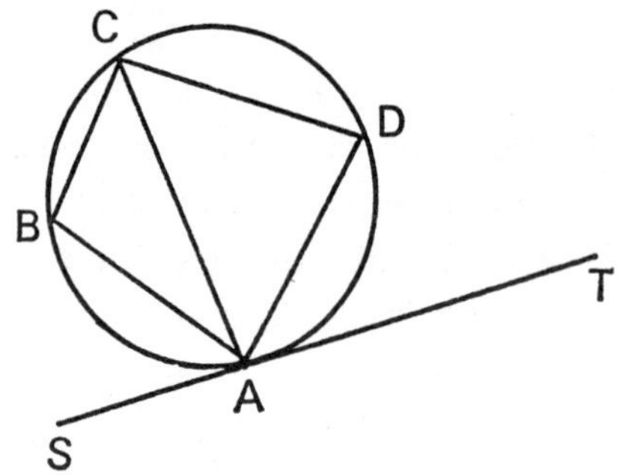

AEB

33 Prove that, if a straight line touches a circle and from the point of contact a chord is drawn, the angles which the chord makes with the tangent are equal to the angles in the alternate segments.

TAN is a tangent touching a circle at *A*. *TBC* is a straight line cutting the circle at *B* and *C* (*B* being nearer to *T*). If angle *CAN* is twice angle *BTA*, prove that *AB* = *BT*. SU

34 Two chords of a circle, AB and CD, intersect at right angles at K. If $AK = 6$ units, $CK = 3$ units, and $KD = 4$ units, find the length of KB.

If E is the midpoint of KD and AE is produced to meet the circle again at F, show that $AE = 4EF$. L

35 In the following diagram, which is not drawn to scale, PA is 12 mm shorter than PD. It is also given that $AB = 156$ mm, $CD = 96$ mm and $PA = x$ mm.

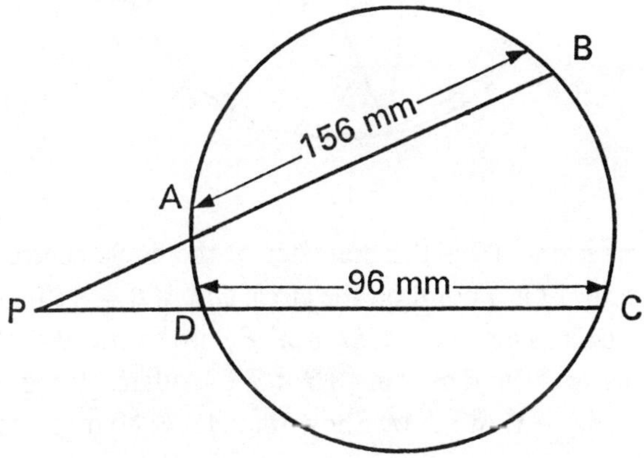

(i) Obtain an equation for x.
(ii) Calculate x. AEB

36 The line TP is the tangent at P to the circle PQR and TQR is the secant such that QR is a diameter. Given that $TP = 60$ mm and $TQ = 20$ mm, calculate

(i) the radius of the circle;
(ii) the angle PTQ;
(iii) the area of the triangle PTR. AEB

37 In the figure (Page 114) the two circles touch at O.
(i) Prove that triangle OEB is similar to triangle DCA.
(ii) If $AC = 30$ mm, $AD = 40$ mm, $EB = 40$ mm and $BD = 25$ mm, find the length of EA, using the fact that

$$DB \, . \, DO = DA \, . \, DE.$$ AEB

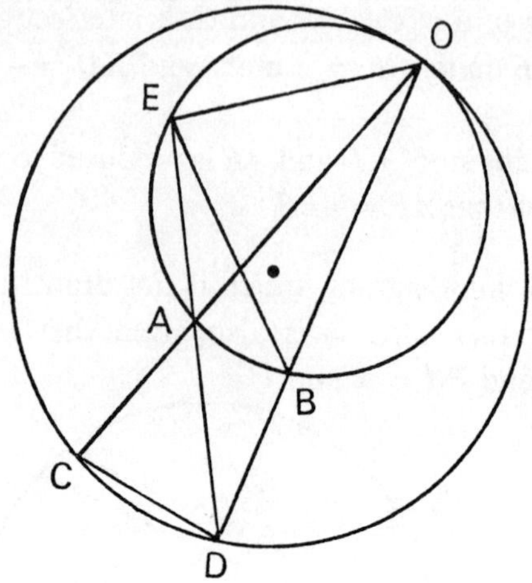

38 In the diagram, AB is the diameter of the circle centre O and radius 100 mm. M is a point on the circle and $MB = 120$ mm. The bisector of angle MBA meets AM at X. PQ is the chord through X perpendicular to AB and meeting AB at S. Calculate, giving reasons, the lengths AM, AX and XM. Show that $AS = 80$ mm and hence calculate PQ. SU

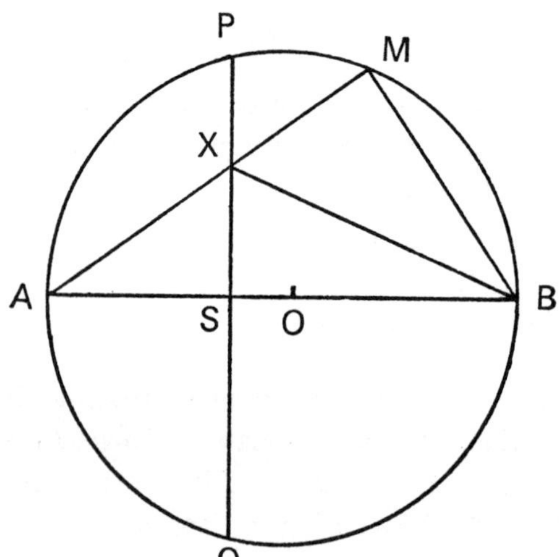

39 Construct two triangles ABC which satisfy the following data:

$$\text{angle } BAC = 57°, \quad AC = 72 \text{ mm}, \quad CB = 66 \text{ mm}.$$

In each case measure and state the length of AB. AEB

40 Triangle PQR is specified by $PQ = 65{\cdot}5$ mm,

$$QR = 82 \text{ mm},$$
$$\angle PQR = 54{\cdot}0°.$$

Make an accurate drawing of the triangle.

Leaving in the diagram any necessary construction lines or arcs, find O the centre of the circle passing through P, Q and R, and measure OP. SC

41 Using ruler and compasses only, construct a quadrilateral $ABCD$ inscribed in a circle of radius 50 mm given that the length of AB is 50 mm, the length of BC is 70 mm and that angle BAD is a right angle.

Measure and state the length of CD.

(All construction lines must be clearly shown). AEB

42 Copy the figure and construct a square $PQRS$ such that P lies on AB, Q lies on AC, and R and S are on BC. Leave all construction lines showing, so that your method is clear. (*Any geometrical instrument may be used for drawing right angles or parallels.*) OC (SMP)

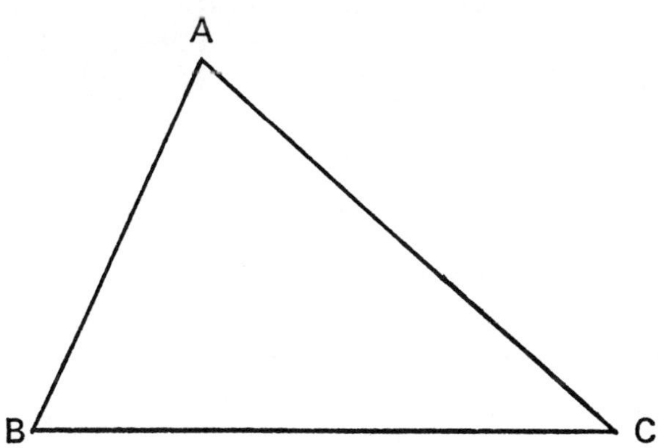

43 Draw a circle of radius 50 mm. Construct a chord AB of length 75 mm. Locate a point C on the circle such that the triangle ABC has the greatest possible area. AEB

44 Construct:

(*a*) a triangle of sides 50 mm, 60 mm and 70 mm;

(*b*) a similar triangle, without measuring, whose sides are two-thirds of the sides of the original triangle;

(*c*) a triangle whose sides are in the ratio 5 : 6 : 7 inscribed in a circle of radius 50 mm and whose vertices lie on the circle.

Measure the sides of the triangle in (*c*) to the nearest millimetre. L

45 Show how to construct an equilateral triangle PQR inside an acute-angled triangle ABC whose sides are unequal, so that RQ is parallel to BC and the vertices P, Q, R lie in the sides BC, CA, AB respectively. L

46 Copy the figure and construct a point A on the line of which a is a segment and a point B on the line of which b is a segment such that the triangle ABC has the shortest possible perimeter. L

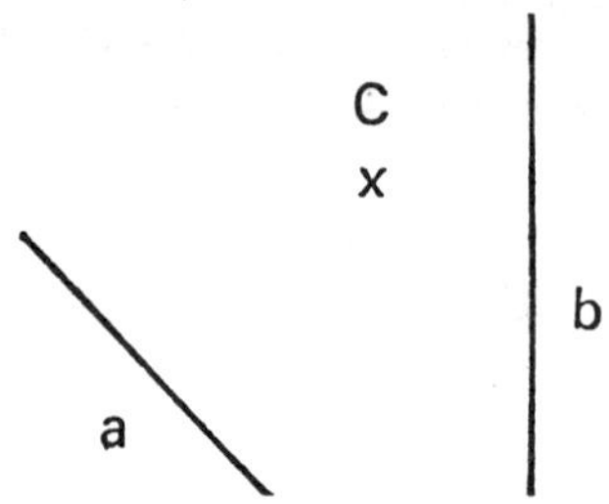

47 A and B are two fixed points. P is a point such that $\angle APB = 120°$.

The locus of P in a plane is:

(*a*) A circle.

(*b*) Two lines parallel to AB.

(*c*) Two circular arcs.

(*d*) An ellipse. OC (SMP)

48 M is the midpoint of the line segment AB. In a given plane containing AB the point P is such that the areas of triangles PAM and PBM are equal (and not equal to zero). The locus of P is:

(*a*) the line through M perpendicular to AB;
(*b*) a line parallel to AB;
(*c*) two lines parallel to AB;
(*d*) the whole plane except points on the line AB. OC (SMP)

49 A, B are two fixed points in space and $AB = 4$ units. P is a variable point in space such that $PA = 5$ units, $PB = 2$ units. The locus of P in space is (*a*) an ellipse, (*b*) a plane, (*c*) a circle, (*d*) none of these. OC (SMP)

50 A, B, C are the vertices of a triangle. The locus (in three dimensions) of a point which is equidistant from A, B and C is:

(*a*) a plane;
(*b*) two lines;
(*c*) a line;
(*d*) none of these. OC (SMP)

51 A and B are two fixed points in a plane. The locus of a variable point P in the plane such that $\angle APB$ has magnitude 50° is

(*a*) a complete circle;
(*b*) part of a circle;
(*c*) a line parallel to AB;
(*d*) parts of two circles;
(*e*) none of these. OC (SMP)

52 A and B are fixed points 40 mm apart. A point P is free to move in a fixed plane containing AB. Sketch the locus of P, and describe it briefly in words, in each of the following cases:

(i) AP is perpendicular to BP.
(ii) The area of triangle APB is constant, equal to 1000 mm^2.

NI

53

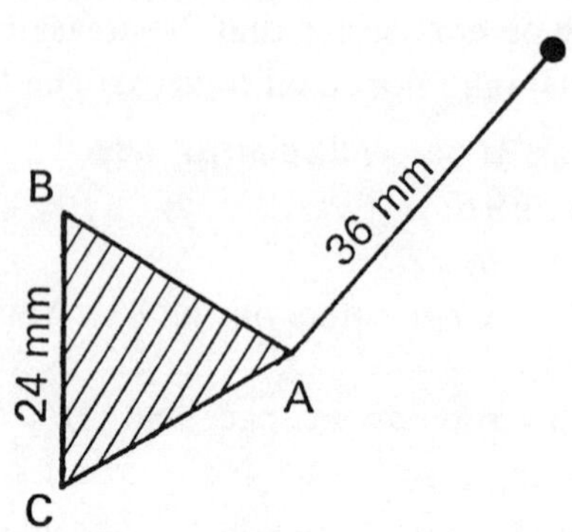

ABC is an equilateral triangle. *P* is a bead attached to *A* by a string of length 36 mm *P* moves in the plane of the triangle so that the string is always taut.

If the string cannot cross the triangle, sketch the locus of *P* on a drawing of triangle *ABC*. OC (SMP)

54

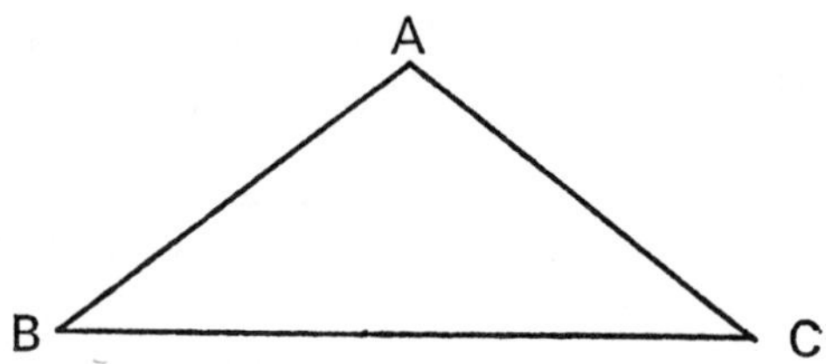

(i) Copy the diagram and draw in the locus of points which are within the triangle and are equidistant from *AB* and *BC*.
(ii) Shade the set of all points within the triangle which are nearer to *BC* than to *AB* and which are less than 25 mm from the point *A*. OC (SMP)

55 A circle is inscribed inside a square *ABCD*. Any point *P* of the circle is joined to any point *Q* of the square and *PQ* is produced to *R*, so that $PR = 2PQ$. Describe and illustrate:

(*a*) the locus of *R* as *Q* moves round the square for any fixed point *P* not a point of contact;

(*b*) the locus of R as P moves round the circle for any fixed point Q not a point of contact;
(*c*) the loci of R for one of the points of contact of the circle with the square. L

56 AB is a straight line segment of length 30 mm. Indicate on a drawing the locus in the plane of a point P: the distance from P

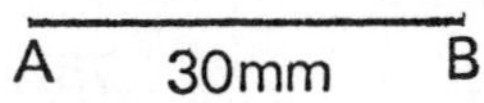

to the nearest point on AB is 20 mm. (An accurately drawn figure is not required.) OC (SMP)

57 The points A and B are 50 mm apart. Make a drawing and construct the following sets in the plane of the paper indicating them clearly on your figure.

(i) $X = \{\text{points } P : AP = 20 \text{ mm}\}$;
(ii) $Y = \{\text{points } P : \angle APB = 90°\}$.

What relation does the line joining B to one of the members of $X \cap Y$ have to the set X? O

58 AB is a chord of length 8 units in a circle with centre C and radius 5 units. M is the midpoint of AB.
Calculate:
(i) $\angle ACB$; (ii) the length CM.

State fully the locus of the midpoints of chords of length 8 units in a circle of radius 5 units. SC

59 O is a fixed point and $S = \{P : OP = 60 \text{ mm}\}$. Draw the locus S. If OP_0 is the initial position of OP and N is the foot of the perpendicular from P to OP_0, draw as accurately as possible the locus T, where

$$T = \{\text{points } Q : Q \text{ lies on } PN \text{ and } PQ = \tfrac{1}{5} \text{ of } PN\}.$$

If L is on OP_0 and $OL = 36$ mm and M is the image of L in O, find the sum of the lengths LQ and MQ for several positions of Q and comment on your results. L

60 The diagram shows a frustum of a right-circular cone. The plane circular faces c and c' are parallel and L, L' are their centres.

$$LM \,||\, L'M', LL' = 100 \text{ mm}, LM = 75 \text{ mm}, L'M' = 125 \text{ mm}.$$

(i) Calculate the distance MM'.

(ii) Calculate the height of the complete cone from which this frustum has been cut.

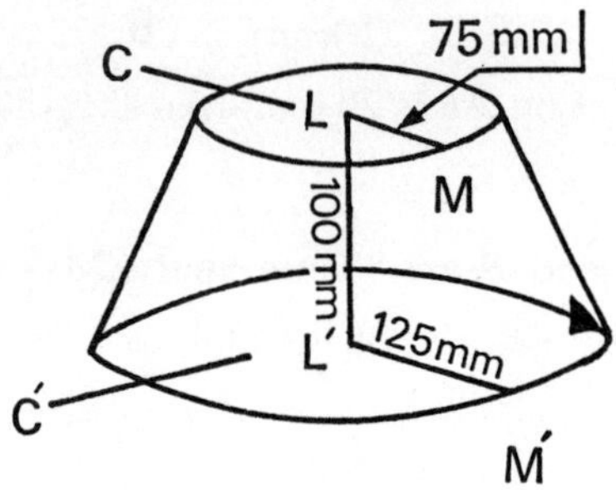

(iii) The frustum is placed with MM' in contact with a horizontal table and rolls without sliding. Describe fully the locus of the point of contact of c with the table. OC (SMP)

61 A rod AB, of length 300 mm is pivoted at A and rotates clockwise, in a horizontal plane, at a constant rate. It takes 60 s to make 1 revolution. An insect starts at A and moves, along the

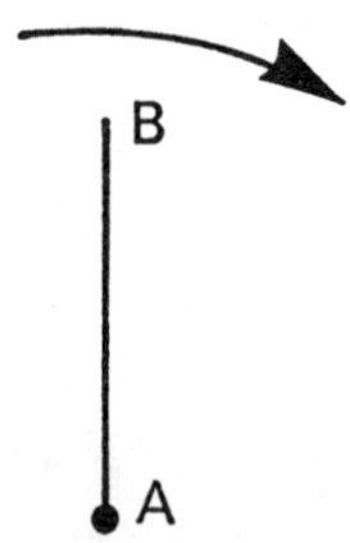

rod, towards B at a constant speed of 5 mm/s. Sketch the path traced out by the insect. C

62 (i) Mark points A and B at a distance apart of 60 mm. Use compasses to find eight points belonging to the set $C = \{P : AP = 2BP\}$, leaving the construction arcs clearly showing. Sketch the locus C.
(ii) If L denotes the set of points on the line AB and $\{X, Y\} = L \cap C$, calculate the distance XY.
(iii) Let $H = \{P : AP > BP\}$, and $K = \{P : AP < 2BP\}$. Mark on your diagram the boundary of H. Indicate by horizontal shading the set $H \cap K$ and by vertical shading the set K', labelling each.

OC (SMP)

63 (i) Using the theorem of Pythagoras obtain (do not merely state) a formula giving the distance from the origin to the point (x, y, z) in space.
(ii) C is the surface of the sphere whose centre is the origin and whose radius is 7 units. Regarding C as a set of points, express it in the form $\{(x, y, z): \qquad \}$.
(iii) Identify the locus $D = \{(x, y, 4)\}$.
(iv) Express $C \cap D$ in the form

$$\{(x, y, 4): \qquad \}$$

and interpret the result geometrically. OC (SMP)

64 Are the following statements true or false?
(*a*) Any square is similar to any rectangle.
(*b*) Any square is similar to any rhombus.
(*c*) Any triangle is similar to any other triangle with the same area.

AEB

65 Is it true or false that the following conditions imply that the triangle ABC is similar to the triangle DEF?
(*a*) Angle A = angle D, $AB = DE$, $AC = DF$.
(*b*) Angle A = angle D, angle B = angle E.
(*c*) $AB = DE$, $AC = 2DF$, $BC = 3EF$.
(*d*) $AB : DE = AC : DF$, angle A = angle D. AEB

66

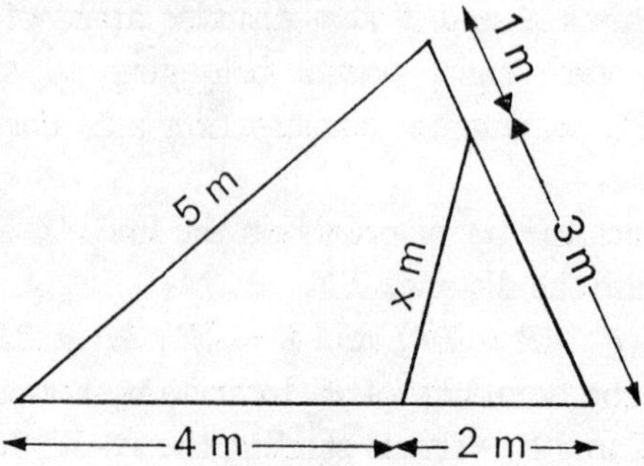

Using a geometric argument, or otherwise, calculate the value of x. C

67

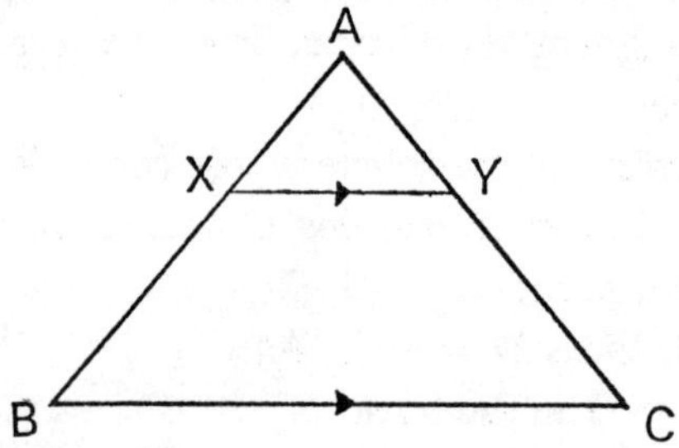

In the triangle ABC (not to scale), $AB = 9$ units, $BC = 12$ units. XY is parallel to BC and $AX = 3$ units. Calculate the length of XY. O

68 A slide projector throws a beam with constant angular width on to a screen set perpendicular to the axis of the beam. If the picture width is 1·2 m the projector must be sited 1·6 m from the screen. Through what distance must the projector be moved forward to reduce the picture width to 1·05 m? SU

69 x units, y units denote the perpendicular distances respectively between the pairs of parallel lines a, b and c, d as shown (Page 123).

If $AB = 10$ units, $BC = 4$ units, find a relationship between x and y.

Evaluate x, if $y = 5$. L

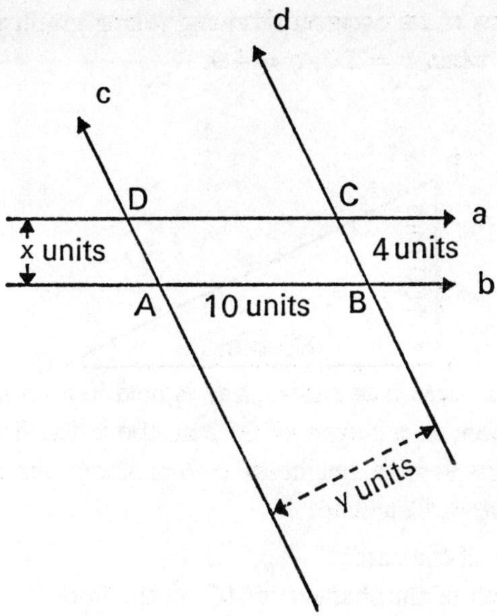

70

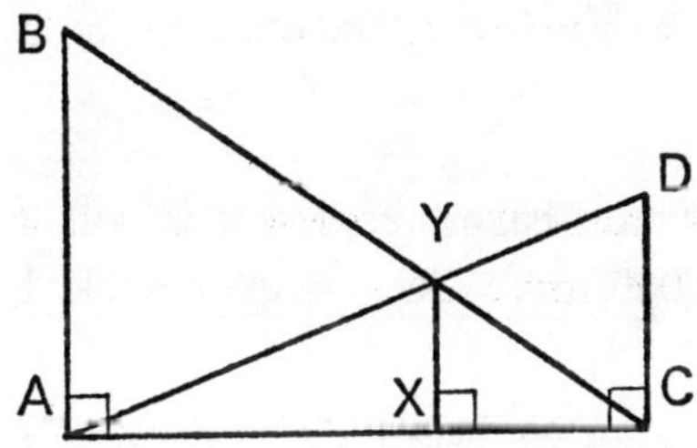

In the diagram AB, XY and CD are at right angles to AC. $AB = p$, $CD = q$, $XY = x$.

(i) Explain why

$$\frac{x}{q} = \frac{AX}{AC},$$

and copy and complete the equation

$$\frac{x}{p} = \frac{\quad}{AC}.$$

(ii) Use these results to simplify

$$\frac{x}{q} + \frac{x}{p}, \quad \text{and show that} \quad \frac{1}{p} + \frac{1}{q} = \frac{1}{x}.$$

(iii) By means of an accurate drawing (using graph paper if you wish) find x when $p = 2{\cdot}7$, $q = 4{\cdot}9$. OC (SMP)

71

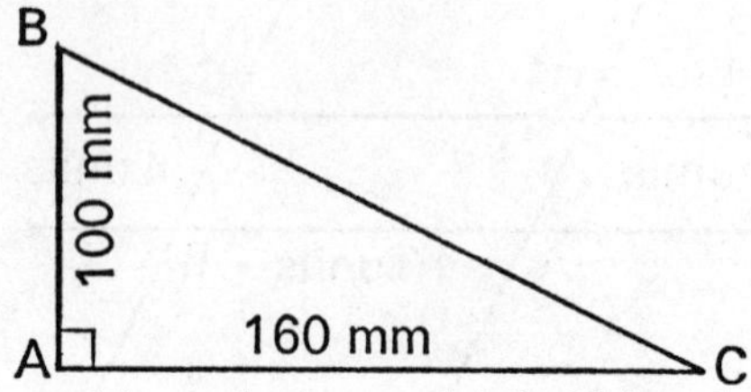

A triangular card is as shown, and is held in a horizontal plane in a dark room at a height of 0·72 m above the floor. A point source of light is at a height of 2·16 m above the floor and is directly above A. Calculate:

(i) the area of the card;

(ii) the length of the shadow of AC on the floor;

(iii) the area of the shadow of the card on the floor.

OC (SMP)

72 The area of an island represented on a map of scale 1 : 100 000 is 20 000 mm². On a map of scale 1 : 50 000 its area would be

(*a*) 5000 mm²; (*b*) 10 000 mm²; (*c*) 80 000 mm²; (*d*) 40 000 mm².

OC (SMP)

73

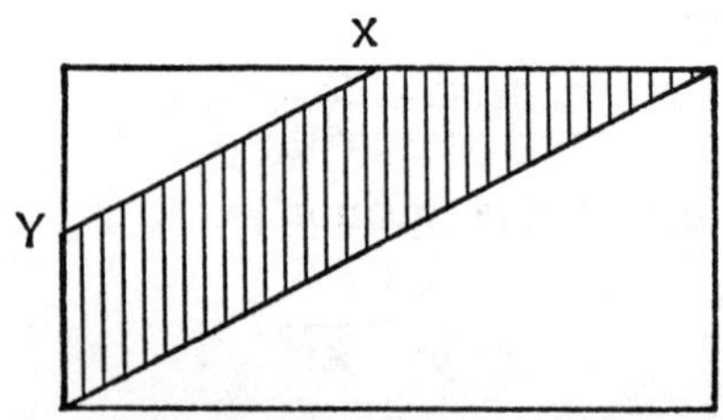

X and Y are midpoints of the sides of the rectangle. The ratio of the shaded area to the area of the whole rectangle is (*a*) $\frac{3}{8}$; (*b*) $\frac{1}{4}$; (*c*) $\frac{1}{3}$; (*d*) none of these. OC (SMP)

74

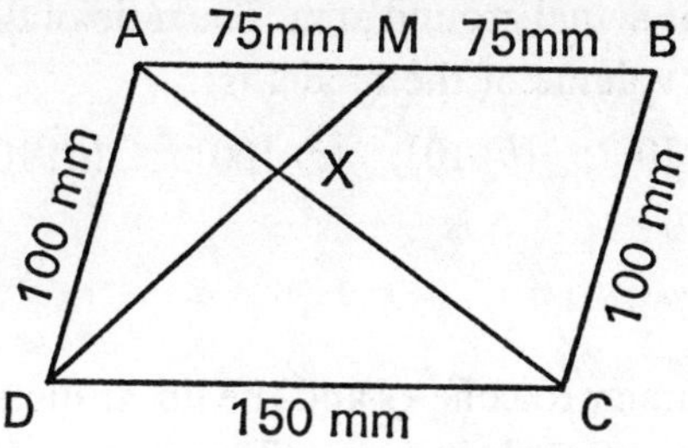

(i) The fraction

$$\frac{\text{Area of } \triangle AMX}{\text{Area of } \triangle CDX}$$

is equal to (*a*) $\frac{1}{2}$; (*b*) $\frac{1}{3}$; (*c*) $\frac{1}{4}$; (*d*) none of these.

(ii) The fraction

$$\frac{\text{Area of } \triangle CDX}{\text{Area of parallelogram } ABCD}$$

is equal to (*a*) $\frac{1}{3}$; (*b*) $\frac{1}{4}$; (*c*) $\frac{1}{6}$; (*d*) none of these. OC (SMP)

75 A triangle has an area of 25 000 mm^2. The points *D*, *E* and *F* are the midpoints of the sides of the triangle. State the area of the triangle *DEF*. OC (SMP)

76 A scalc model of a ship is one-two-hundredth as long as the ship itself. Copy and complete the following table:

	Ship	Model
Height of mast	............m	100 mm
Area of deck	............m^2	90 000 mm^2
Volume of hold	16 000 m^3	............mm^3
No. of cabins	200	

NI

77 In a scale model of a building, the ground area is one-hundredth of the actual ground area. The ratio of the volume of the building to the volume of the model is:

(*a*) 100^3; (*b*) 10^3; (*c*) 100^{-3}; (*d*) 10^{-3}.

OC (SMP)

78 Cone P is similar to cone Q and the linear dimensions of P are three times those of Q. Is it true or false that

(*a*) the surface area of P is 9 times the surface area of Q?

(*b*) the volume of P is 9 times the volume of Q? AEB

79 A plane intersects a right-circular cone and is parallel to the base of the cone. If V is the vertex of the cone and VA the altitude, then let B be the point where the plane cuts VA. It is given that $VB : BA = 3 : 2$. Are the following statements true or false?

(*a*) The ratio of the volume of the small cone (the upper part of the section) to the volume of the whole cone is 8 : 27.

(*b*) The ratio of the surface area of the small cone to the surface area of the whole cone is 9 : 25.

(*c*) The ratio of the volume of the small cone to the volume of the frustum of the cone (the lower part of the section) is 27 : 125.

AEB

80 A model of a boat is made on a scale of 1 to 10.

(i) If the boat is 20 m long, how long is the model?

(ii) If there are k m^2 of deck area in the model, what is the deck area on the boat?

(iii) The boat's fuel tank has a capacity of 10 m^3. Calculate the capacity of the model's fuel tank.

(iv) If the boat has a speed of x m/s, can you say anything about the speed of the model? OC (SMP)

81 A circular cylinder is of length 240 mm and cross-sectional area 160 mm^2. A second such cylinder has length 180 mm and cross-sectional area 120 mm^2. State, with reason, whether the cylinders are geometrically similar. OC (SMP)

82 A spherical balloon of radius 100 mm is blown up, still remaining spherical, so that it occupies eight times the original volume. Find its new radius. OC (SMP)

83 A conical flask of height 100 mm has a capacity of 100 000 mm^3. Calculate the height of a similar conical flask which has a capacity of 500 000 mm^3. AEB

Chapter Ten

1 Given two normal dice, are the following statements true or false?
(*a*) The probability of throwing two sixes is less than that of throwing a six and a five.
(*b*) The probability of throwing a total score of 10 is greater than that of throwing a total score of 11.
(*c*) The probability of throwing a total score of five is $\frac{1}{9}$. AEB

2 Are the following statements true or false?
If a penny is tossed three times then
(*a*) the probability of a head each time is less than that of a head, a tail and a head, in that order;
(*b*) the probability of a head each time is less than that of a head and two tails, in any order;
(*c*) the probability of a head first and at least one more head is $\frac{1}{2}$.
AEB

3 State the probability that a throw of a die will result in a score of 3 or more. OC (SMP)

4 A card is selected at random from a pack of playing cards. State the probability
(i) that the card is a club;
(ii) that the card is either a club or an ace (or both).
OC (SMP)

5(*a*) A is a set containing four elements. $\bar{A}$ is the set of all ordered pairs of elements of A, i.e. pairs (a, b), where $a \in A$ and $b \in A$. How many elements are there in $\bar{A}$?
(*b*) If A is the set $\{0, 1, 2, 3\}$, what is the probability that an element (a, b) of $\bar{A}$ picked at random is such that $a < b$? AEB

6 A bag contains 30 discs: 10 red, 10 green, 10 yellow.
(i) If three are drawn out in succession and not replaced, what is the probability of drawing 2 reds and 1 yellow in that order?
(ii) If each disc is replaced after drawing what would the answer be now? OC (SMP)

7 100 discs, numbered from 1 to 100, are placed in a bag and one is drawn out at random. State the probability that the number on the disc includes the digit 9. C

8 A bag contains 10 marbles, of which 5 are red, 3 are blue and 2 are green. They are drawn out at random, one by one, and are not replaced. Find the probability that:
(i) the first one drawn will be blue;
(ii) the first one drawn will be either red or green;
(iii) the first one drawn will be red and the second will be green. NI

9 When I throw a dart at a dart-board, trying to score as much as possible, there is a probability of $\frac{1}{2}$ that I score over 12. If I throw two darts at the board, what is the probability that
(*a*) I score over 12 both times;
(*b*) I score over 12 at least once. O

10 In a class of 40 boys, 3 have the first name John and 4 have the surname Smith. Calculate the probability that a boy chosen at random should have the name John Smith. Calculate also the probability that each of the boys with the name John has the name John Smith.

If, further, 2 boys have the surname Brown, calculate the probability that a boy chosen at random should have either the name John Smith or the name John Brown. AEB

11 Two cards are drawn at random from nine cards numbered 1 to 9. What is the probability that both two-digit numbers, which can be formed by placing the cards side by side, are prime numbers? L

12 (i) A man has large numbers of £1 and £5 notes. Write down, in table form, the different ways in which he can pay a bill of £33. State the probability that he uses at least twenty £1 notes.
(ii) A bag X contains 3 red balls and 3 blue balls and a bag Y contains 4 yellow balls. A ball is taken from X and placed in Y and then one is taken from Y. Given that the selections are random, find the probability that the ball taken from Y is blue. C

13 There are two candidates for a by-election. A random sample survey of eligible voters contained 52 per cent and 48 per cent favouring the first and second candidates respectively. In the election, 55 per cent and 60 per cent of those favouring the first and second candidates respectively voted out of a total electorate of 80 000. Assuming that the random sample was truly representative, find which candidate was elected and by what majority. L

14 Three men agree to meet outside the Town Hall at a specified time. If the probabilities of each man being unable to keep the appointment are independent and have values $\frac{1}{2}$, $\frac{3}{8}$, $\frac{3}{4}$, find the probabilities (*a*) that all three meet, (*b*) only two of them meet. L

15 During a school year, a half-holiday may be given on any afternoon from Monday to Friday. Assuming that any one of these five days is equally likely, find the probability that two half-holidays given in one school year occur

(*a*) both on Monday afternoons;
(*b*) both on afternoons of the same day of the week;
(*c*) neither on Monday afternoons. L

16 If all birthdays are equally likely to occur in any month of any year, show that the probability that the birthdays of two randomly chosen people do not occur in the same month is 11/12.

Find the probability that three randomly chosen people do not have birthdays in the same month. L

17 For simplicity, assume that every day can be described as either fine or wet. If it is fine today, the probability that it will be fine tomorrow is 0·7. If it is wet today, the probability that it will be wet tomorrow is 0·6.

(i) Copy and complete the following table, showing the probabilities of tomorrow's weather, given today's:

		Tomorrow	
		Fine	Wet
Today	Fine	0.7	
	Wet		

(ii) Calculate the probability that, if Monday is fine, (*a*) both Tuesday and Wednesday will be fine; (*b*) Wednesday will be fine, regardless of Tuesday's weather.

(iii) M is the matrix formed by the entries in the table; N is the corresponding matrix for the probabilities of the-day-after-tomorrow's weather, given today's. Express N in terms of M.

OC (SMP)

18 (i) A bag of 6 chocolates all looking alike has 4 with soft centres and 2 with hard centres. What is the probability that the first one eaten will be soft-centred?

(ii) What is the probability that the second one eaten will be soft-centred: (*a*) if it is known that the first one was soft, (*b*) if it is known that the first one was hard?

(iii) Use the results of part (ii) to find the probability that the second one eaten will be soft, if it is not known whether the first was hard or soft.

(iv) If nothing is known about the first two eaten, what do you think will be the probability that the third one eaten will be soft-centred?

OC (SMP)

19 In a road safety survey, 1000 vehicles were examined. 62 of these were found to have defective tyres, 30 had defective steering and 45 had defective brakes. Assuming that this sample does accurately represent all the vehicles in this country, find the probability that a vehicle chosen at random

(i) has defective brakes;
(ii) has defective brakes but neither of the other two defects;
(iii) has all three defects;
(iv) has no defects.

If the owner of a defective vehicle is warned if his car has one or two of these defects, but is fined £20 if his car has all three defects, what is the total amount of fines that one would expect to be imposed after 10 000 vehicles had been inspected at random? AEB

20 A school blouse is made in three sizes, small, medium and large. In a class of 24 girls, 5 can wear the large size, of whom 3 can also wear the medium size (but none the small size). Altogether 18 of the class can wear the medium size, 7 can wear the small size, and all can wear at least one size.

(i) Draw a Venn diagram to illustrate this.
(ii) If one girl is chosen at random from the class, find the probability that she can wear
(*a*) a large-size blouse;
(*b*) a medium size but not a large size;
(*c*) both a medium size and a small size.
(iii) If a girl wearing a small-size blouse is chosen, find the probability that she cannot wear a medium-size blouse. OC (SMP)

21 (i) A die is thrown and a coin is tossed. X denotes the set $\{1, 2, 3, 4, 5, 6\}$ and Y denotes the set {heads, tails}. List the elements of the set $Z = \{(p, q): p \in X, q \in Y\}$.

State the probability of obtaining an even number on the die with a tail on the coin.

(ii) A large board is divided into 75 mm squares. The figure *ABCD* shows four of these squares. A coin, of diameter 30 mm, is thrown on to the board so that its centre lies within *ABCD*.

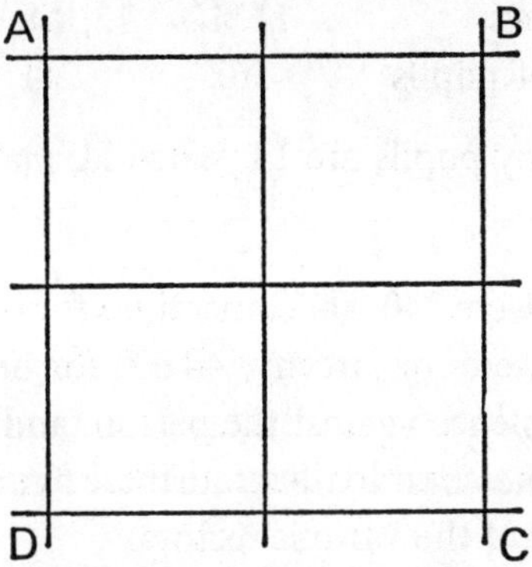

Indicate by shading, on a sketch of *ABCD*, the regions within which the centre of the coin must lie if the coin does not cover any part of any line. What is the probability that the coil will not cover any part of a line? What is the probability that it will not cover any part of the line in either of two successive throws? C

22 Of 100 pupils 25 prefer French, 35 prefer German, 40 prefer Spanish. Illustrate with a pie-chart and state the sector angles.
OC (SMP)

23 Ninety children on a picnic were offered the choice of four types of sandwich. 31 chose ham, 23 beef, 14 cheese and the rest tomato. Construct a pie-chart to illustrate this choice. If the cost of the four types of sandwich per packet was 5p, 6p, 4p and $3\frac{1}{2}$p respectively, what was the average cost per child of providing one packet each? SU

24 In a school, the number of pupils in respective age groups are shown in the following table:

Age in years	11, 12, 13, 14	15, 16	17, 18
Number of pupils	321	162	57

Illustrate this data by means of a pie-chart and give a table showing clearly the angle of each slice.

Given, in addition, the following information:

Age in years	11, 12	13, 14, 15	14, 15
Number of pupils	162	241	160

calculate how many pupils are 14 years old, making your method clear. C

25 In 1967, there were 240 000 convictions for indictable offences: of these, 140 000 were for larceny, 48 000 for breaking and entering, 17 000 for violence against the person, and the rest for other offences. Draw a pie-chart to illustrate these figures, marking in the sizes of the angles of the various sectors. L

26 Construct a frequency table of occurrence of the digits 0 to 9 from the last digits in column 0 of the first page of logarithms from the top line 10 to line 49. Represent the table in two ways by a bar-chart and a pie-chart. L

27 Each week there are numerous classified advertisements in a newspaper. The following is a list of some of the types of advertisement which appear in the Appointments Vacant section, showing the number of columns devoted to them in one issue. Illustrate the list in a suitable way, e.g. a bar-chart.

Type	*No. of columns*
Librarians	1
Fellowships	2
Universities	10
Colleges of Education	8
Service of Youth	3
Child Care	2
Special Education	7

AEB

28 Find the mean value of: 10, 13, 14, 15, 18.

Deduce the mean value of:

(*a*) 710, 713, 714, 715, 718.
(*b*) −6, −3, −2, −1, 2.
(*c*) 50, 65, 70, 75, 90. L

29 A traffic enquiry was undertaken to compare the contributions of private and public transport to the problem of road congestion. 100 successive cars travelling along a certain road were observed, the number of *passengers* in each car being noted (i.e. excluding the driver). The classified results were as follows:

No. of passengers per car	0	1	2	3	4	5
No. of cars	70	20	5	3	2	0

(i) Represent the information in the above table in an appropriate graphical form.
(ii) Calculate the mean number of passengers per car.
(iii) State the probability, at a given instant during the census, that the next car to pass would carry at least 2 passengers.
(iv) Allowing a 15 m length of road to each car, calculate the mean length of road per *car-occupant*. NI

30 A skilled player of the game of 'shove ha'penny' was asked to test his skill in propelling his disc so as to stop as close as possible to a mark at a distance of 400 mm. His results for 50 trials, measured to the nearest mm, were as follows:

373	376	378	362	405	409	363	396	392	427
427	423	406	401	380	447	425	395	397	369
396	407	410	406	384	388	362	412	393	390
384	414	408	393	401	416	426	393	376	387
402	409	384	418	403	405	426	403	395	404

Tabulate the results in classes of 10 mm width, commencing with the class 360–369 inclusive, and plot a histogram to exhibit the frequency distribution so obtained. Calculate (i) the mean of the *classified* distribution, treating each class as located at its middle-point; (ii) the median of the given distribution. O

31 In an examination, 250 candidates had total marks distributed as follows:

0–100 marks : 50 candidates
100–200 marks : 115 candidates
200–300 marks : 85 candidates.

Calculate a mean mark, stating clearly any assumptions you have made. L

32 The height distribution of a class of 30 children was as follows:

Mid-interval height (mm)	1400	1450	1500	1550	1600
Frequency	2	7	11	6	4

Calculate an estimate of the mean height of the class. L

33 In each of five towns, the heights of a sample of the male population were recorded and the mean calculated. The results were as follows:

Town	*Sample Size*	*Mean Height*
A	150	1800 mm
B	200	1770 mm
C	400	1810 mm
D	350	1830 mm
E	400	1810 mm

What is the mean height of the complete sample over all the towns?

How many towns show mean heights below the overall mean? SU

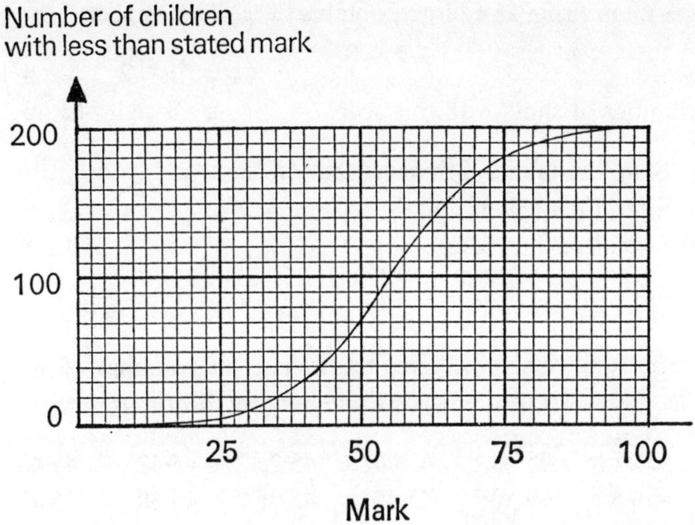

34 The diagram above shows the cumulative frequency graph for the marks of a set of 200 children who took an examination with a top mark of 100.

From the graph estimate:

(i) the median mark;
(ii) the interquartile range;
(iii) the pass mark, if 140 children passed. O

35 A random sample of 100 householders in a village were asked how many refugee children they would be prepared to accommodate. The answers were classified as follows:

No. of children	0	1	2	3	4	5	6 or more.
No. of householders	23	20	38	14	3	2	0.

Find the median and the mean of this distribution.

There was no time to question the other householders, but it was known that there were 376 householders in the village. Estimate the number of children that the village could accommodate. L

36 A man, firing at a target, obtains the following scores.

Score	0	1	2	3	4	5
Number of shots with this score	2	8	11	12	6	1

(i) State the mode of this distribution.
(ii) State the median.
(iii) Calculate the mean. OC (SMP)

37 The following table gives the weights in grammes of 40 golf balls, measured to the nearest one-hundredth of a gramme:

45·61	45·08	45·00	45·26	45·42	45·48
45·38	45·50	45·45	45·05	45·38	45·47
45·29	45·29	45·42	44·79	45·20	44·76
45·34	45·66	45·34	45·29	45·48	45·31
44·92	45·46	45·41	44·98	45·69	45·37
45·21	45·55	45·44	45·68	45·02	45·53
45·04	45·02	45·37	45·28		

Beginning at 44·695 g and using a class interval of 0·1 g construct a histogram for this data. Which is the modal class of this distribution? SU

38 A bag is found to contain nails of the following sizes:

Length	12 mm	18 mm	24 mm	30 mm	36 mm	48 mm
No. of nails	15	30	50	45	40	20

State the modal class.

Determine the class which contains the median of the distribution.

If one nail is chosen at random from the bag, what is the probability that it is 18 mm long? C

39 A man played several games of skittles. The scores he obtained are shown in the following table.

Score	0	1	2	3	4	5	6	7	8	9
Frequency	2	0	3	3	6	5	5	4	2	0

(i.e. the number of times the above score was obtained)

Find:

(i) the mode; (ii) the median; (iii) the mean score.

C

40 The results of an examination taken by 100 candidates are given in the following table.

Mark obtained	0–19	20–39	40–59	60–79	80–99
Number of candidates:	10	15	35	27	13

(i) Draw a histogram to illustrate these results.
(ii) What is the modal group of marks? AEB

41 100 oranges were tested for their vitamin C content, with the following results:

Amount of Vit. C in milligrams, to the nearest milligram	25	26	27	28	29	30	31	32	33	34	35
No. of oranges	1	6	4	13	18	21	16	12	6	2	1

(*a*) Find the mean and median vitamin C content.
(*b*) What is the probability that an orange selected at random from this batch has a vitamin C content less than the mean? (You may assume that in any group the vitamin C content of the oranges is evenly distributed.) AEB

42 The table shows an analysis, at a certain date, of a country's merchant fleet according to age of ships. Form a cumulative frequency table and draw a cumulative frequency graph. Use your graph to estimate, to the nearest year, the median and the quartiles of the distribution. Explain why it is not possible to calculate a mean age.

Age of ships (years)	Number
Under 5	85
5 and under 10	85
10 and under 15	81
15 and under 20	80
20 and under 25	60
25 and under 30	33
Over 30	16

O

43 A group of 100 soldiers, who were considered reasonable marksmen, each fired one shot from a rifle at a target. The distance from the centre of the target was measured for each shot, giving the following table:

Distance mm (to nearest millimetre)	0	20	40	60	80	100	120	140	160
No. of shots:	27	6	0	1	4	14	40	6	2

(i) Draw a cumulative frequency curve to represent this information.

(ii) Find the mean, mode and median distances from the centre of the target.

(iii) Which of the three measures gives the best representation of the data?

(iv) If this experiment were designed to test the suitability of the rifle for general use, design a further experiment in order to test the conclusions of the above. State carefully what you would measure and how you would reach your conclusions. AEB

44 The table below shows the cumulative mark distribution of 560 candidates in an examination. Construct a cumulative frequency curve, labelling your axes clearly. How many candidates fail if the pass mark is 45? What must the pass mark be if 60 per cent of the candidates are to pass? Determine the median of the distribution.

Mark	10	20	30	40	50	60	70	80	90	100
Number of Candidates less than or equal to given mark	18	43	78	130	240	372	462	523	552	560

SU

45 A group of 100 children were given two similar tests with the following results:

Mark	0	1	2	3	4	5	6	7	8	9	10	11	12	13	14	15
Frequency (1)	0	0	1	4	6	11	8	10	14	7	11	5	8	8	3	4
Frequency (2)	1	1	6	8	2	8	6	13	14	13	4	8	5	7	3	1

On the same graph paper and on the same scales, plot the cumulative frequency curves for Test (1) and Test (2) for frequencies of children obtaining a certain mark or below that mark.

Estimate the median mark for each test and comment briefly on any differences observed between the two curves. L

46 In an experiment the lengths of 100 white mice were measured to the nearest mm and the frequencies tabulated as follows:

Length in mm	*Frequency*	*Length in mm*	*Frequency*
20–24	1	45–49	26
25–29	4	50–54	7
30–34	15	55–59	1
35–39	20	60–64	1
40–44	25		

(i) Find the (arithmetic) mean length.

(ii) Construct a cumulative frequency table and draw the cumulative frequency curve.

(iii) Find the semi-interquartile range and explain, in a few words, its significance. AEB

47 Give expressions for five consecutive integers whose median is n. Show that their mean is also n.

Show that the mean of the squares of these five integers exceeds the median of the squares by an amount which is independent of n. L

48 Write down an ordered set of 5 integers whose mean is 4 and whose median is 3. OC (SMP)

Chapter Eleven

1 Express in binary notation: (*a*) 17; (*b*) 17·5. OC (SMP)

2 Solve the equation $11x = 1001$, the numbers being binary, giving the solution in binary. OC (SMP)

3 How can you tell by inspection that a number expressed in the binary scale is divisible by 4? C

4 Write the decimal number 19·375 as a binary number. AEB

5 Write the decimal number 32·375 as a binary number. AEB

6 Express 56 in the scale of 3. OC (SMP)

7 Express 213_4 as a number written to base 10. OC (SMP)

8 Is it true or false that the representation of any number which is a multiple of 4 (in base 10):

(*a*) ends in 0 when the base is 2;
(*b*) ends in 1 when the base is 3;
(*c*) ends in 0 when the base is 4;
(*d*) never ends in 0 when the base is 5. AEB

9 Express 234_5 as a numeral to base ten. OC (SMP)

10 Compile a table with five rows and five columns each labelled 0, 1, 2, 3, 4 for multiplication of numbers in base 5. SU

11 The following simultaneous equations are written with numbers to base 5.

$$2x + 3y = 12,$$
$$x + y = 3.$$

Solve these equations showing all your written calculations in base 5. AEB

12 To ensure that a number is understood to be in decimal notation we write, for example, 24_{10}. Similarly 12_5 is to be read as meaning that the number is in the scale of 5.

If $p = 12_5$, $q = 24_5$ and $r = 24_{10}$, which of the following statements are true and which false?

(*a*) $q < r$; (*b*) $q = 2p$; (*c*) $p + q = 42_5$; (*a*) $5q = 240_5$.

OC (SMP)

13 (*a*) Express the denary number 283 in the scale of 7.
(*b*) Express the binary number 101101 in the scale of 8. AEB

14 Express 735_8 in the binary scale. C

15 (i) Express 37_8 in binary.
(ii) Find the value of n if $154_n = 88_{10}$.
(iii) Find the sum and the difference of 325_6 and 144_6 giving your answers in the scale of 6. OC (SMP)

16 Express 265_{10} (i) in the binary scale; (ii) in the scale of 8.
(iii) If $212_n = 25_9$, what is n? OC (SMP)

17 Copy the table below. Convert the numbers A, B, C into each of the other scales to complete the table.

	A	B	C
Scale of 10	49		
Scale of 8		127	
Scale of 2			11101

L

18 Evaluate the following denary (base ten) expressions and convert your answers to base 8.

(i) 11^3 (ii) 22^3 (*Part* (*ii*) *follows from part* (*i*).)

SU

19 1326 is the product of two factors in *any* base greater than six. Find the factors and hence the prime factors of 1326_7, expressed in base ten. L

20 Find the product of 102 and 12, stating the number bases for which your result is not true.

If $102_n \times 12_n = 2001_n$, find the number base n. L

21 In the table below is represented the last digit when each of the denary numbers (i.e. to base 10) in the first column is expressed to bases 2, 3 and 5. If the denary numbers have been expressed in ascending order of magnitude, find

(*a*) the missing denary number;

(*b*) the last digit of the total of the six numbers for each base 2, 3 and 5;

(*c*) the eight pairs of denary numbers in the table whose sums have 0 as the last digit to base 3. L

Denary Number	Base 2	Base 3	Base 5
23	1	2	3
25	1	1	0
	0	2	2
35	1	2	0
52	0	1	2
53	1	2	3

22 In which bases are the following calculations carried out?

$$\text{(i)}\ \begin{array}{r} 471 \\ +263 \\ \hline 754 \end{array} \qquad \text{(ii)}\ \begin{array}{r} 141 \\ -22 \\ \hline 114 \end{array} \qquad \text{(iii)}\ 4503 \div 24 = 156.$$

SU

23 In the following addition, the numbers are not in base 10, and there is one digit missing.

$$\begin{array}{rcccc} & & 6 & * & 5 \\ + & & 3 & 6 & 4 \\ \hline & 1 & 2 & 3 & 1 \\ \hline \end{array}$$

Give

(*a*) the number base;

(*b*) the missing digit. O

Chapter Twelve

1 Simplify

$$\begin{pmatrix} 3 \\ -2 \\ -1 \end{pmatrix} + \begin{pmatrix} -2 \\ 5 \\ -3 \end{pmatrix}.$$

OC (SMP)

2 If A is the row matrix $(4 \quad 3)$ and B is the column matrix $\begin{pmatrix} -1 \\ 3 \end{pmatrix}$, calculate (if possible) AB. OC (SMP)

3 State which of the following have no meaning and simplify the others.

(*a*) $(1 \quad 2) \begin{pmatrix} 3 & 4 \\ 5 & 6 \end{pmatrix}$ (*b*) $\begin{pmatrix} 1 \\ 2 \end{pmatrix} \begin{pmatrix} 3 & 4 \\ 5 & 6 \end{pmatrix}$

(*c*) $\begin{pmatrix} 3 & 4 \\ 5 & 6 \end{pmatrix} \begin{pmatrix} 1 \\ 2 \end{pmatrix}$ (*d*) $\begin{pmatrix} 3 & 4 \\ 5 & 6 \end{pmatrix} (1 \quad 2)$ L

4 Given that $\mathbf{A} = \begin{pmatrix} 3 & 1 \\ -1 & 2 \end{pmatrix}$, $\mathbf{B} = \begin{pmatrix} 1 & 0 \\ -3 & 2 \end{pmatrix}$,

$$\mathbf{C} = \begin{pmatrix} 1 & 1 \\ 0 & -3 \end{pmatrix}.$$

Show that $A(B + C) = AB + AC$.

Deduce also that $\mathbf{AB} \neq \mathbf{BA}$ and either by using this fact or by direct evaluation show that $A^2 - B^2 \neq (A + B)(A - B)$. SU

5 A and B are 2×2 matrices and O is the zero matrix. Indicate which of the following are true and which are false:

(*a*) $A \,.\, B = O \Leftrightarrow A = O$ and $B = O$;
(*b*) $A = O \Rightarrow A \,.\, B = O$;
(*c*) $A \,.\, B = O \Leftrightarrow A = O$ or $B = O$;
(*d*) $A^2 = O \Rightarrow A = O$. OC (SMP)

6 If $A = \begin{pmatrix} a_1 & a_2 \\ a_3 & a_4 \end{pmatrix}$, find matrices B and C such that

(i) $BA = \begin{pmatrix} a_1 - a_3 & a_2 - a_4 \\ a_3 & a_4 \end{pmatrix}$,

(ii) $AC = \begin{pmatrix} 2a_2 & a_1 \\ 2a_4 & a_3 \end{pmatrix}$. AEB

7 If A and B are any 2×2 matrices, are the following statements true or false?

(*a*) $AB = 0 \Rightarrow A = 0$ or $B = 0$ or both.

(*b*) $AB = \begin{pmatrix} 1 & 0 \\ 0 & 1 \end{pmatrix} \Rightarrow A = B^{-1}$.

(*c*) $(A + B)^2 = A^2 + 2AB + B^2$.

(*d*) $(A + B)^{-1} = A^{-1} + B^{-1}$. AEB

8 If $2\begin{pmatrix} x \\ y \end{pmatrix} = \begin{pmatrix} 8 \\ -6 \end{pmatrix}$, find x and y. SC

9 If

$$\begin{pmatrix} h & 3 \\ 0 & 0 \end{pmatrix} \begin{pmatrix} 2 \\ -1 \end{pmatrix} = \begin{pmatrix} 5 \\ 0 \end{pmatrix},$$

find the value of h. C

10 Find x and y if

$$\begin{pmatrix} 2 & 1 \\ 0 & -5 \end{pmatrix} \begin{pmatrix} x \\ 1 \end{pmatrix} = \begin{pmatrix} 1 \\ y \end{pmatrix}.$$

OC (SMP)

11 Find x and y if

$$\begin{pmatrix} 0 & 2 \\ -3 & 1 \end{pmatrix} \begin{pmatrix} x \\ y \end{pmatrix} = \begin{pmatrix} -6 \\ 9 \end{pmatrix}$$

OC (SMP)

12 Calculate x and y if

$$\begin{pmatrix} x \\ y \end{pmatrix} = \begin{pmatrix} 2 & 1 \\ 3 & -1 \end{pmatrix} \begin{pmatrix} 1 \\ 3 \end{pmatrix}.$$

OC (SMP)

13 (i) State the product of

$$\begin{pmatrix}1 & 0\\0 & 1\end{pmatrix} \text{ and } \begin{pmatrix}3 & 5\\7 & 1\end{pmatrix}.$$

(ii) Find x and y if

$$(x, y) \times \begin{pmatrix}2 & 0\\-5 & 3\end{pmatrix} = (20, 6).$$ OC (SMP)

14 Solve

$$\begin{pmatrix}2 & 0\\3 & 1\end{pmatrix}\begin{pmatrix}x\\y\end{pmatrix} = \begin{pmatrix}6\\10\end{pmatrix}.$$ OC (SMP)

15 **T** is the transformation $\begin{pmatrix}x\\y\end{pmatrix} \to \begin{pmatrix}0 & -2\\2 & 0\end{pmatrix}\begin{pmatrix}x\\y\end{pmatrix}$.

(i) Write down the images of the points whose position vectors are

$$(a)\ \begin{pmatrix}2\\1\end{pmatrix}, \quad (b)\ \begin{pmatrix}-1\\3\end{pmatrix}.$$

(ii) Find the $\begin{pmatrix}x\\y\end{pmatrix}$ which is mapped on to $\begin{pmatrix}4\\2\end{pmatrix}$.

(iii) The transformation **T** is carried out geometrically in two stages, the first being a rotation of 90° anti-clockwise about the origin. What is the second stage? NI

16 (i) Given that

$$\begin{pmatrix}3-a & 3\\-1 & -2\end{pmatrix}\begin{pmatrix}-3\\x\end{pmatrix} = \begin{pmatrix}-3\\x\end{pmatrix},$$

find a and x.

(ii) T is the matrix

$$\begin{pmatrix}2 & 3\\-1 & -2\end{pmatrix}.$$

Write down the result of pre-multiplication of each of the column-vectors

$$\begin{pmatrix}-4\\4\end{pmatrix} \text{ and } \begin{pmatrix}4\\-4\end{pmatrix} \text{ by } T.$$

P is the point $(-4, 4)$ and *Q* the point $(4, -4)$. Show, on a sketch the points *P* and *Q*. Show, also, their respective images P' and Q' under the transformation defined by *T*.

Describe a single geometrical operation which maps *P* on to P' and *Q* on to Q'. C

17 Given that

$$\begin{pmatrix} 3 & 1 \\ 1 & 0 \end{pmatrix}\begin{pmatrix} 4 & a \\ a & 2 \end{pmatrix} = \begin{pmatrix} 15 & b \\ c & 3 \end{pmatrix},$$

find the value of each of *a*, *b* and *c*. C

18 (*a*) If *X* is a 2×2 matrix, find four distinct solutions of the equation $X^2 = X$.

(*b*) Solve the equation

$$\begin{pmatrix} 5 & 2 \\ 3 & 7 \end{pmatrix}\begin{pmatrix} x \\ y \end{pmatrix} = \begin{pmatrix} a \\ b \end{pmatrix},$$

for each of the following values for $\begin{pmatrix} a \\ b \end{pmatrix}$

(i) $\begin{pmatrix} 7 \\ 10 \end{pmatrix}$, (ii) $\begin{pmatrix} 3 \\ -4 \end{pmatrix}$, (iii) $\begin{pmatrix} 4 \\ 14 \end{pmatrix}$, (iv) $\begin{pmatrix} 6 \\ 3 \end{pmatrix}$.

AEB

19 Find three different 2×2 matrices, *X*, which satisfy the equation

$$\begin{pmatrix} 2 & -1 \\ -1 & \frac{1}{2} \end{pmatrix} X = \begin{pmatrix} 1 & 0 \\ -\frac{1}{2} & 0 \end{pmatrix}$$

AEB

20 Write down the 2×2 matrix which transforms the vectors $\begin{pmatrix} 1 \\ 0 \end{pmatrix}$ and $\begin{pmatrix} 0 \\ 1 \end{pmatrix}$ into the vectors $\begin{pmatrix} 2 \\ 1 \end{pmatrix}$ and $\begin{pmatrix} 3 \\ 2 \end{pmatrix}$ respectively. Find the transforms of $\begin{pmatrix} 7 \\ -4 \end{pmatrix}$ and $\begin{pmatrix} 12 \\ -7 \end{pmatrix}$. L

21 A'_r is the transpose of $A_r = \begin{pmatrix} a_r & b_r \\ c_r & d_r \end{pmatrix}$. Show that

$$(A_1A_2)' = A'_2A'_1$$

Use this result to show that $(A_1(A_2A_3))' = ((A_1A_2)A_3)'$. L

22 The inverse of the matrix $\begin{pmatrix} 1 & 1 \\ 0 & 1 \end{pmatrix}$ is:

(*a*) $\begin{pmatrix} 1 & -1 \\ 0 & 1 \end{pmatrix}$; (c) $\begin{pmatrix} 0 & 1 \\ 1 & -1 \end{pmatrix}$;

(*b*) $\begin{pmatrix} 1 & 0 \\ -1 & 1 \end{pmatrix}$; (*d*) $\begin{pmatrix} -1 & 1 \\ 1 & 0 \end{pmatrix}$. OC (SMP)

23 State the inverse of $\begin{pmatrix} 20 & 12 \\ 5 & 3 \end{pmatrix}$, or give a reason why it has not got an inverse. OC (SMP)

24 Assuming

$$\begin{matrix} 2x - 5y = 1 \\ 3x - 7y = 2 \end{matrix} \Leftrightarrow \begin{pmatrix} 2 & -5 \\ 3 & -7 \end{pmatrix}\begin{pmatrix} x \\ y \end{pmatrix} = \begin{pmatrix} 1 & 0 \\ 0 & 1 \end{pmatrix}\begin{pmatrix} 1 \\ 2 \end{pmatrix},$$

show that $\begin{pmatrix} 14 & -35 \\ 15 & -35 \end{pmatrix}\begin{pmatrix} x \\ y \end{pmatrix} = \begin{pmatrix} 7 & 0 \\ 0 & 5 \end{pmatrix}\begin{pmatrix} 1 \\ 2 \end{pmatrix}$

and $\begin{pmatrix} 1 & 0 \\ 15 & -35 \end{pmatrix}\begin{pmatrix} x \\ y \end{pmatrix} = \begin{pmatrix} -7 & 5 \\ 0 & 5 \end{pmatrix}\begin{pmatrix} 1 \\ 2 \end{pmatrix}$.

Hence, or otherwise, find the inverse of $\begin{pmatrix} 2 & -5 \\ 3 & -7 \end{pmatrix}$ and the value of $\begin{pmatrix} x \\ y \end{pmatrix}$.

L

25 Write down the inverse of

$$\begin{pmatrix} 3 & 2 \\ -4 & 1 \end{pmatrix}.$$

Solve simultaneously the equations $3x + 2y = 6$
and $-4x + y = 14$.

OC (SMP)

26 $$\mathbf{A} = \begin{pmatrix} 5 & 4 \\ 3 & 2 \end{pmatrix}, \quad \mathbf{B} = \begin{pmatrix} 6 & 4 \\ 3 & 2 \end{pmatrix}.$$

(i) Calculate the determinants of the matrices **A** and **B**.
(ii) Which of the matrices has an inverse?
What is the inverse in this case? NI

27 Calculate the determinant of the matrix

$$\begin{pmatrix} 3 & 2 \\ 4 & 3 \end{pmatrix}.$$

Write down the inverse of this matrix.
Use your result to find the solution set of the equations

$$3x + 2y = 8,$$
$$4x + 3y = 10\tfrac{1}{2}.$$ L

28 In the equation

$$\begin{pmatrix} 1 & 2 \\ 2 & -2 \end{pmatrix} \begin{pmatrix} x \\ y \end{pmatrix} = k \begin{pmatrix} x \\ y \end{pmatrix},$$

k is a number. This equation always has the solution $\begin{pmatrix} x \\ y \end{pmatrix} = \begin{pmatrix} 0 \\ 0 \end{pmatrix}$ whatever the value of k. By trying to find the general solution in terms of k, or otherwise, show that there are two values of k for which the equation has solutions distinct from $\begin{pmatrix} 0 \\ 0 \end{pmatrix}$, and find these values of k. AEB

29 The elements a, b, c, d in that order of the matrix $\begin{pmatrix} a & b \\ c & d \end{pmatrix}$ have a pattern such that each element after the first is one less than twice the element that precedes it.

Express b, c, d in terms of a and find the value of the determinant $\begin{vmatrix} a & b \\ c & d \end{vmatrix}$ in its simplest form in terms of a. L

30 If **P** and **Q** are respectively the matrices

$$\begin{pmatrix} -\frac{1}{2} & \frac{\sqrt{3}}{2} \\ -\frac{\sqrt{3}}{2} & -\frac{1}{2} \end{pmatrix} \text{ and } \begin{pmatrix} -\frac{1}{2} & -\frac{\sqrt{3}}{2} \\ \frac{\sqrt{3}}{2} & -\frac{1}{2} \end{pmatrix}.$$

evaluate the products $\mathbf{P}^2$, $\mathbf{Q}^2$, **PQ** and **QP**.

Show that **P**, **Q** and the identity matrix $\mathbf{I} = \begin{pmatrix} 1 & 0 \\ 0 & 1 \end{pmatrix}$ form a group under the operation of multiplication. (The associative property of matrix multiplication may be assumed.) State the inverse element of each member of the group. L

31 (i) What geometrical transformation is associated with the matrix $\begin{pmatrix} 0 & 1 \\ 1 & 0 \end{pmatrix}$?

(ii) What is the inverse matrix? OC (SMP)

32 If $\mathbf{Q} = \begin{pmatrix} 0 & -1 \\ 1 & 0 \end{pmatrix}$, name the geometrical transformation $\mathbf{Q}\begin{pmatrix} x \\ y \end{pmatrix}$. Identify $\mathbf{Q}^2$, $\mathbf{Q}^3$ and $\mathbf{Q}^4$ as geometrical transformations and construct a table under the operation of matrix multiplication.

L

33 $\mathbf{T} = \begin{pmatrix} 0 & 1 \\ -1 & 0 \end{pmatrix}$ operates on the vector $\begin{pmatrix} x \\ y \end{pmatrix}$. Name the transformation effected by each of

(*a*) $\mathbf{T}\begin{pmatrix} x \\ y \end{pmatrix}$ (*b*) $\mathbf{T}^2\begin{pmatrix} x \\ y \end{pmatrix}$ (*c*) $\mathbf{T}^4\begin{pmatrix} x \\ y \end{pmatrix}$. L

34 (*a*) Evaluate the matrix product

$$\begin{pmatrix} 1 & 0 \\ 0 & -1 \end{pmatrix}\begin{pmatrix} -1 & 0 \\ 0 & 1 \end{pmatrix}\begin{pmatrix} -1 & 0 \\ 0 & -1 \end{pmatrix}$$

and suggest a geometrical interpretation of the result.

(*b*) Find the multiplicative inverse of the matrix $\begin{pmatrix} 1 & 2 \\ -2 & 0 \end{pmatrix}$ and hence find the values of *a*, *b*, *c* and *d* given that

$$\begin{pmatrix} 1 & 2 \\ -2 & 0 \end{pmatrix}\begin{pmatrix} a & b \\ c & d \end{pmatrix} = \begin{pmatrix} 3 & 1 \\ -1 & 2 \end{pmatrix}.$$

AEB

35 Draw a diagram to show the position of the image of the square $A\,(1,\ 0)$, $U\,(1,\ 1)$, $B\,(0,\ 1)$, $O\,(0,\ 0)$ obtained by pre-multiplying the position column-vectors of its vertices by the matrix $\begin{pmatrix} 1 & -1 \\ 1 & 1 \end{pmatrix}$. Describe the transformation geometrically.

OC (SMP)

36 A quadrilateral has vertices (1, 0), (3, 1), (1, 3) and (0, 1). Under the transformation $\begin{pmatrix} 1 & -1 \\ 1 & 1 \end{pmatrix}$, find (*a*) the vertices, (*b*) the area, of the new quadrilateral. Hence, or otherwise, find the area of the original quadrilateral.

L

37 Two matrices $\mathbf{S}_1$ and $\mathbf{S}_2$ are given by $\mathbf{S}_1 = \begin{pmatrix} 1 & -1 \\ 0 & 1 \end{pmatrix}$ and $\mathbf{S}_2 = \begin{pmatrix} 1 & 0 \\ 1 & 1 \end{pmatrix}$.

(*a*) Show in separate diagrams the transformations effected by $\mathbf{S}_1$, $\mathbf{S}_2$, $\mathbf{S}_2\mathbf{S}_1$ and $\mathbf{S}_1\mathbf{S}_2$, operating on the vector $\begin{pmatrix} x \\ y \end{pmatrix}$.

(*b*) Show that $\mathbf{S}_1\mathbf{S}_2\mathbf{S}_1 = \mathbf{S}_2\mathbf{S}_1\mathbf{S}_2$.

(*c*) Apply the transformation $\mathbf{S}_1\mathbf{S}_2\mathbf{S}_1$ to the triangle with vertices (1, 1), (1, 3), (2, 1) and show in the same diagram the triangle and its transform. State the geometrical effect of the transformation.

L

38 What geometrical transformation is effected by pre-multiplication by $\begin{pmatrix} \cos\theta & -\sin\theta \\ \sin\theta & \cos\theta \end{pmatrix}$?

OC (SMP)

39 (i) Calculate the coordinates of the image of the point $A(4, 3)$ obtained by pre-multiplying its column vector $\begin{pmatrix}4\\3\end{pmatrix}$ by the matrix $\begin{pmatrix}0{\cdot}6, & -0{\cdot}8\\0{\cdot}8, & 0{\cdot}6\end{pmatrix}$.
(ii) Show that this mapping is a rotation about the origin O and calculate its angle.
(iii) Calculate the image of $B(2, 5)$ under the same rotation and hence the area of triangle OAB. OC (SMP)

40 The position vector of the point (x, y) is written as the column matrix $\begin{pmatrix}x\\y\end{pmatrix}$. A geometrical transformation is represented by the equation

$$\begin{pmatrix}x'\\y'\end{pmatrix} = \begin{pmatrix}a & b\\c & d\end{pmatrix}\begin{pmatrix}x\\y\end{pmatrix}.$$

(i) Write down the coordinates of the images of (1, 0) and (0, 1) under this transformation.
(ii) Show that the image of (1, 0) under a rotation of $+30°$ about the origin is $\left(\frac{\sqrt{3}}{2}, \frac{1}{2}\right)$ and find the image of (0, 1) under the same rotation.
(iii) Using your answers to (i) and (ii), or otherwise, write down the matrix M of this rotation.
(iv) Calculate M^2 and write down the coordinates of the images of (1, 0) and (0, 1) under this transformation. Explain your result geometrically. OC (SMP)

41 Find the solution set of

$$0{\cdot}8x - 0{\cdot}6y = 1$$
$$0{\cdot}6x + 0{\cdot}8y = 2$$

and describe the transformation which takes the vector $\begin{pmatrix}1\\2\end{pmatrix}$ into the vector $\begin{pmatrix}x\\y\end{pmatrix}$. L

42 A transformation in which (x', y') is the image of (x, y) is defined as follows:

$$\begin{pmatrix} x' \\ y' \end{pmatrix} = \begin{pmatrix} 2 & 0 \\ 0 & 2 \end{pmatrix} \begin{pmatrix} x \\ y \end{pmatrix}.$$

Which of the following statements are true and which false?

(*a*) The image of (2, 3) is (4, 6).

(*b*) The transformation consists of a translation of 2 units parallel to Ox and 3 units parallel to Oy.

(*c*) The transformation is an enlargement, centre O.

(*d*) The matrix M such that

$$\begin{pmatrix} x \\ y \end{pmatrix} = M \begin{pmatrix} x' \\ y' \end{pmatrix} \text{ is } \begin{pmatrix} \frac{1}{2} & 0 \\ 0 & \frac{1}{2} \end{pmatrix}.$$

OC (SMP)

43 The unit square, whose vertices are the points (0, 0), (1, 0), (0, 1) and (1, 1), is denoted by U, and

$$M_1 = \begin{pmatrix} 1 & 0 \\ 0 & 2 \end{pmatrix}, \quad M_2 = \begin{pmatrix} 2 & 2 \\ 1 & 4 \end{pmatrix}, \quad M_3 = \begin{pmatrix} -1 & 1 \\ 0 & 0 \end{pmatrix}.$$

When the column vectors $\begin{pmatrix} 0 \\ 0 \end{pmatrix}$, etc., of the vertices of U are pre-multiplied by M_1, M_2 and M_3, the resulting images of the square are called U_1, U_2 and U_3 respectively.

(i) Show U_1, U_2 and U_3 on separate sketches, making clear the coordinates of each point.

(ii) Calculate the matrix which transforms U_1 into U_2.

OC (SMP)

44 A matrix $\mathbf{M} = \begin{pmatrix} a & b \\ c & d \end{pmatrix}$ defines a transformation of the plane into itself under which the points (1, 2) and (3, 4) are images of each other thus $\begin{pmatrix} 1 \\ 2 \end{pmatrix} = \mathbf{M}\begin{pmatrix} 3 \\ 4 \end{pmatrix}$ and $\begin{pmatrix} 3 \\ 4 \end{pmatrix} = \mathbf{M}\begin{pmatrix} 1 \\ 2 \end{pmatrix}$. Write down a pair of simultaneous equations for a and b and a further pair for c and d. Hence determine the elements of $\mathbf{M}$. Verify that $\mathbf{M}^2 = \mathbf{I}$ where $\mathbf{I}$ is the unit matrix.

SU

45 A is the point (1, 0), B is the point (0, 1) referred to rectangular axes OX, OY. The transformation matrix $\begin{pmatrix} 2 & 1 \\ 0 & 2 \end{pmatrix}$ is applied to the vertices of the triangle OAB.

Show that the origin is invariant under this transformation.

What are the coordinates of the vertices of the transformation triangle $OA'B'$?

What transformation matrix would convert the triangle $OA'B'$ back into the triangle OAB? L

46 Determine the 2 × 2 matrix, A, which transforms

$$\begin{pmatrix} 1 \\ 0 \end{pmatrix} \text{ into } \begin{pmatrix} 29 \\ 4 \end{pmatrix} \text{ and } \begin{pmatrix} 0 \\ 1 \end{pmatrix} \text{ into } \begin{pmatrix} 7 \\ 1 \end{pmatrix}.$$

Express the product

$$\begin{pmatrix} 1 & k \\ 0 & 1 \end{pmatrix} \begin{pmatrix} 1 & 0 \\ t & 1 \end{pmatrix}$$

as a single matrix.

Hence describe **two** transformations which, when carried out in succession, are equivalent to the transformation given by the matrix A. C

47

	Cereals	*Other crops*
Farm A	0	50
Farm B	150	50

hectares

	Before	*After*
Cereals	3·6	4·0
Other crops	3·0	3·2

tonnes/hectare

The matrix on the left shows the area of land (in hectares) at farms A and B which is devoted to cereals and other crops. The right-hand matrix indicates the yield (in tonnes/hectare) of these crops before and after the application of a new fertiliser.

Multiply the two matrices together, state appropriate units for the product and label the rows and columns of the product to indicate what each of its entries represents. NI

48 A certain island lives by the tourist trade and allows no visitors' cars. It has just two towns, Anna (A) and Bonna (B). Both these are on the coast and are connected by a bus service and a train service. There are also two sea services, one from A via the island of Cuna (C) to B and back direct to A; the other to and fro between A and the isle of Dyna (D). Show how all these data are incorporated in the matrix **M** shown, explaining the distinction between the row A and the column A:

$$\begin{array}{c} \\ A \\ B \\ C \\ D \end{array} \begin{array}{c} \begin{array}{cccc} A & B & C & D \end{array} \\ \begin{pmatrix} 0 & 2 & 1 & 1 \\ 3 & 0 & 0 & 0 \\ 0 & 1 & 0 & 0 \\ 1 & 0 & 0 & 0 \end{pmatrix} \end{array}.$$

Form the square of **M** (i.e. the product **M** $\times$ **M**) in the usual way and interpret the non-zero numbers which now appear in the main diagonal (i.e. top left to bottom right). If a tourist wishing to do a day trip out and back can only fit in two journeys in that time, explain, using $\mathbf{M}^2$ or otherwise, which base of operations gives him most choice for planning his trip. O

49 The country of Albion has four local airstrips A, B, C, D and two international airports G, H. Regular services exist or not between these, as shown by 1 or 0 in the matrix **M**. Flights from G and H to airports U, V, W in Gaul are given by matrix **N**.

$$\text{Matrix } \mathbf{M} \quad \begin{array}{c} \\ A \\ B \\ C \\ D \end{array} \begin{array}{c} \begin{array}{cc} G & H \end{array} \\ \begin{pmatrix} 1 & 0 \\ 0 & 1 \\ 1 & 1 \\ 1 & 1 \end{pmatrix} \end{array} \qquad \text{Matrix } \mathbf{N} \quad \begin{array}{c} \\ G \\ H \end{array} \begin{array}{c} \begin{array}{ccc} U & V & W \end{array} \\ \begin{pmatrix} 1 & 0 & 1 \\ 1 & 1 & 0 \end{pmatrix} \end{array}.$$

Form the product matrix **MN** and interpret it.

Local services in Gaul go from U, V, W to internal airports X, Y, Z as shown by matrix **P**.

$$\text{Matrix } \mathbf{P} \quad \begin{array}{c} \\ U \\ V \\ W \end{array} \begin{array}{c} X \quad Y \quad Z \\ \begin{pmatrix} 1 & 0 & 1 \\ 1 & 1 & 0 \\ 0 & 0 & 1 \end{pmatrix} \end{array}$$

A traveller wishes to travel by air between these countries. Find, by any method, (*a*) which of the journeys from *A* or *B* or *C* or *D* to *X* or *Y* or *Z* have no air route, (*b*) which of them are connected by more than one route. O

50 *ABC* is an equilateral triangle of side 25 mm.

If $\overrightarrow{AB}$ is the vector **b** and $\overrightarrow{AC}$ is the vector **c**, draw accurately on a copy of the diagrams

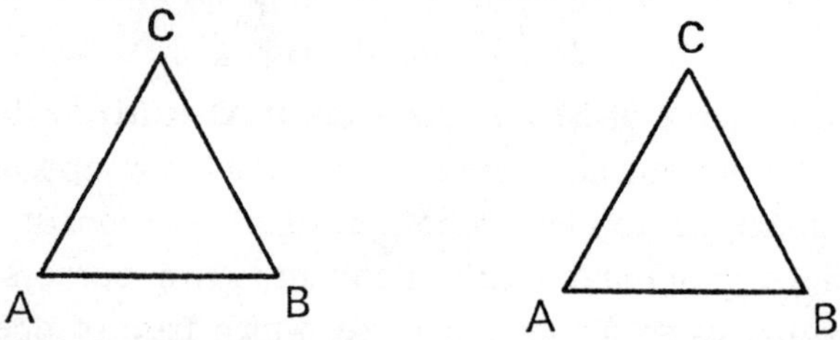

(i) the line segment *AP* which represents the vector $\frac{1}{2}\mathbf{b} + 2\mathbf{c}$;
(ii) the line segment *AQ* which represents the vector $2\mathbf{b} - \mathbf{c}$. C

51

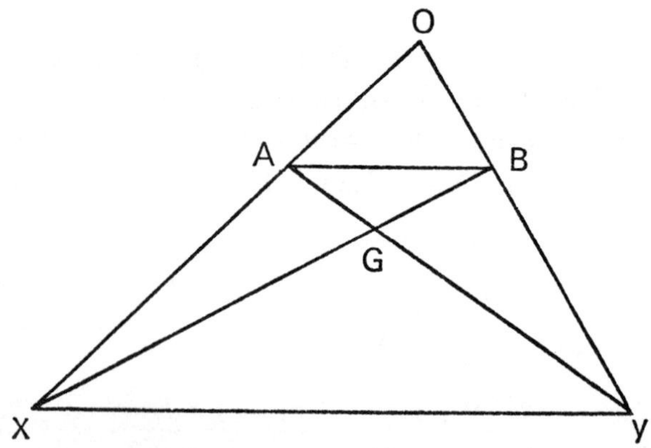

In the diagram, $\overrightarrow{OA} = \mathbf{a}$, $\overrightarrow{OB} = \mathbf{b}$, $\overrightarrow{OX} = 3\mathbf{a}$, $\overrightarrow{OY} = 3\mathbf{b}$.

Find $\overrightarrow{AB}$, $\overrightarrow{XY}$, $\overrightarrow{AY}$, $\overrightarrow{AG}$ and $\overrightarrow{OG}$. L

52 O is the origin, A is the point (5, 7), B is the point (−2, −1), and P is a point (x, y). The directed line segments OA, OB, OP, represent the vectors **a**, **b** and **p**. Given that $\mathbf{a} - \mathbf{b} = \mathbf{p}$, find the coordinates of P. C

53 Express $\overrightarrow{AB}$ in the figure in terms of **a** and **b**, where $\overrightarrow{OA} = \mathbf{a}$, $\overrightarrow{OB} = \mathbf{b}$.

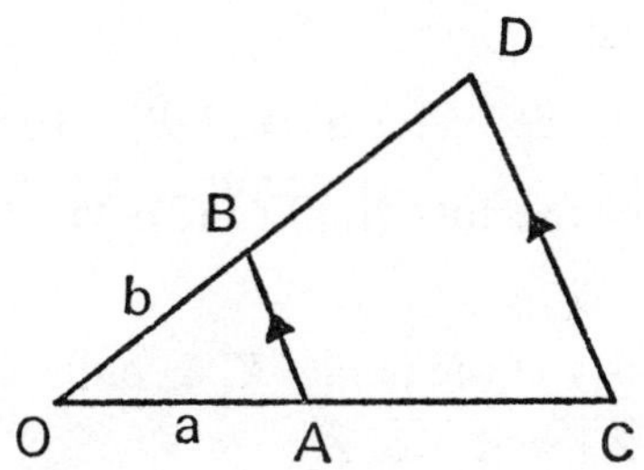

Given $\overrightarrow{AC} = 2\mathbf{a}$ and $\overrightarrow{BD} = 2\mathbf{b}$, express $\overrightarrow{CD}$ in terms of **a** and **b**, and hence give two relations between $\overrightarrow{AB}$ and $\overrightarrow{CD}$. L

54 From the information given in the figure, express $B \rightarrow A$ in terms of **a** and **b**.

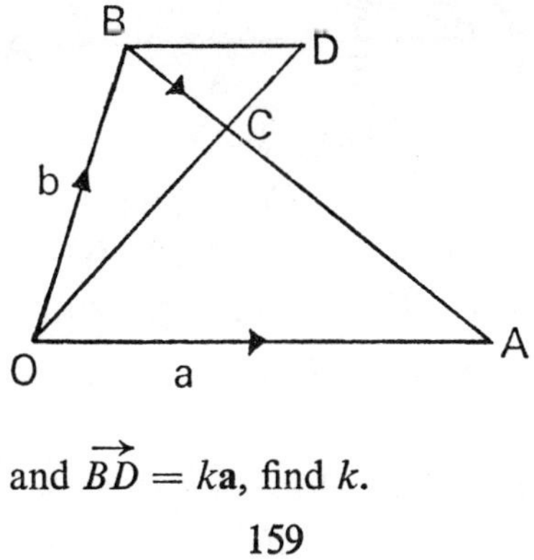

If $\overrightarrow{BA} = 4\overrightarrow{BC}$ and $\overrightarrow{BD} = k\mathbf{a}$, find k. L

55 In the triangle ABC, M is the midpoint of BC and N the midpoint of AC. Vectors $\mathbf{p}$ and $\mathbf{q}$ are defined as $\mathbf{p} = \overrightarrow{AB}$ and $\mathbf{q} = \overrightarrow{BC}$. BN is produced to D such that $BD/BN = 4/3$. Express $\overrightarrow{AM}$ and $\overrightarrow{DC}$ in terms of $\mathbf{p}$ and $\mathbf{q}$ and hence show that AM is parallel to DC and that their lengths are in the ratio $3:2$. SU

56 In the triangle OAB, X is the point on OA such that $\overline{OX} = \frac{2}{3}\overline{OA}$ and Y is the midpoint of $\overline{AB}$. The point Z on OB produced is such that $\overline{OB} = \overline{BZ}$.

Given that $\overrightarrow{OA}$ is the vector $\mathbf{a}$ and $\overrightarrow{OB}$ is the vector $\mathbf{b}$, state, in terms of $\mathbf{a}$ and $\mathbf{b}$, the vectors (i) $\overrightarrow{OX}$; (ii) $\overrightarrow{OY}$; (iii) $\overrightarrow{OZ}$; (iv) $\overrightarrow{XY}$; (v) $\overrightarrow{YZ}$.

Deduce a property of the points X, Y and Z and state the ratio of the lengths of $\overline{XY}$ and $\overline{YZ}$. C

57

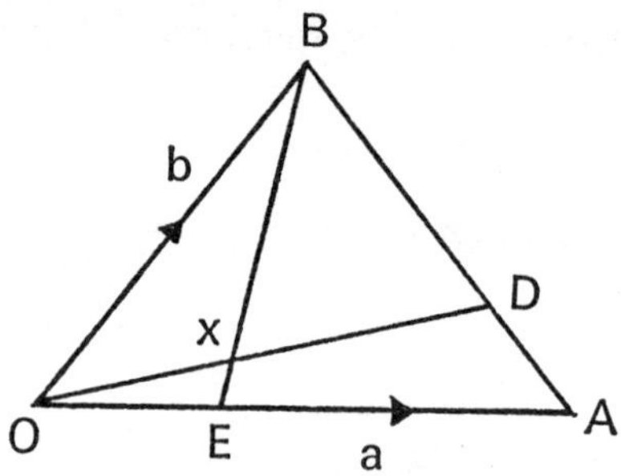

OA is the vector **a** and **OB** is the vector **b**. The points D and E are such that $\overline{AD} = \frac{1}{3}\overline{AB}$ and $\overline{OE} = \frac{1}{3}\overline{OA}$.
Express, in terms of **a** and **b**, the vectors **OD** and **BE**.

If $\overline{OX} = k.\ \overline{OD}$ and $\overline{BX} = l.\ \overline{BE}$, express the vector **OX** in two different ways and hence deduce

(i) the values of k and l;
(ii) the vector **OX** in terms of **a** and **b** only. C

58 In a triangle ABC, M is the midpoint of AC. N is a point on AB such that $AN = 3NB$ and D is the midpoint of CN. Vectors $\mathbf{p}$ and $\mathbf{q}$ are defined by $\mathbf{p} = \overrightarrow{AB}$ and $\mathbf{q} = \overrightarrow{AC}$. Express $\overrightarrow{AM}$, $\overrightarrow{AN}$ and $\overrightarrow{ND}$ in terms of $\mathbf{p}$ and $\mathbf{q}$. Hence show that MD is parallel to AB and that $MD/AB = 3/8$. SU

59 The diagram shows part of a tessellation of equilateral triangles extending in all directions of the plane. $\overrightarrow{OH}$, $\overrightarrow{OL}$, $\overrightarrow{OK}$ represent vectors $\underline{u}$, $\underline{v}$, $\underline{w}$ respectively which describe translations of the plane.

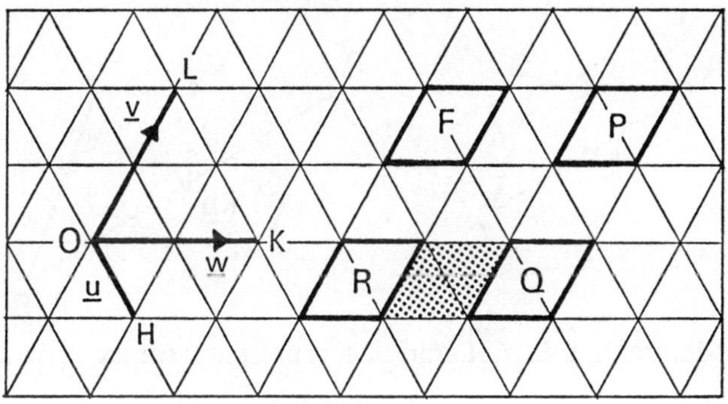

(i) Express $\underline{w}$ in terms of $\underline{u}$ and $\underline{v}$.

(ii) Use the vectors $\underline{u}$, $\underline{v}$, $\underline{w}$ to describe translations which will map F on to P; F on to R; F on to Q.

(iii) Find in terms of $\underline{v}$ and $\underline{w}$, a vector which maps F into the shaded part. SC

60 Unit vectors $\mathbf{i}$ and $\mathbf{j}$ are at right angles to each other. $\mathbf{p} = 3\mathbf{i} + 4\mathbf{j}$, $\mathbf{q} = 5\mathbf{i}$, $4\mathbf{r} = \mathbf{p} + \mathbf{q}$, $2\mathbf{s} = \mathbf{p} - \mathbf{q}$. Show that (*a*) $|\mathbf{p}| = |\mathbf{q}|$ (*b*) $|\mathbf{r}| = |\mathbf{s}|$ (*c*) $\mathbf{r}$ is perpendicular to $\mathbf{s}$ (*d*) $|\mathbf{r} + \mathbf{s}| = |\mathbf{r} - \mathbf{s}|$ (*e*) $\mathbf{r} + \mathbf{s}$ is perpendicular to $\mathbf{r} - \mathbf{s}$.

Show also that, for all real k, $|\mathbf{r} + k\mathbf{s}| = |\mathbf{r} - k\mathbf{s}|$. L

61 The unit vectors **i** and **j** are at right angles. Show that $\mathbf{p} = 24\mathbf{i} + 7\mathbf{j}$ and $\mathbf{q} = 20\mathbf{i} + 15\mathbf{j}$ have the same modulus. Find $\mathbf{p} - \mathbf{q}$ in terms of **i** and **j**, and the modulus of $\mathbf{p} - \mathbf{q}$. Hence find the acute angle between **p** and **q**. Check your answer for the angle by some other method. L

62 (*a*) Relative to an origin O, vectors $\underline{a}$, $\underline{b}$ and $\underline{c}$ are given as follows:

$$\underline{a} = \begin{pmatrix} 2 \\ 3 \end{pmatrix}, \quad \underline{b} = \begin{pmatrix} 4 \\ 7 \end{pmatrix} \quad \text{and} \quad \underline{c} = \begin{pmatrix} 8 \\ 11 \end{pmatrix}.$$

Find real numbers m and n such that $\underline{c} = m\underline{a} + n\underline{b}$.

(*b*)

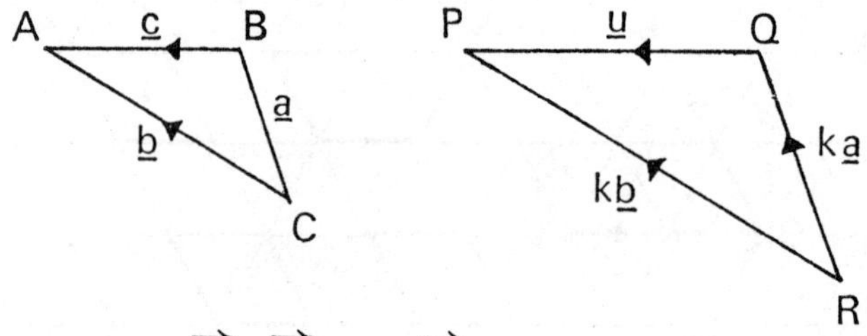

In the diagram, $\overrightarrow{CB}$, $\overrightarrow{CA}$ and $\overrightarrow{BA}$ represent vectors $\underline{a}$, $\underline{b}$ and $\underline{c}$ respectively.

$\overrightarrow{RQ}$, $\overrightarrow{RP}$ and $\overrightarrow{QP}$ represent vectors $k\,\underline{a}$, $k\,\underline{b}$ and $\underline{u}$ respectively.

(i) Express $\underline{c}$ in terms of $\underline{a}$ and $\underline{b}$.

(ii) Express $\underline{u}$ in terms of $\underline{a}$, $\underline{b}$ and k.

(iii) State one relation between the sides of triangle ABC and the sides of triangle PQR.

(iv) Draw a sketch of the triangles ABC and PQR when $k = -1$, naming the vertices. SC

63 $ABCD$ is a quadrilateral with $\overrightarrow{AB} = \mathbf{a}$, $\overrightarrow{BC} = \mathbf{b}$, $\overrightarrow{CD} = \mathbf{c}$, and $\overrightarrow{DA} = \mathbf{d}$. Write down an equation connecting **a**, **b**, **c** and **d**.

W, X, Y, Z are the midpoints of AB, BC, CD, DA respectively. Express $\overrightarrow{WX}$ in terms of **a** and **b** and express $\overrightarrow{ZY}$ in terms of **c** and **d**. Show that $\overrightarrow{WX}$ and $\overrightarrow{ZY}$ are equivalent vectors, and deduce what kind of quadrilateral $WXYZ$ is. L

64 Points X and Y are taken on the sides AB and AC respectively of triangle ABC so that $AX = \frac{1}{3}AB$ and $AY = \frac{1}{3}AC$. M is the mid-point of BC. The directed segments $\overrightarrow{AX}$ and $\overrightarrow{AY}$ represent vectors **x** and **y** respectively.

(i) What vectors are represented by $\overrightarrow{XY}$, $\overrightarrow{AB}$, $\overrightarrow{AC}$, $\overrightarrow{BC}$ and $\overrightarrow{AM}$?

(ii) Find also a vector which is represented by $\overrightarrow{XC}$.

(iii) If BY meets CX at L, use similar triangles to show that $\overrightarrow{XL}$ represents $\frac{1}{4}(3\mathbf{y} - \mathbf{x})$.

(iv) Hence show that $\overrightarrow{AL} = \frac{1}{2}\overrightarrow{AM}$. What conclusion can you draw about the relative positions of A, L and M? NI

65 Draw in the centre of a page a triangle of approximately the size and shape shown. The vector **a** is the position vector of A with respect to O as origin, and **b** is that of B. Mark on your figure the points C, D, E, F, G, H of which the position vectors respectively are

$$\mathbf{c} = \mathbf{a} + \mathbf{b}, \quad \mathbf{d} = \mathbf{b} - \mathbf{a}, \quad \mathbf{e} = \tfrac{1}{2}\mathbf{a},$$
$$\mathbf{f} = -\tfrac{1}{2}\mathbf{b}, \quad \mathbf{g} = \tfrac{1}{2}\mathbf{b}, \quad \mathbf{h} = \tfrac{1}{2}\mathbf{a} + \tfrac{1}{2}\mathbf{b}.$$

State, and establish by vector methods, relations between (i) $\overline{OH}$, $\overline{HC}$, and $\overline{EF}$, (ii) $\overline{EG}$ and $\overline{HB}$, (iii) $\overline{AG}$ and $\overline{AD}$. O

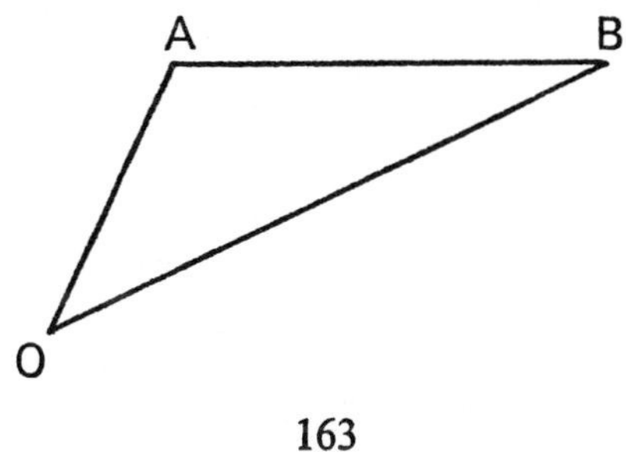

Chapter Thirteen

Note: Point symmetry is taken to mean rotational symmetry.

1 Indicate on diagrams of the following letters of the alphabet any points or lines of symmetry they may have. If a letter has none, write 'None' under that letter.

A H N P

AEB

2 Which of the following words, when printed in the type shown, have point symmetry?

pod mum dıd oxo

OC (SMP)

3 List the types of symmetry possessed by an equilateral triangle, and in a sketch show all the axes of symmetry for such a triangle.

SU

4 Complete the following figure in such a way that *A* is a point of symmetry, that the dotted line is a line of symmetry and that the figure has no other point of symmetry.

If your figure has any other lines of symmetry draw and label them. AEB

5 (i) Which one or more of the following figures always have point symmetry about the point of intersection of the diagonals:

(*a*) a rhombus; (*b*) a rectangle; (*c*) a trapezium; (*d*) a kite?
(ii) Which of these figures always have line symmetry about both diagonals? OC (SMP)

6 Name two types of quadrilateral which have two and only two axes of symmetry. OC (SMP)

7 If $\mathscr{E} =$ {quadrilaterals},
and $P =$ {quadrilaterals with point symmetry},
and $Q =$ {quadrilaterals with line symmetry},
draw a quadrilateral which is a member of $P' \cap Q$.

OC (SMP)

8 What is the name of a quadrilateral with
(*a*) two diagonals as axes of symmetry;
(*b*) one centre of symmetry? AEB

9 Draw a quadrilateral which has just one axis of symmetry and this axis does *not* pass through a vertex. O

10 Are the following statements true or false?
(*a*) A quadrilateral with one line of symmetry only is necessarily a parallelogram.
(*b*) A triangle with one line of symmetry only is necessarily isosceles.
(*c*) A quadrilateral with one point of symmetry only is necessarily a parallelogram.
(*d*) No quadrilateral has two points of symmetry. AEB

11 Is the following statement true or false?
If a figure has two intersecting lines of symmetry, it must have a centre of symmetry. AEB

12 A square $ABCD$ has the line $y = x$ as an axis of symmetry, and the vertices A, B and C have coordinates (0, 6), (6, 0) and (12, 6) respectively.

(i) Using 5 mm squared paper, make a sketch of square $ABCD$.
(ii) What are the coordinates of the vertex D?
(iii) Find the equation of the axis of symmetry perpendicular to the given one.
(iv) If the axis of symmetry in (iii) cuts the x-axis in the point P and the y-axis in the point Q, compare the area of triangle OPQ with that of square $ABCD$. SC

13

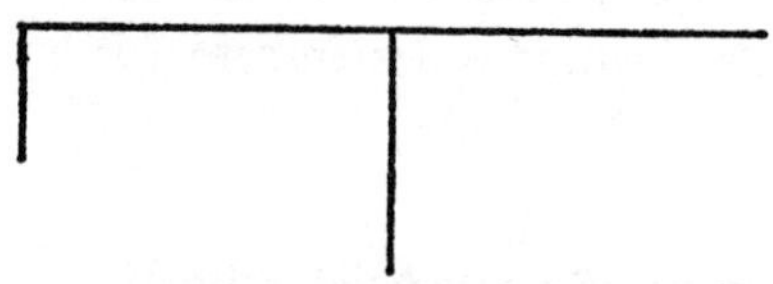

What is the least number of line segments which must be added to the diagram to give it **one** axis of symmetry?

Indicate on a copy of the diagram where the segment(s) must be drawn. OC (SMP)

14 The diagram shows a regular pentagon.
(i) State the number of axes of symmetry in the plane of the pentagon.
(ii) Draw one of these axes on a copy of the diagram.

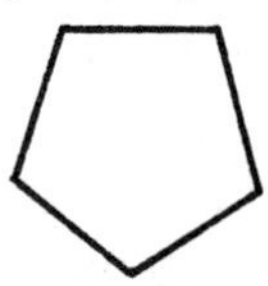

OC (SMP)

15 $ABCDEF$ is a regular hexagon of side 20 mm.
(i) How many axes of symmetry has it?
(ii) What number expresses the order of rotational symmetry?
(iii) Calculate to two significant figures the area of the circle which passes through the vertices of the hexagon. O

16

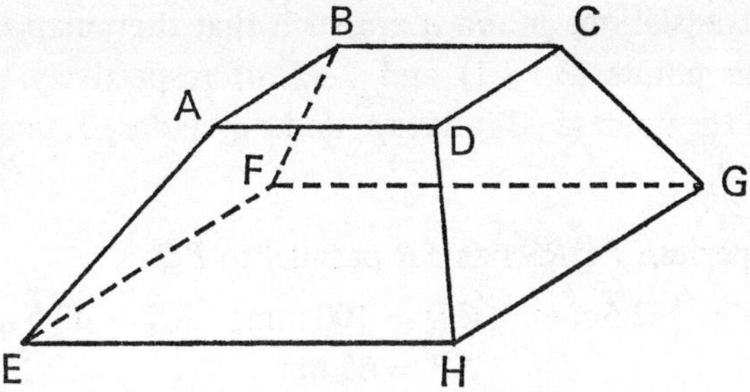

The top and base of the solid are parallel squares. The four sloping faces are congruent, and the four sloping edges are equal.
(i) State the number of planes of symmetry.
(ii) Describe, or indicate clearly on a copy of the diagram, the position of one of these. OC (SMP)

17 A rectangular door-mat 1 m by 0·5 m may be used either way up, and it fits exactly the hole cut into the floor behind a door. In how many ways may the mat be placed in the hole? List the different types of symmetry possessed by the mat, and show in a sketch the axes of symmetry. SU

18 What are the coordinates of A', the image of A(3, −2) under the translation vector $\begin{pmatrix} -1 \\ 6 \end{pmatrix}$? SC

19 Under a translation T, the point $P(4, 5)$ maps on to the point $Q(1, 2)$. Under T, the point Q maps on to the point R. State the coordinates of R. OC (SMP)

20 Under a translation the image of the point (3, 4) is (1, 7). What is the image of (1, −3)? OC (SMP)

21 A and B are the images of O under the translation p and q respectively. Show on a copy of the figure
(i) the image, C, of O under the translations p followed by q;
(ii) the image, D, of O under the translations p followed by the inverse of q. OC (SMP)

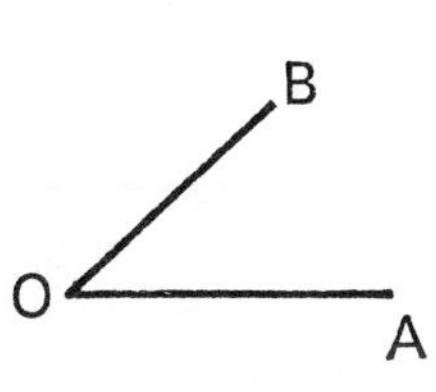

22 Two translations p and q are such that they map the origin on to the points (3, -1) and (-2, 4) respectively. Give the images of the point (5, 3) under p, under q, under pq, under qp and under pq^{-1}. OC (SMP)

23 A trapezium $PQRS$ has SR parallel to PQ.

$$PQ = 152{\cdot}5 \text{ mm}, \quad QR = 100 \text{ mm}; \quad RS = 47{\cdot}5 \text{ mm}$$
$$SP = 65 \text{ mm}$$

The translation which maps S on to P maps R on to T.

(i) State with reasons the lengths of RT and TQ.

(ii) Construct accurately triangle QRT and hence $PQRS$.

(iii) Measure the distance between the parallel sides, and find the area of the trapezium. OC (SMP)

24 The line m represents a mirror. Copy the diagram and sketch

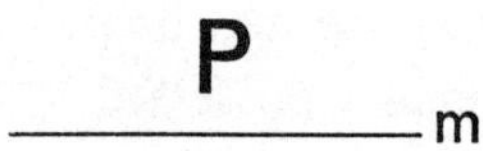

the image of the letter P after reflection in m. SC

25 Mark on a copy of the diagram the reflection of (3, -1) in the line $y = x$, stating its coordinates. OC (SMP)

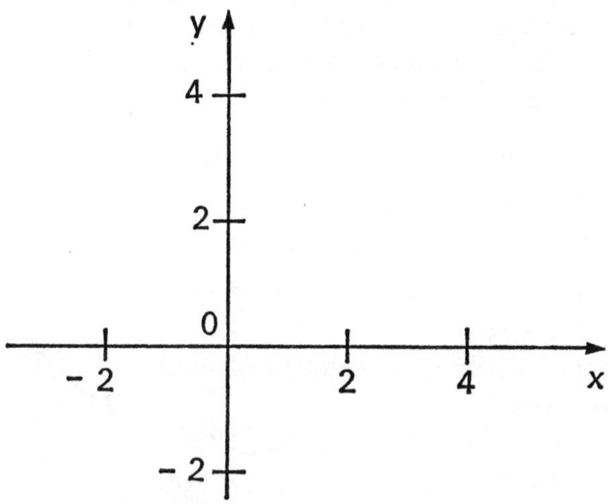

26 Under a reflection, a triangle ABC is transformed into a triangle $A'B'C'$. The positions of A, B', C' and X are shown, X being the point at which AC produced meets the axis of reflection. Copy the diagram and construct the position of B. C

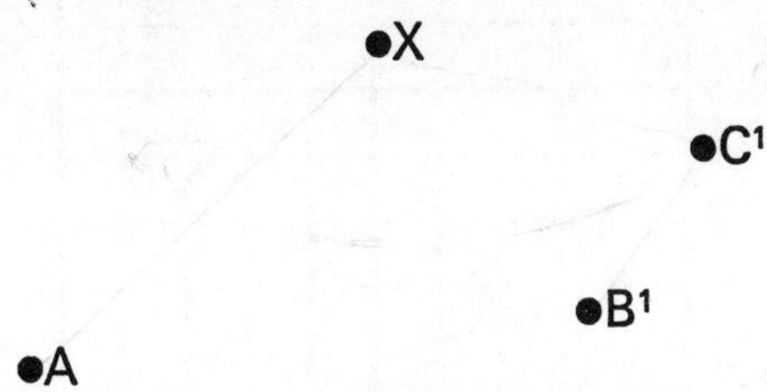

27 State the coordinates of the reflection of the point (3, 2) in the line $x = 1$. OC (SMP)

28 If P means 'reflect in Ox', and Q means 'reflect in the line $x = 4$', and if Z is the point $(-1, 3)$, which of the following statements are true and which false?

(*a*) $P(Z) = (-1, -3)$;
(*b*) $Q(Z) = (-1, 1)$;
(*c*) $PQ(Z) = (-9, 3)$;
(*d*) $PQ = QP$;
(*e*) $P^2 = I$ (where I is the identity transformation). OC (SMP)

29 If P means 'reflect in the y-axis'; and Q means 'translate +3 units parallel to the x-axis'; and if PQ means 'first Q, then P',

(i) find PQ (2, 4);
(ii) find (x, y) if $QP(x, y) = (1, 3)$. OC (SMP)

30

A is the point (1, 6), B is (5, 6) and C is (5, 8).
P denotes reflection in the line $x = 6$.
Q denotes reflection in the line $y = 3$.
T denotes the translation $\begin{pmatrix} -2 \\ 4 \end{pmatrix}$.

(i) Copy the diagram neatly on to the top left-hand quarter of a piece of 5 mm squared paper.

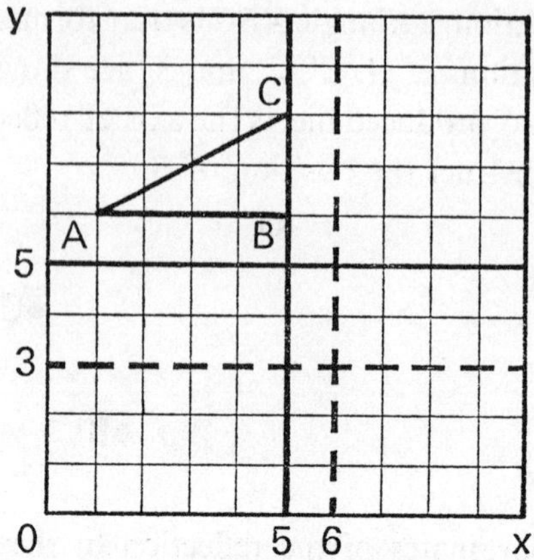

(ii) Show the positions of the triangles $A_1B_1C_1$, $A_2B_2C_2$ and $A_3B_3C_3$ where

$A_1B_1C_1$ is the mapping of triangle ABC under $\boldsymbol{P}$;
$A_2B_2C_2$ is the mapping of triangle ABC under $\boldsymbol{Q} \circ \boldsymbol{P}$;
$A_3B_3C_3$ is the mapping of triangle $A_2B_2C_2$ under $\boldsymbol{T}$.

(iii) Describe fully the single transformation equivalent to $\boldsymbol{Q} \circ \boldsymbol{P}$.
(iv) What single transformation maps triangle ABC on to triangle $A_3B_3C_3$?
(v) If the mapping of (iv) is accomplished by reflection in a line m followed by reflection in a line n, what is the angle between lines m and n?

SC

31

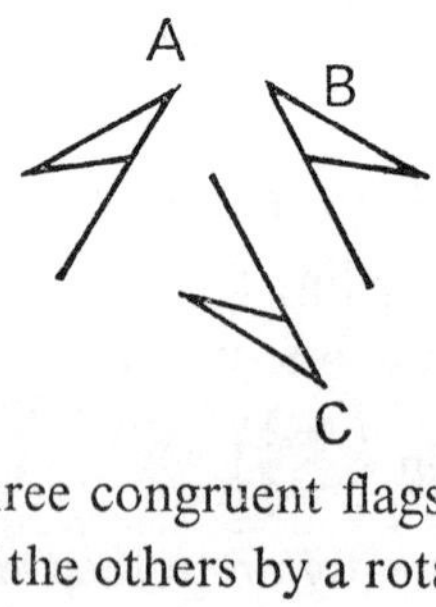

A, *B*, *C* represent three congruent flags. Which one cannot be mapped on to *either* of the others by a rotation in the plane of the flags?

OC (SMP)

32 If K stands for an anti-clockwise rotation of 240° about the origin, describe K^2 and K^{-1}. OC (SMP)

33 O is the centre of a rotation which transforms B into B' and C into C'. Given that OB' is parallel to BC, state the size of the angle of rotation. C

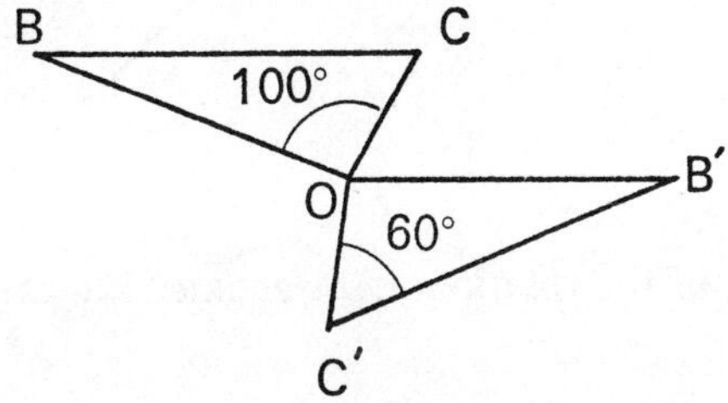

34 A triangle ABC is rotated through 180° in the plane of the triangle about the midpoint D of BC. If A' is the image of A after rotation, name the shape of $ABA'C$ when the triangle ABC has

(*a*) unequal sides;
(*b*) angle $BAC = 90°$;
(*c*) $AB = AC$;
(*d*) angle $BAC = 90°$ and $AB = AC$, L

35 Is the following statement true or false?
If a semicircular plate OHK is given an anti-clockwise rotation

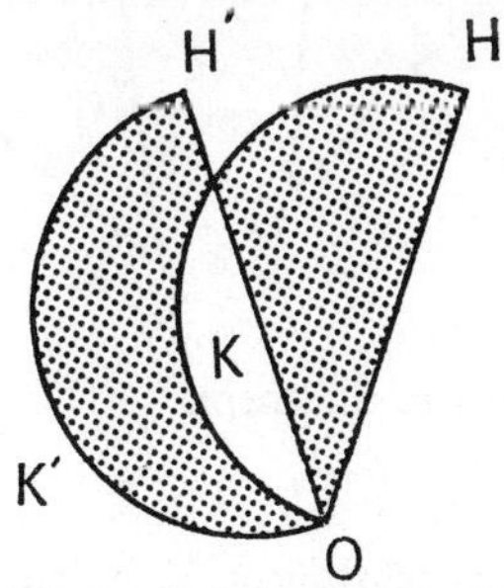

about O so that $OH'K'$ is its new position, as shown in the diagram, then the shaded parts are equal in area. SC

36 A rotation transforms the points P, Q into P', Q' respectively, as shown in the diagram. Copy the diagram and find by drawing,

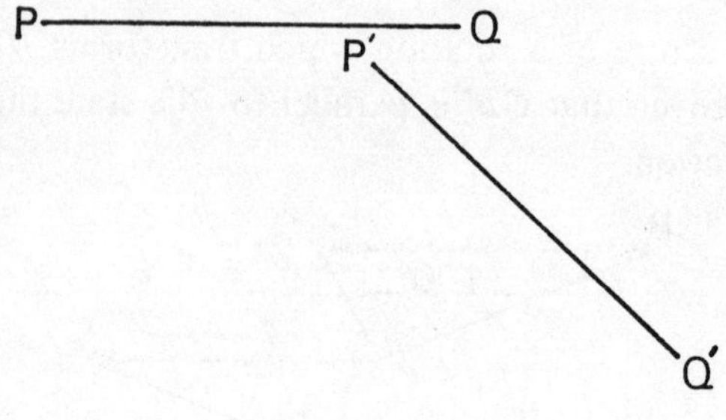

the fixed point of the rotation. (*Any* geometrical instruments may be used.) OC (SMP)

37 Triangle $A'B'C'$ is the image of triangle ABC under a rotation. Copy the diagram and find by drawing, the centre of this rotation.

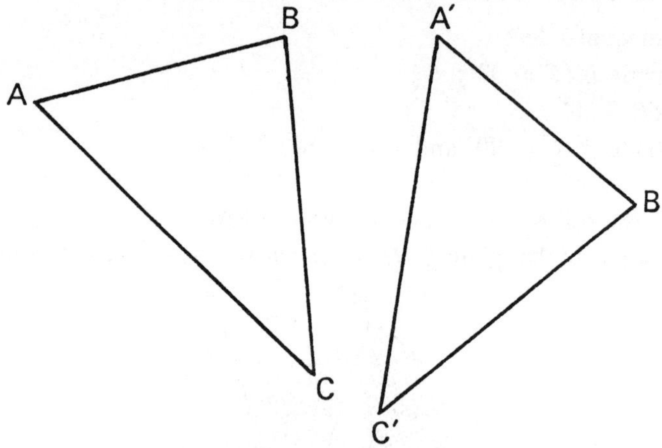

Mark this centre R on the diagram. OC (SMP)

38 $ABCDE$ is a regular pentagon, O its centre.

(i) State the clockwise angle of rotation about O under which $A \to C$.

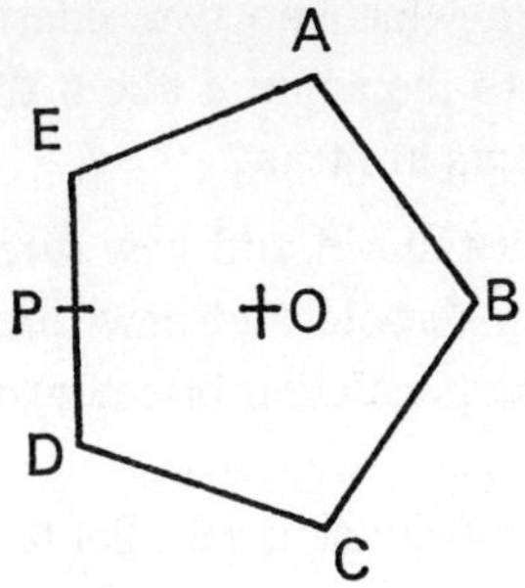

(ii) P is the midpoint of DE. Insert on a copy of the diagram the point P', the transform of P under this rotation. Write down the acute angle between CP and EP'.
(iii) If $OA = 200$ mm, calculate the length of OP, using your tables. OC (SMP)

39 The triangle $A'B'C$ is the image of the triangle ABC under a clockwise rotation of 20° about C.

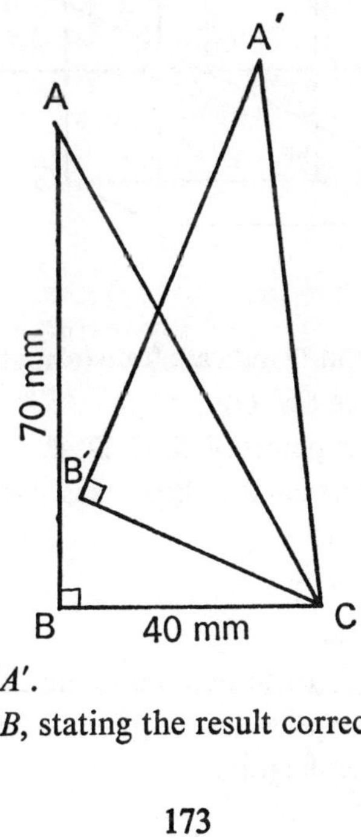

(i) Calculate $\angle CAA'$.
(ii) Calculate $\angle ACB$, stating the result correct to the nearest $\frac{1}{2}°$.
OC (SMP)

40 A triangle ABC in which no two sides are equal is given a clockwise turn equal to the angle A about the vertex B. Which of the following statements are true?

(*a*) The angle between the old and new directions of AC is A.
(*b*) The angle between the old and new directions of BC is B.
(*c*) $B \in$ the mediator (perpendicular bisector) of AA', where A' is the new position of A.
(*d*) No side of the new triangle is parallel to a side of the original triangle. OC (SMP)

41

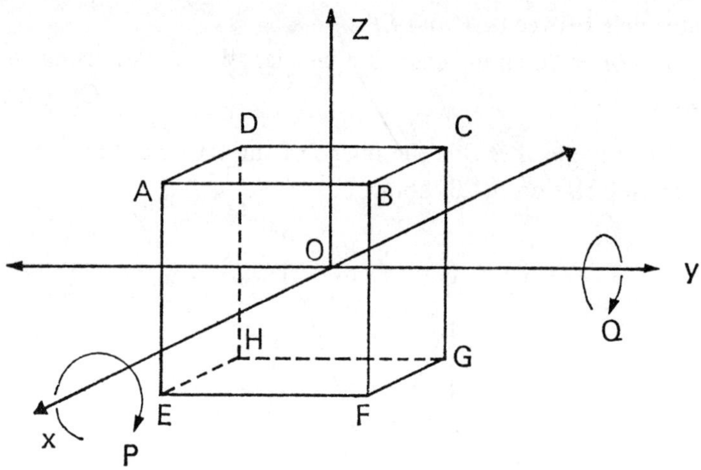

In the diagram P and Q indicate transformations which are half-turns about fixed axes Ox, Oy.

The positions of the points A, B, C, D, E, F, G, H are corners of a cube which is such that the three axes pass through the mid-points of opposite faces.

(i) Find $P(A)$ and $Q(E)$.
(ii) Find $Q(P(A))$ and $Q(P(B))$.
(iii) Use the result of (ii) to determine the single transformation (call this R) which is equivalent to QP, and indicate this transformation clearly on the diagram. OC (SMP)

42 In the figure $ABCD$ is a square and lengths are as shown. A clockwise quarter-turn about the centre of $ABCD$ is denoted by θ.

(i) State with reasons the images under θ of the point A and the segment AP.

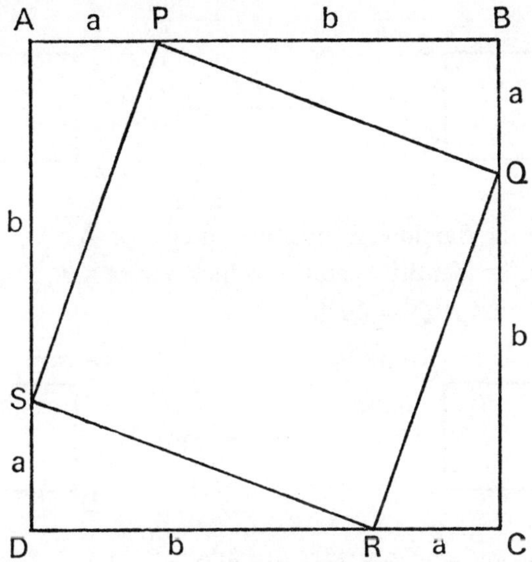

(ii) State the images of P under θ^2, θ^3 and θ^4.

(iii) State one or more properties of a square which justify you in concluding that $PQRS$ is a square.

(iv) Express in terms of a and b the areas $ABCD$ and APS. *Deduce* the area $PQRS$. OC (SMP)

43 The operation P applied to a square of card $ABCD$ (lettered as shown on Page 176) means 'rotate through 90° *clockwise* about the centre'. The operation Q means 'turn over about whichever diagonal is running from bottom left to top right'. The results of P and Q are as shown in the diagram. PQ means 'first P, then Q'.

(i) Draw similar pairs of diagrams to illustrate the effect of P^2, QP.

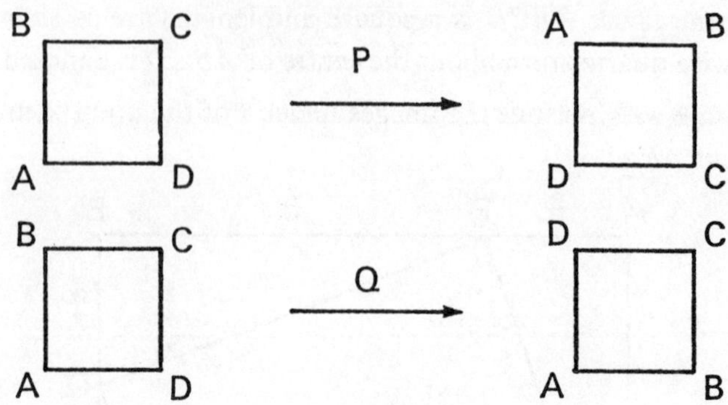

(ii) What is the lowest positive integer k for which $P^k = I$, where I is the identity operation which leaves $ABCD$ unchanged?
(iii) Show that $P^2Q = QP^2$.

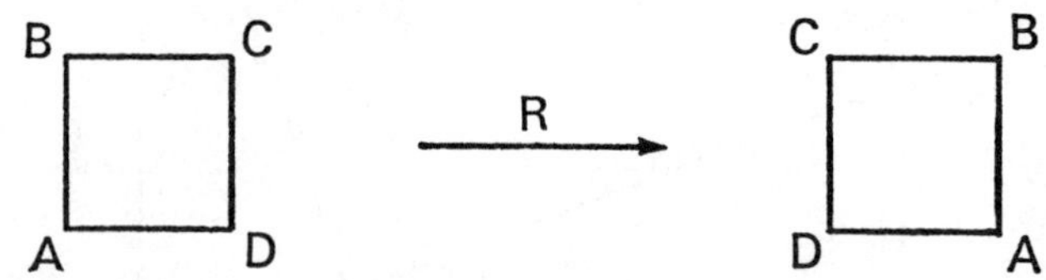

(iv) The result of a third operation R is as shown.
Express R in terms of P and Q. OC (SMP)

44 (i) What is the result of a half-turn of a plane about a point M_1 of the plane followed by a half-turn about another point M_2 of the plane?

If M_1 and M_2 are the midpoints of the sides AB, AC of a triangle identify the image of B under these successive half-turns.
(ii) D is a point *not* in the plane ABC; M_3 and M_4 are the midpoints of DB, DC. Explain why M_3M_4 is equal and parallel to M_1M_2. What can you deduce about M_1M_4 and M_2M_3?
(iii) M_5, M_6 are the midpoints of BC, AD, the remaining edges of the pyramid $ABCD$. Can you say anything about M_1M_4 and M_5M_6? OC (SMP)

45 B is the point $(-5,\ 0)$ and R is the transformation which gives a 90° clockwise rotation (↻) about the origin. T is the translation which increases x-coordinates by 2 and decreases y-coordinates by 3.

If $RT(B) = C$ and $TR(B) = D$, write down the coordinates of C and D. C

46

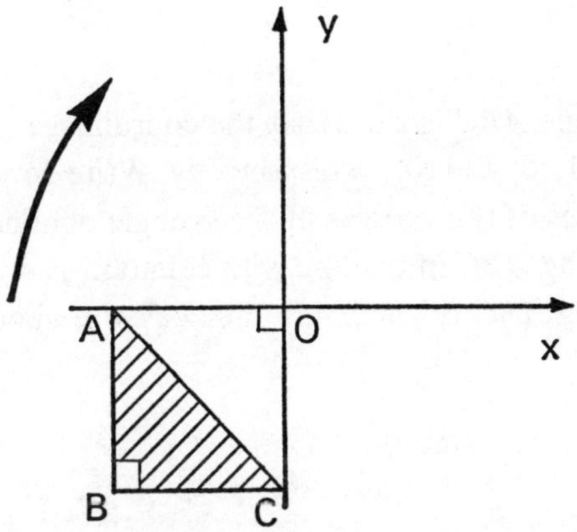

The isosceles triangle ABC is given a quarter-turn clockwise about O and is then reflected in the x-axis. Sketch on a copy of the diagram below, the final position of the triangle, marking A, B and C clearly. C

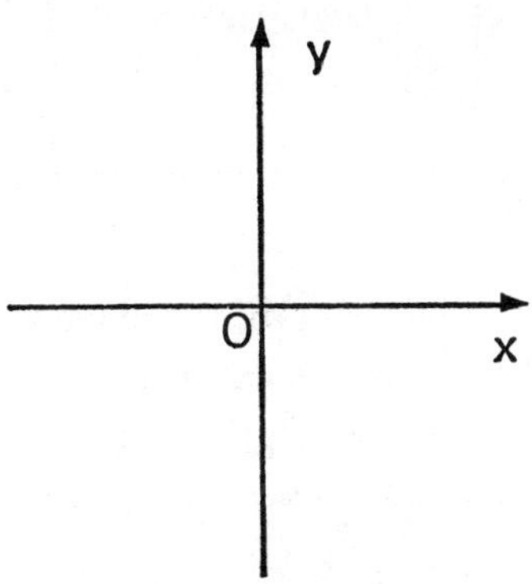

47 If P denotes reflection in the x-axis and Q denotes rotation about the origin through a quarter-turn anti-clockwise, find

(*a*) $PQ(2, 3)$;

(*b*) (x, y) if $QP(x, y) = (3, 1)$. L

48 m_1 and m_2 are perpendicular straight lines meeting at O. Name the single transformation in the plane of m_1 and m_2 which is equivalent to reflection in m_1 followed by reflection in m_2.

OC (SMP)

49 The triangle ABC is such that the coordinates of A, B and C are $(1, 0)$ $(-1, 0)$ and $(0, 1)$ respectively. Write down or calculate the coordinates of the vertices of the triangle obtained:

(i) by reflecting ABC in the line with equation $y = x$;

(ii) by rotating ABC through 45° anticlockwise about the origin.

AEB

50

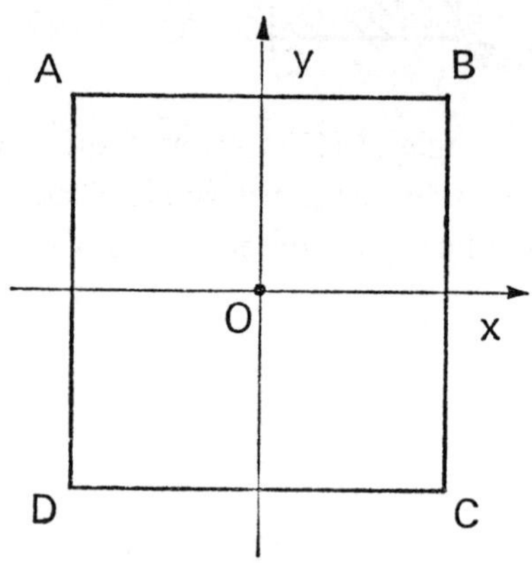

P denotes a positive quarter-turn, in the plane, about O;

Q denotes the reflection in the axis Ox.

(i) Sketch on a copy of the diagram (Page 179) the image of the square, correctly lettered, under the transformation QP (i.e. P followed by Q).

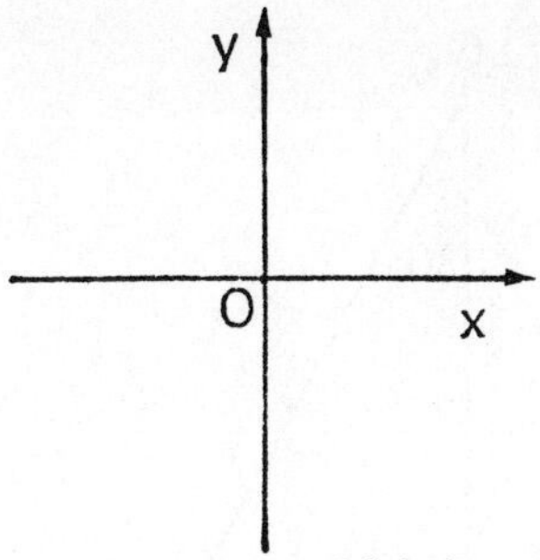

(ii) State a single transformation which is equivalent to QP.

OC (SMP)

51 Which one or more of the following transformations map the point (2, 1) on to the point (−1, 2)?
(*a*) A rotation about the origin through 90° in an anti-clockwise direction;
(*b*) A reflection in the y-axis followed by a reflection in the line $y = x$;
(*c*) A reflection in the line $y = x$ followed by a reflection in the y-axis.

OC (SMP)

52 A triangle has its vertices at the points with coordinates (1, 1), (2, 3) and (−1, 4). It is transformed by first reflecting in the x-axis and then by rotating the resulting points through 90° anti-clockwise about the origin. Calculate the coordinates of the vertices of the triangle in the transformed position.

A square, whose vertices had been at the points P, Q, R and S, is transformed by the above transformations into a square whose vertices are at the points with coordinates (0, 5), (3, 5), (3, 8), (0, 8). Calculate the coordinates of P, Q, R and S.

AEB

53 Copy in the middle of your paper the diagram which shows a triangle $A_1B_1C_1$ with $\angle A_1 = 60°$, $\angle B_1 = 90°$ and $\angle C_1 = 30°$.

It is given a clockwise rotation through 60° about A_1 and $A_1 \to A_2$, $B_1 \to B_2$ and $C_1 \to C_2$. The triangle $A_2B_2C_2$ is then given a reflection in the line B_2C_2 which sends $A_2 \to A_3$, $B_2 \to B_3$ and $C_2 \to C_3$. Finally $A_3 \to A_4$, $B_3 \to B_4$ and $C_3 \to C_4$ when triangle

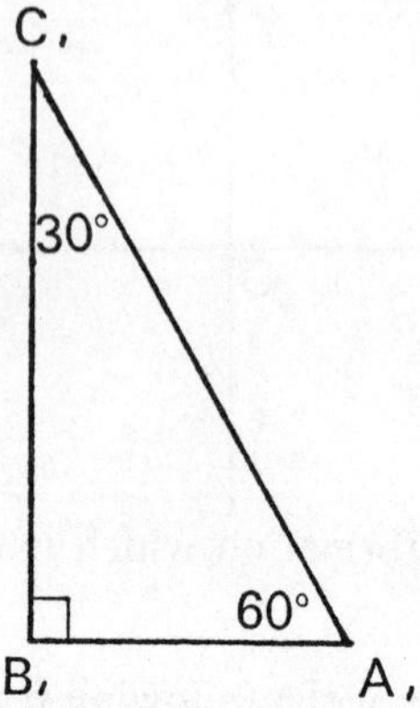

$A_3B_3C_3$ is given an anti-clockwise rotation through 60° about C_3.
(i) Mark clearly on your diagram the points A_2, B_2, C_2. A_3, B_3, C_3, A_4, B_4 and C_4. Take special care in labelling your points where one point has more than one label. Shade the triangle $A_4B_4C_4$.
(ii) Describe single transformations under which
(*a*) $A_2B_2C_2 \rightarrow A_4B_4C_4$.
(*b*) $A_1B_1C_1 \rightarrow A_4B_4C_4$. NI

54 In the regular pentagon *ABCDE*, centre *O*, two types of transformation are carried out:

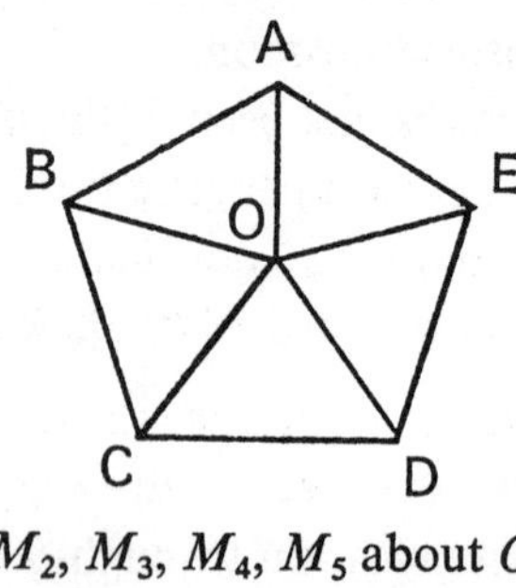

(*a*) Reflection: M_1, M_2, M_3, M_4, M_5 about *OA*, *OB*, *OC*, *OD*, *OE* respectively;
(*b*) Rotation: R_1, R_2, R_3, R_4, R_5 of *OA* into *OB*, *OC*, *OD*, *OE*, *OA* respectively.

Show that $M_1M_2 = R_2 \neq M_2M_1$ and find the R-transformation equivalent to M_2M_1. Find four other pairs of M-transformations equivalent to R_2. L

55 A line segment A_0B_0 in a rectangular cartesian framework is transformed by any one of the following operations:

(i) I; unchanged as A_0B_0,
(ii) X; reflected in the x-axis into A_1B_1,
(iii) Y; reflected in the y-axis into A_2B_2,
(iv) H; half-turn about the origin into A_3B_3.

Find which operations superimpose each of the following quadrilaterals on itself

(*a*) $A_0A_1B_3B_2$,
(*b*) $A_0A_2B_3B_1$,
(*c*) $A_0B_2A_3B_1$,
(*d*) $A_0B_2B_3B_1$,
(*e*) $A_0A_1A_3A_2$. L

56 The square $A'B'C'D'$ (side 40 mm) is the image of $ABCD$ (side 20 mm) under an enlargement. $CD' = 10$ mm.

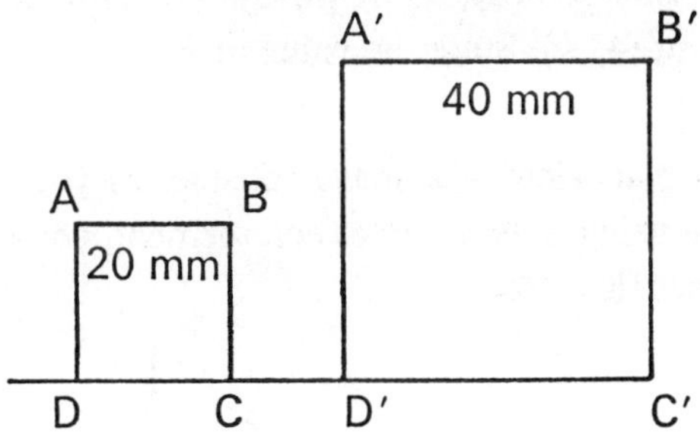

State the position of X, the centre of enlargement, giving its exact distance from D. OC (SMP)

57 The triangle XYZ (Page 182) is an enlargement of the triangle ABC.

(i) Construct on a copy of the diagram, the centre E of the enlargement.

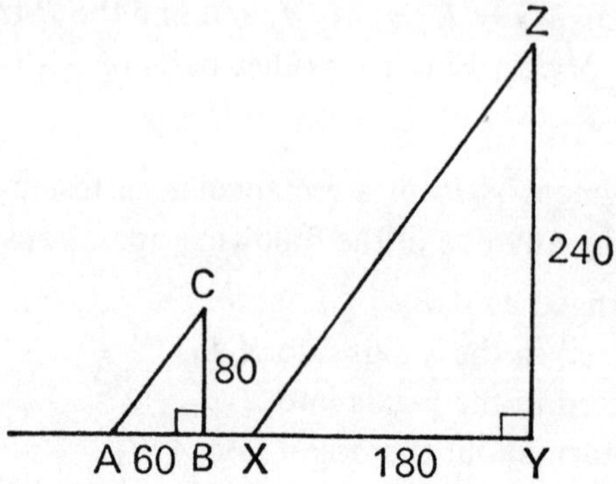

(ii) If all the given dimensions are in millimetres and $\overline{BX} = 20$ mm, calculate $\overline{EA}$. C

58 On a copy of the diagram construct the centre of enlargement of the circles C_1 and C_2, whose centres O_1 and O_2 have been marked. OC (SMP)

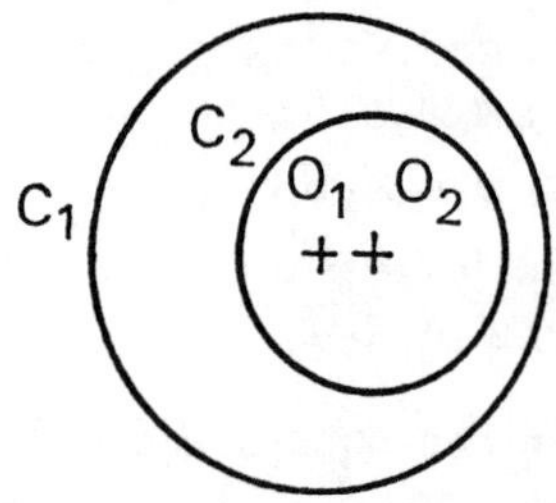

59 Under an enlargement, centre (0, 3), the point (2, 5) is mapped on to the point (4, k). State the value of k. C

60 Here is a plan view of a space capsule. In your book, sketch this plan, and using A as centre of enlargement, construct a similar plan four times the area. L

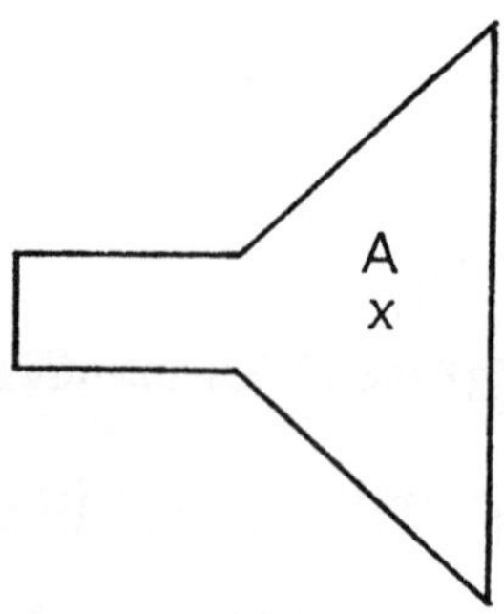

61

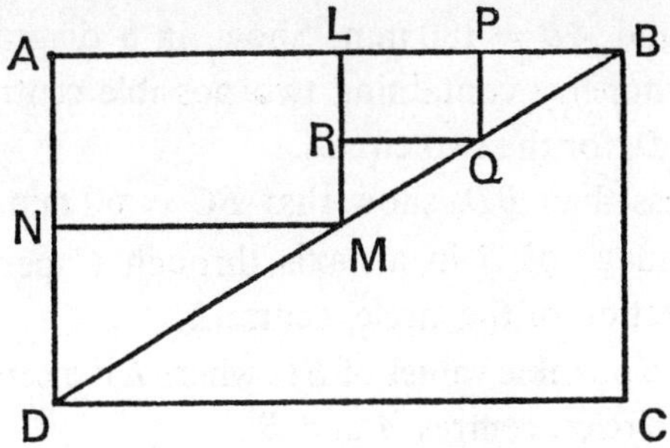

ABCD, *ALMN* and *LPQR* are rectangles. *M* is the midpoint of *BD*, and *Q* is the midpoint of *BM*, the rectangles being consequently similar.
(i) State the centre of the enlargement under which *ABCD* is the image of *ALMN*.
(ii) Give a reason why *DR* and *CQ* when produced meet on *AB*.
OC (SMP)

62 $A_1B_1C_1D_1$ is a parallelogram and A_2, B_2, C_2 are the midpoints of A_1D_1, A_1C_1, C_1D_1. A_3, B_3, C_3 are the midpoints of A_2D_1, A_2C_2, C_2D_1 and so on. Show that D_1 is the centre of enlargement of triangles $A_tB_tC_t$ ($t = 1, 2, 3, \ldots$). L

63 On 5 mm squared paper, plot the points *A*(2, 4), *B*(4, 4), *C*(4, 6) and *D*(2, 6). Join these points to form a square *ABCD*.
(i) With P(0, 5) as centre and scale factor 3, construct the image *A'B'C'D'* of the square *ABCD* under the given dilation, and state the coordinates of *C'*.
(ii) Taking *A* as centre and scale factor −3, construct the image *A"B"C"D"* of *ABCD* under the dilation [*A*, −3] and give the coordinates of *C"*.
(iii) Find also the coordinates of the centre *Q*, on *C'C"*, of a rotation which maps *C"* on to *C'*. SC

64 The radii of two circles, centres A and B are 30 mm and 15 mm respectively and $AB = 180$ mm. Show, in a diagram, that AB is an axis of symmetry containing two possible centres of enlargement, C and D, for the two circles.

If BC is less than BD, show that $BC = 60$ mm and find BD.

B' is the image of B in an axis through C perpendicular to AB after reflection of the circle, centre B.

Find the two possible values of BE, where E is a centre of enlargement for the circles, centres A and B'.

Show that C and D are also the centres of two circles, for which A and B are centres of enlargement, and find the ratio of the radii of these two circles. L

65 In the figure $PQRS$ is a square, $LMNP$ is a rectangle and MR is parallel to LS.

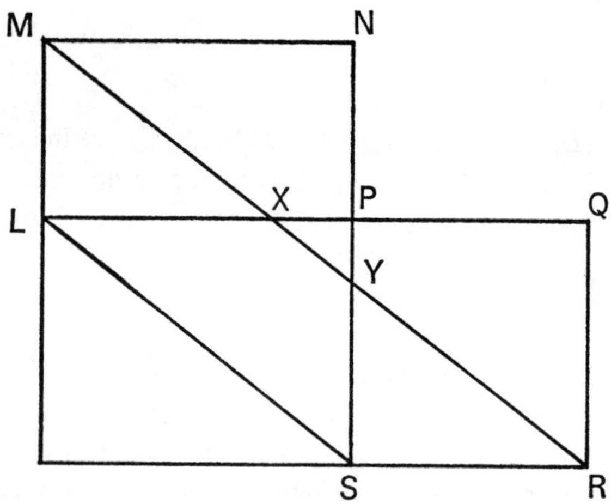

By describing **three** successive shears which transform the square into the rectangle $LMNP$, or otherwise, show that they have the same area.

Given, in addition, that $SR = 150$ mm and $MN = 200$ mm, calculate (i) LM; (ii) LS; (iii) the distance between the lines MR and LS. C

66 The rectangle $ABCD$ is sheared into the position $A'B'CD$. Say what symmetry, if any, the figure $A'B'CD$ has. OC (SMP)

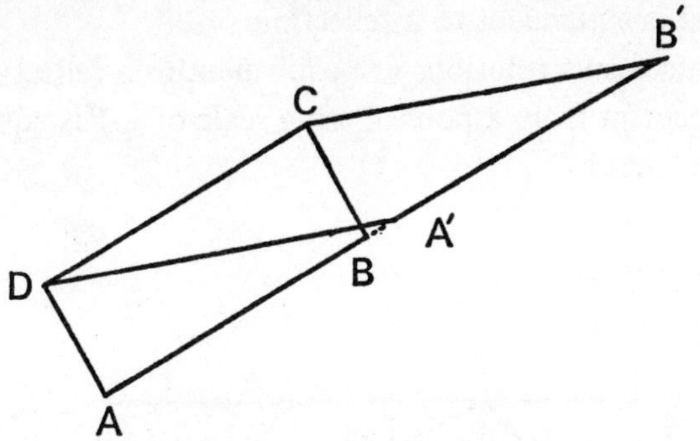

67 (i) Show that the shear described by pre-multiplying by

$$\begin{pmatrix} 1 & 0 \\ -2 & 1 \end{pmatrix}$$

transforms the point P, whose coordinates are given by the column vector $\begin{pmatrix} 2 \\ 4 \end{pmatrix}$, into a point P' on the x-axis. If it also transforms Q, whose coordinates are given by $\begin{pmatrix} -3 \\ -5 \end{pmatrix}$, into Q', find the coordinates of Q'. Draw a diagram showing the positions of P, Q, P', Q'.

(ii) Find the value of b for which the shear

$$\begin{pmatrix} 1 & b \\ 0 & 1 \end{pmatrix} \text{ transforms } \begin{pmatrix} -3 \\ 1 \end{pmatrix}$$

into a point M on the y-axis. If it also transforms P' into L, find the coordinates of L and M.

(iii) State the area of triangle OLM, where O is $\begin{pmatrix} 0 \\ 0 \end{pmatrix}$, and name any other figures in the diagram with the same area, giving your reasons. OC (SMP)

68 Indicate for each of the following statements whether it is necessarily true (T), necessarily false (F) or neither of them (N):

(*a*) Two successive reflections are equivalent to a rotation.
(*b*) A translation followed by a reflection in an axis parallel to the translation is equivalent to a reflection.
(*c*) Two successive rotations are equivalent to a reflection.
(*d*) Enlargement from a point O on a scale of -1 is equivalent to a half turn about O. OC (SMP)

69

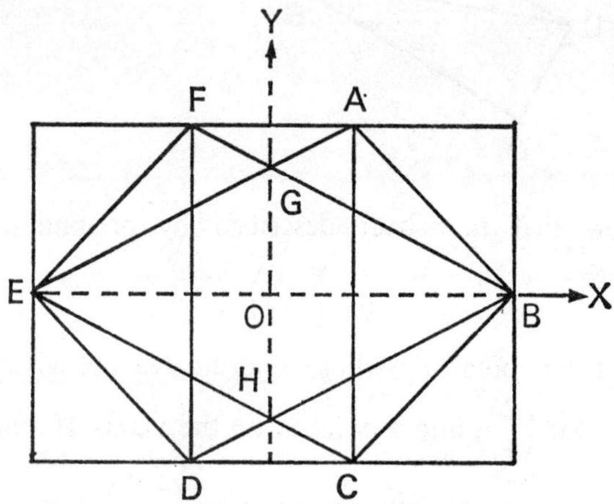

State which of the statements (*a*), (*b*), (*c*), (*d*), (*e*) are true and which are false.

The diagram shows a tiling of six congruent squares. The points A, B, C, D, E, F, vertices of squares, are joined to form a figure which has two axes of symmetry, OX and OY through E, O, B and H, O, G respectively.

(*a*) $EFBC$ is a parallelogram.
(*b*) A half-turn about O, in the plane of the figure, maps triangle AGB on to triangle CHB.
(*c*) Triangle GEF is the image of triangle GBA under a reflection in the *y-axis*.
(*d*) A translation represented by $\overrightarrow{EH}$ maps F on to B.
(*e*) If A is the image of G under a certain dilatation, centre E, then the image of O by this dilatation lies on the line CA. SC

70 State which of the statements (*a*), (*b*), (*c*), (*d*), (*e*) are true and which are false.

T_1 denotes the transformation which maps the point $(a,\ b)$ to the point $(b,\ a)$.

T_2 denotes the transformation which maps the point $(a,\ b)$ to the point $(a+b,\ b)$.

(*a*) T_1 represents reflection in the line $y = x$.

(*b*) Under T_1 the origin is the only point which is mapped to itself.

(*c*) Under T_2 each point on the x-axis is mapped to itself.

(*d*) The image of $(1,\ 2)$ under $T_2 \circ T_1$, T_2 after T_1, is $(2,\ 3)$.

(*e*) The image of $(1,\ 2)$ under $T_2 \circ T_1$ is the same as the image of $(1,\ 2)$ under $T_1 \circ T_2$. SC

71 State a simple geometrical transformation which, when applied twice in succession, maps the point $(1,\ 3)$ on to the point $(4,\ 12)$. OC (SMP)

72

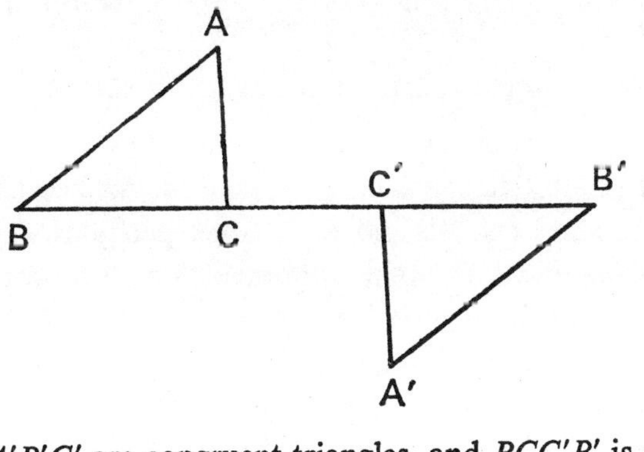

ABC, *A'B'C'* are congruent triangles, and *BCC'B'* is a straight line.

(*a*) Describe a single transformation which would map *A*, *B*, *C* on to *A'*, *B'*, *C'* respectively.

(*b*) What can you state about the relation between the lines *AA'* and *CC'*? OC (SMP)

73 In the triangle ABC, P and Q are the midpoints of the sides BC and BA, CQ cuts AP at M. Describe as fully as possible the single operations which transform (i) triangle BPQ into triangle BCA; (ii) triangle PMQ into triangle AMC, the triangles being named with their vertices in corresponding order. Use what you find to write down the ratio $QM : QC$. If the area of the triangle ABC is 30 000 mm^2 calculate the areas of the triangles BPQ and QMP. State with reason whether it is possible for these triangles to be equiangular, the equal angles being in the order indicated.

OC (SMP)

74 An invariant point of a transformation of the plane is a point which is mapped on to itself by the transformation. For instance, if the transformation is a rotation about a point P, then P is an invariant point, and, in this case, the only invariant point of this transformation. Some transformations do not have any invariant points, some have one as we have seen, and some have more than one.

Describe in geometrical terms the transformation of the plane given by

$$\begin{pmatrix} x' \\ y' \end{pmatrix} = \begin{pmatrix} 0 & -1 \\ 1 & 0 \end{pmatrix} \begin{pmatrix} x \\ y \end{pmatrix} + \begin{pmatrix} 1 \\ 1 \end{pmatrix},$$

where the point with coordinates (x, y) is mapped on to the point with coordinates $(x'\ y')$, and find (either geometrically or algebraically) the invariant point or points of this transformation.

AEB

Chapter Fourteen

1 Sets of natural numbers satisfying the equation $a^2 + b^2 = c^2$ are known as Pythagorean Triples. Copy and complete the following table of such triples.

a	b	c
3	4	5
5	12	—
7	24	—
—	8	10
—	40	41
10	24	—
12	—	37

2 In a certain triangle ABC, $AC^2 = AB^2 - BC^2$. Which one or more of the following statements is (are) necessarily true?

(*a*) A is a right angle.
(*b*) B is a right angle.
(*c*) AC is the shortest side.
(*d*) AB is the longest side. OC (SMP)

3 Let T be the set of all right-angled triangles and let S be the subset of all right-angled triangles each with hypotenuse 40 mm long. Write down two statements about *all* the elements of S which do *not* apply to *all* the elements of T. AEB

4 Are the following statements true or false?

(*a*) It is possible to draw a triangle with sides of length 3, 4 and 5 units which is not right-angled.

(*b*) It is possible to draw a triangle with sides of length 1, 2 and 4 units.

(*c*) It is possible to draw a triangle with sides of length 2, 3 and 4 units. AEB

5 Two of the three sides of a right-angled triangle are respectively 100 mm and 60 mm. Find (*a*) the set of possible values of the smallest angle, (*b*) the set of possible values of the area of the triangle. L

6 Calculate the distance between the points (–2, 1) and (2, 4). OC (SMP)

7 A rhombus *ABCD* has each side 130 mm. If the diagonal *AC* is 100 mm, calculate *BD*. SU

8 Give the length of the diagonal of a rectangular container whose dimensions are 4 m × 3 m × 2 m. [You may leave your answer as a square root.] OC (SMP)

9

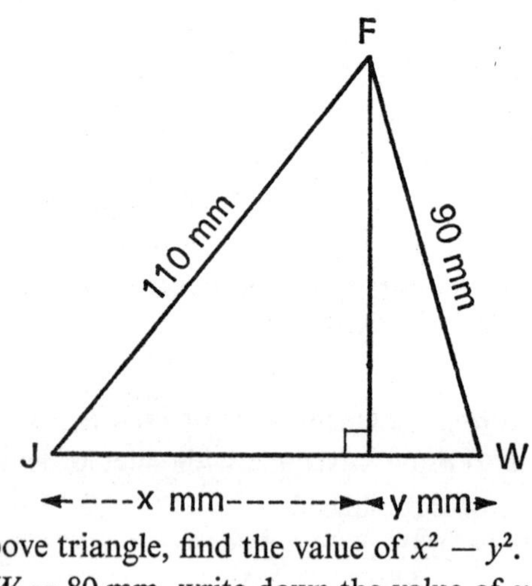

(i) In the above triangle, find the value of $x^2 - y^2$.
(ii) If also $JW = 80$ mm, write down the value of $x - y$. C

10 In the triangle ABC, $AB = 130$ mm, $AC = 80$ mm, $BC = 150$ mm. The foot of the perpendicular from A to BC is D, $BD = x$ mm, $CD = y$ mm, $AD = z$ mm.
(i) Calculate $x^2 - y^2$.
(ii) By using this result, or otherwise, calculate x, z and the area of the triangle ABC. OC (SMP)

11 (i) A and B are the points $(a, 0)$, $(b, 0)$, and M is the midpoint of AB. What are the coordinates of M?
(ii) Express $OA^2 + OB^2 - 2OM^2$ in terms of a and b.
(iii) C is the point $(0, c)$. Express CA^2 and CB^2 in terms of a, b, c. Hence find an expression for $CA^2 + CB^2 - 2CM^2$, simplifying your answer as much as you can. OC (SMP)

12 In the diagram, $OP = PP_1 = P_1P_2 = P_2P_3 = \ldots . = 1$ unit and the right angles are indicated. Calculate OP_1, OP_2, OP_3, leaving square root signs in your answer.

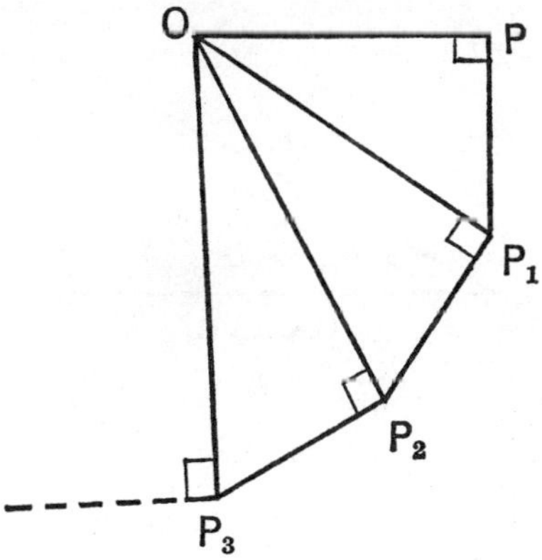

Write down the values of OP_4 and OP_n, the hypotenuses of the 4th and nth right-angled triangles respectively, where the sequence is continued indefinitely.

Find two pairs of values m, n such that the hypotenuses OP_m, OP_n are in the ratio 2 : 1. L

13

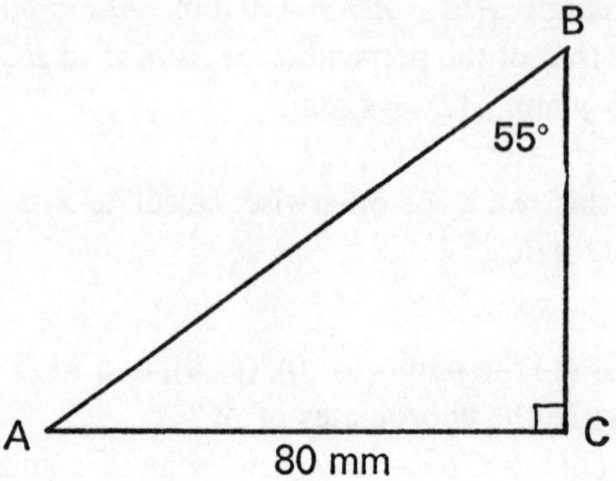

The length AB, in mm, is (*a*) 80 sin 55°; (*b*) $\frac{80}{\sin 55°}$;

(*c*) $\frac{80}{\cos 55°}$; (*d*) 80 tan 55°.

OC (SMP)

14 Is the statement about r true or false.

In the figure, angle ACB is a right angle. If $BC = 100$ mm, angle $ABC = z°$ and $AB = r$ mm

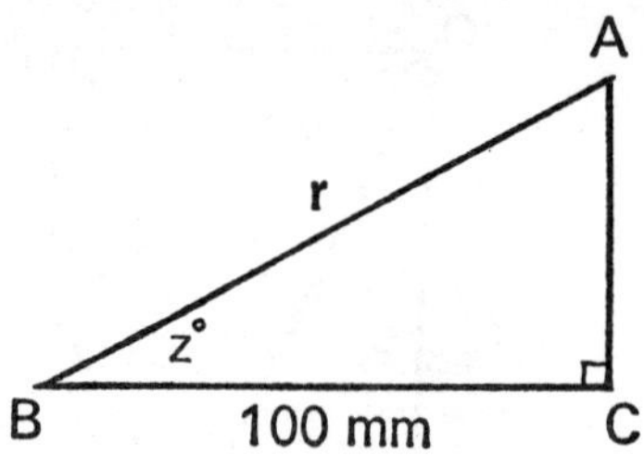

then $r = \frac{100}{\cos z°}$.

SC

15 Calculate the angle $x°$ correct to one-tenth of a degree.

OC (SMP)

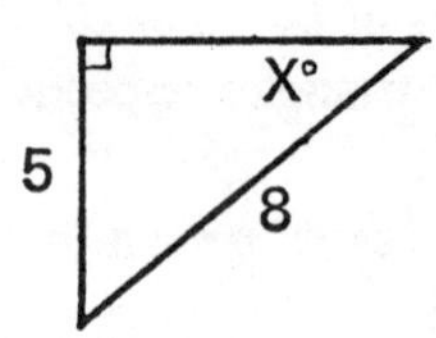

16 The altitude AD of a triangle ABC is 125 mm. If $CD = 75$ mm and $DB = 150$ mm, calculate angle CAB correct to the nearest degree. SU

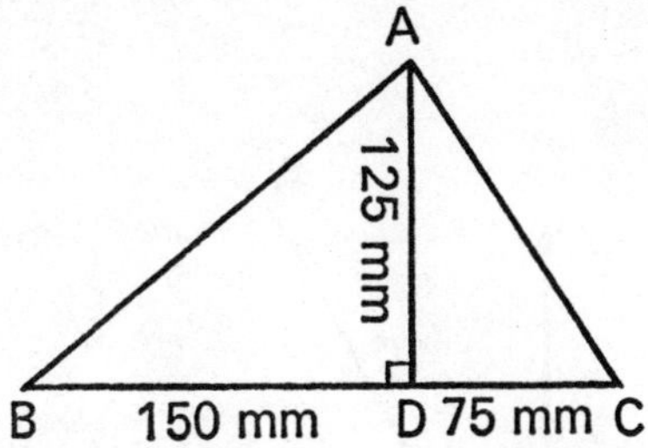

17 State the ratio of the length of the shortest side to the length of the hypotenuse of a right-angled triangle having one angle of 32°.

If the length of the shortest side is 75 mm, find the length of the hypotenuse. OC (SMP)

18 B is 10 km from A in the direction $x°$ east of north. C is 5 km

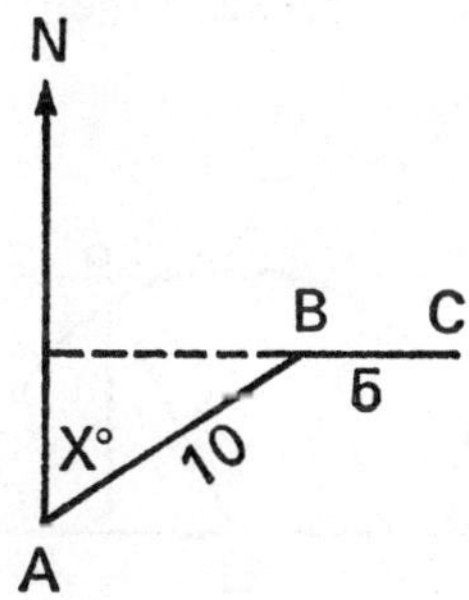

due east of B. It follows that C is $(10 \sin x° + 5)$ km east of A. Is this statement true or false? SC

19 Calculate the coordinates of P. (Decimal answers should be stated correct to one decimal place.) OC (SMP)

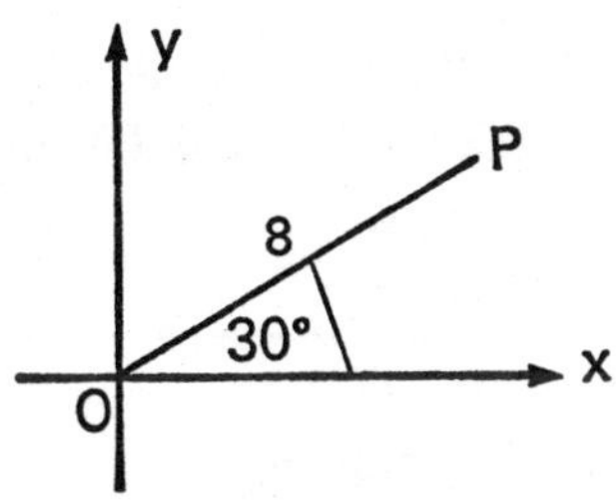

20 The map coordinates (on a kilometre grid) of Guildford station and Horsham station respectively are (499,150), (518,131). Find the bearing of Guildford station from Horsham station.

OC (SMP)

21

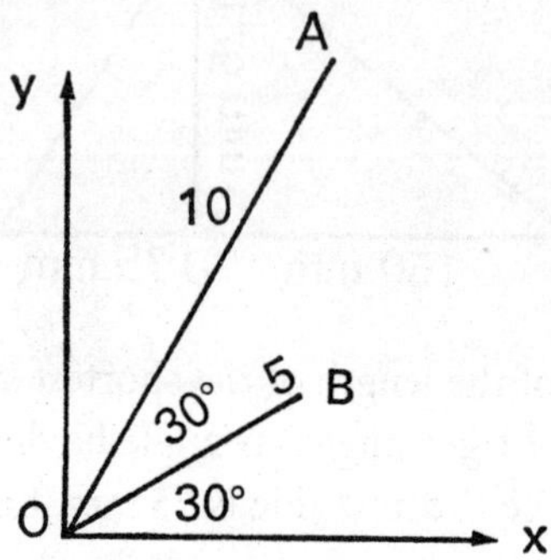

(i) State which of A or B has the greatest x-coordinate. (The diagram is not drawn to scale.)
(ii) Calculate the difference between their y-coordinates.

OC (SMP)

22

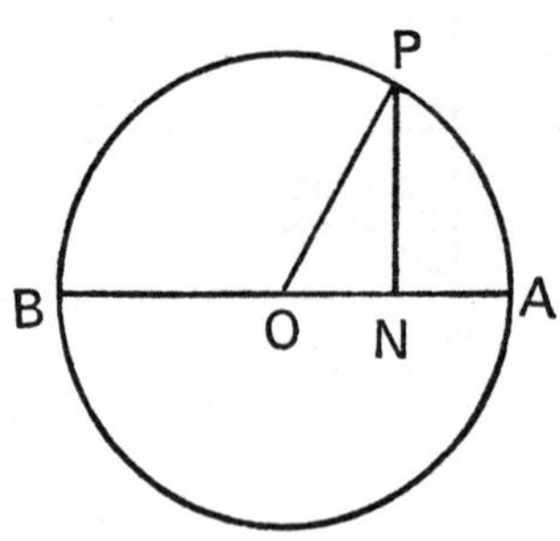

In the figure O is the centre of the circle and r is its radius. $\angle AOP$ is 60°, and PN is perpendicular to BA. ON is equal to

(*a*) $r \sin 60°$;
(*b*) $r \cos 60°$;
(*c*) $r \sin 30°$;
(*d*) $r(1 - \sin 60°)$.

OC (SMP)

23

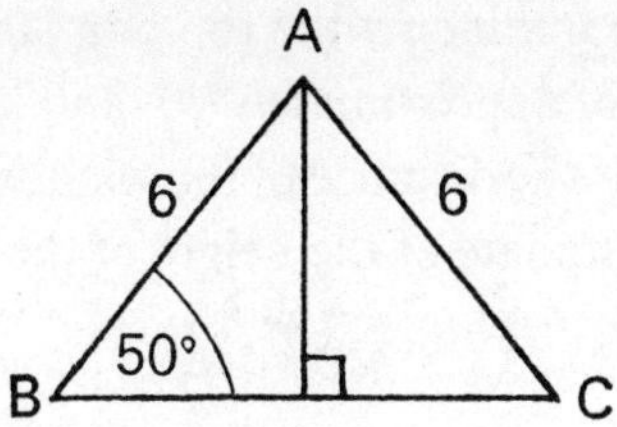

Find an expression for the length of BC. OC (SMP)

24 Calculate the length of YZ. C

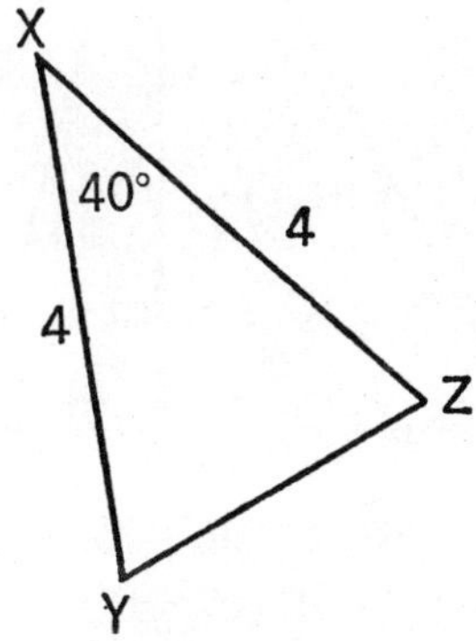

25 Triangle AOB is such that $AO = OB = 100$ mm. Find the angle AOB

(*a*) if $AB = 50$ mm;

(*b*) if O is 50 mm from AB. L

26 Calculate the length of the side of a regular pentagon whose vertices lie on a circle of radius 67·5 mm. AEB

27 Write down, but do not evaluate, an expression for the length of XY. C

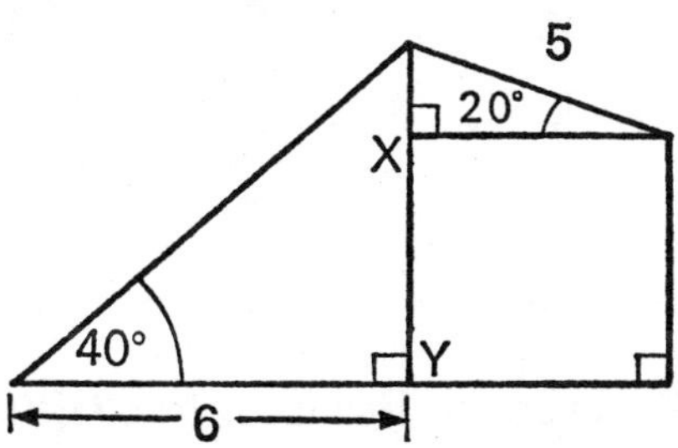

28 From a first-floor window the top of a lamp-post is seen at an angle of elevation of approximately 20° and its base at an angle of depression of 46°. If the distance of the window from the lamp-post is 3 m, obtain an estimate of the height of the lamp-post. AEB

29

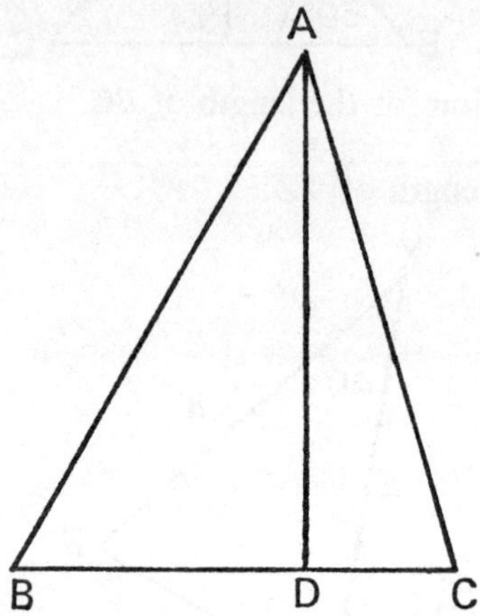

In the diagram, $AB = 40$ mm, $BC = 30$ mm, angle $ABC = 60°$ and AD is perpendicular to BC.
Find (*a*) BD; (*b*) AD; (*c*) AC, correct to three significant figures.
L

30

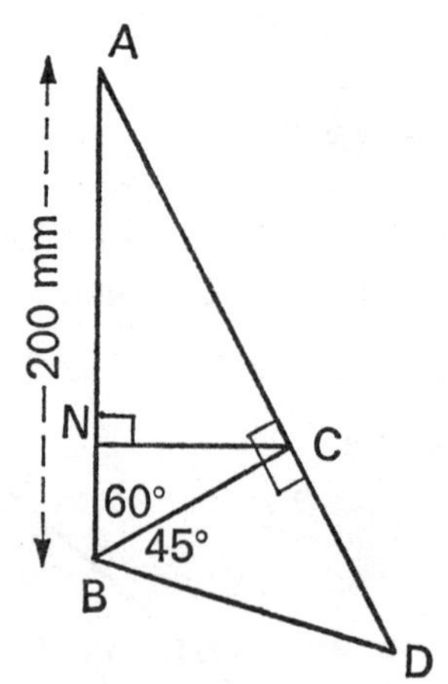

Calculate the length of: (i) CD; (ii) AN. C

31 A and B are two points 300 m apart on a straight and level road running East to West, B being to the east of A. X is a point on the road 200 m from A. S and T are landmarks, both North of X such that angle $TAB = 41° 24'$ and angle $SAB = 49° 48'$. Calculate: (i) TX; (ii) ST; (iii) angle TBA. SU

32 A ship P is 8·7 km South of a lighthouse L and is travelling towards it. A second ship Q is anchored 4·8 km West of L. What is the bearing of P from Q? How far will P be from the lighthouse when its bearing from Q is S 80° E? SU

33 Three anti-aircraft gunnery positions A, B and C are situated so that B is 32 km due north of A and C is 16 km due east of B. An aircraft flies directly over position A and 5 min later is sighted on a bearing 060° from B and 339° from C. Assuming that the aircraft has been flying on a constant course, at a constant altitude and at a constant speed, calculate the course and speed of the aircraft. AEB

34 In the triangle ABC, it is given that $BC = 125$ mm and $AB = 175$ mm. The inscribed circle touches BC at D, where $BD = 75$ mm.

(i) Calculate the length of AC.

(ii) The angle ABC is calculated to be $57° 7'$. Using this result, or otherwise, calculate the radius of the inscribed circle.

(iii) Hence, or otherwise, calculate the angle ACB. AEB

35 A parachutist P, descending vertically with a constant speed, is directly over a point A on an airfield. An observer O, stationed 750 metres from A and on the same level as A, notes that at a given instant the angle of elevation of P is 64°. Make a sketch diagram and *calculate* the height of the parachutist above A.

After an interval of one minute the angle of elevation of P from O changes to 58°. How much longer, to the nearest half-minute, will he take to reach the ground? SC

36 An aircraft is flying in a horizontal straight line at a steady speed over horizontal ground. An observer estimates its height as

450 m. At a certain instant it passes directly over a radar set. Exactly 8 second later this measures its angle of elevation as 12°. (The angle of elevation is the angle between a straight line from the set to the aircraft and a horizontal line through the set.)
(i) Accepting the observer's estimate of its height, calculate its speed in m/s.
(ii) If the estimate of the aircraft's height is liable to be 20 per cent out, find the greatest speed consistent with the data.
(iii) If in fact the speed was 240 m/s calculate the true height of the aircraft.

Give all answers correct to two significant figures.

OC (SMP)

37 (i) Find sin 73·2°.
(ii) Find (to the nearest 0·1°) the angles x and y if

(*a*) $0° \leqslant x \leqslant 180°$ and $\cos x = -0{\cdot}821$;
(*b*) $0° \leqslant y \leqslant 180°$ and $\tan y = \quad 0{\cdot}821$. NI

38 Write down the values of the following, the angles being measured in radians:

(i) $\sin \frac{1}{2}\pi$; (ii) $\cos \pi$. O

39 The value of sin 240° is equal to (*a*) −0·5; (*b*) 0·866; (*c*) sin 120°; (*d*) −sin 60°; (*e*) cos 150°. O

40

Calculate the length of the side *AB*.

C

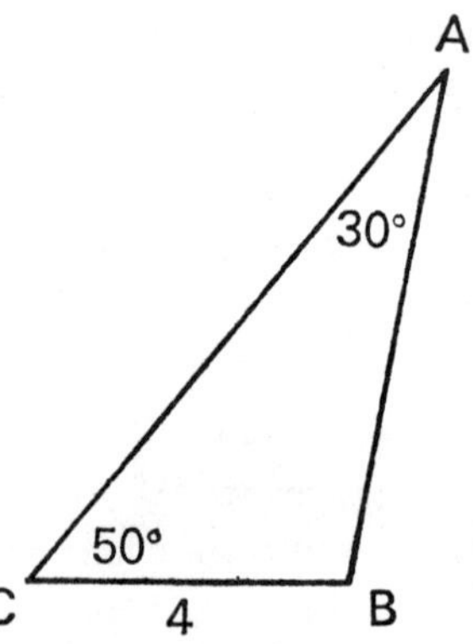

41 In triangle *ABC*, $a = 2$, $b = 5$ and $B = 150°$. Find sin *A*. SC

42 Two ground radar stations B and C, 31 kilometres apart on the same horizontal level, simultaneously observe an aircraft A vertically above the line BC. The angles of elevation of A from B and C are 8° and 5° respectively.
Calculate:

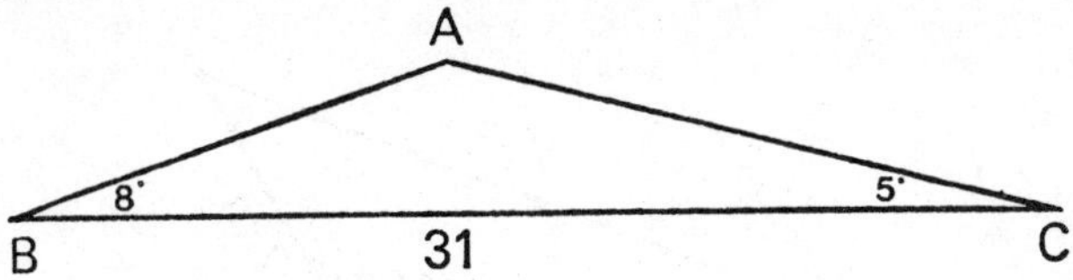

(i) the distance AB to the nearest kilometre;
(ii) the height of the aircraft above the ground correct to the nearest tenth of a kilometre. SC

43
A fishery cruiser leaves a port P and steams 16 km in the direction 037°(N37°E) to a position A where it changes course and steams 13 km to a position B as shown in the diagram.

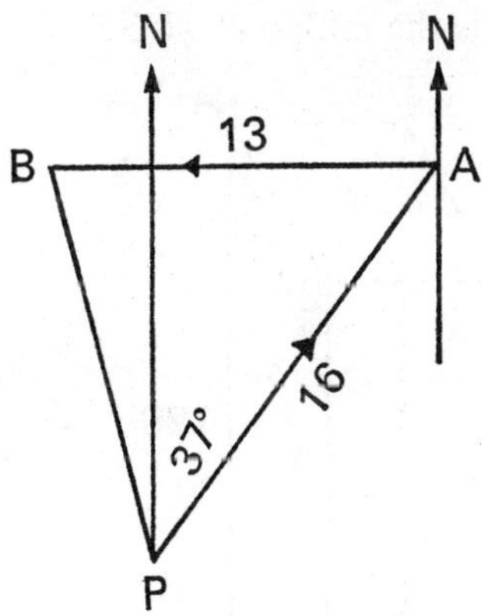

(i) State the size of angle PAB in degrees.
(ii) Calculate the distance represented by PB to the nearest tenth of a kilometre.
(iii) Using the sine rule, calculate to the nearest degree the size of angle PBA and hence obtain the direction the ship should steer to reach port P. SC

44 Two circles with centres X and Y intersect at A and B. The radii AX and AY of the circles are 60 mm and 80 mm, and XY = 120 mm. Calculate the angle AXY and the length of AB. (You may assume that XY and AB intersect at right angles.) SU

45

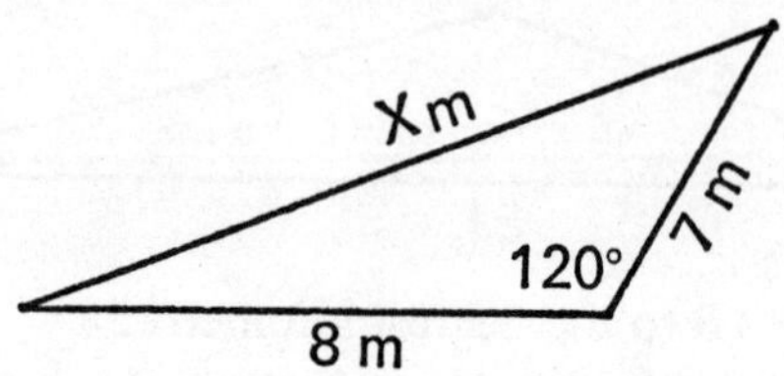

In the calculation of x by means of the cosine formula, a student uses $\cos 120° = \frac{1}{2}$ instead of $-\frac{1}{2}$.

(i) Find the error in his calculation of x^2.

(ii) What is the error in his calculation of x? C

46 $ABCD$, $EFGH$ is a cuboid with a square base. $GE = 50$ mm, $AE = 120$ mm, X is the midpoint of GE.

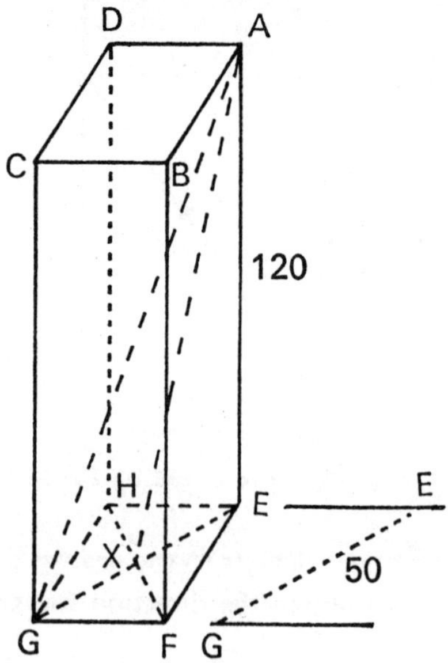

Find:

(*a*) the length of AG;
(*b*) the size of the angle which AG makes with the base $EFGH$;
(*c*) the area of triangle AGX;
(*d*) the length of GF keeping it as a surd;
(*e*) the volume of the given cuboid. SC

47 The figure represents a cube with edges 50 mm long. $ABCD$ is horizontal and E is the midpoint of the vertical edge through C. The line AE is inclined at $x°$ to the horizontal.

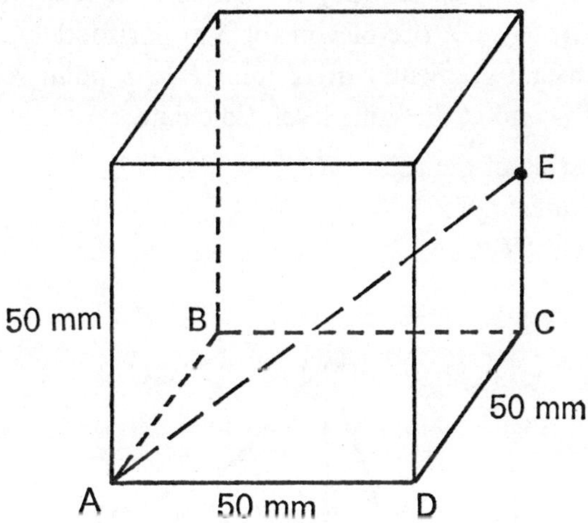

(i) Mark clearly, on a copy of the figure, the angle $x°$ which measures the inclination of AE to the horizontal.
(ii) Calculate $\sin x°$, giving your answer as a fraction. C

48 A right pyramid $VABCD$ stands on its square base $ABCD$ on a horizontal plane, A being due north of B. The point P lies in the plane $ABCD$ and is 50 m from A at a bearing of 255° from A. The bearing of B from P is 135°. By drawing the perpendicular from P to AB, or otherwise, calculate the length of AB.

If the perpendicular height of the pyramid through V is 20 m calculate the angle between the edge VA and the horizontal plane. AEB

49 The horizontal base $ABCD$ of a pyramid is a square of side 100 mm. The vertex H is 100 mm vertically above the centre of the base. P is the midpoint of HD and L is the point of the base vertically below P. By using coordinates or otherwise, calculate:

(i) the length of AL;
(ii) the inclination of the plane ABP to the base;
(iii) the area of triangle ABP. OC (SMP)

50 Two points P and Q lie on a plane hillside, Q being due north of P and higher by 60 m. They are joined by a road of constant gradient 1 in 5 (i.e. a rise of 1 m for 5 m horizontally). Another road of constant gradient 1 in 12 joins P to a point R which is due east of Q and at the same level. Calculate:

(i) the bearing of the road PR;
(ii) the distance QR;
(iii) the angle QPR. OC (SMP)

51

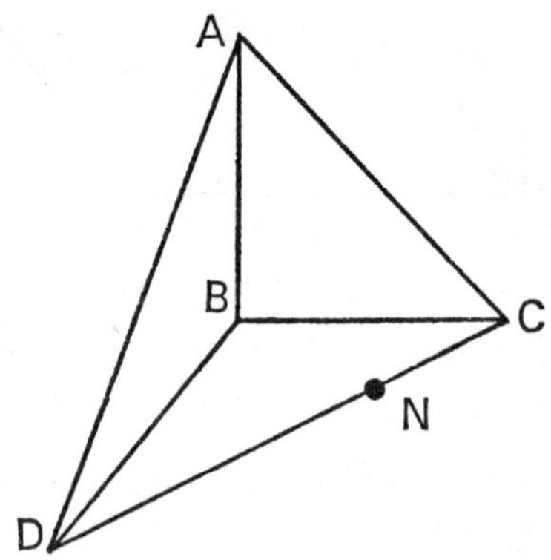

The triangle ABC is situated with BC horizontal and AB vertical. The triangle is rotated through a quarter-turn about AB so that C moves to D. N is the point on DC nearest to B.

(i) State the value of $\angle BCN$.
(ii) If $AB = 6\sqrt{2}$ m, and $BC = 3$ m, evaluate tan $\angle ANB$.

OC (SMP)

52 A piece of cardboard in the shape $OECN$ as shown has $OE = OC = ON = 4$ units, angle $EOC = 20°$, and angle $CON = 40°$ Find the lengths EC and CN.

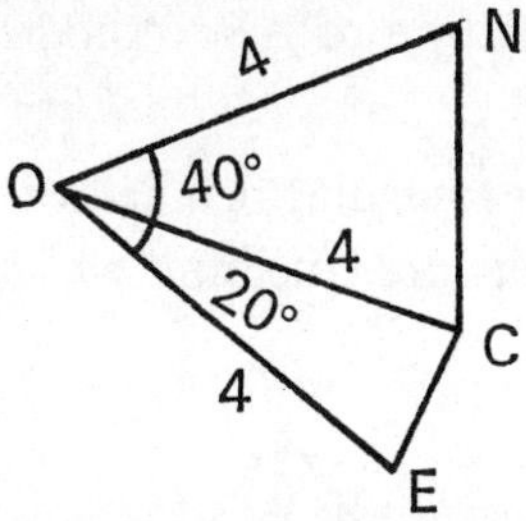

If the cardboard is folded about OC until the new angle ECN is a right-angle, find the new length EN, and the new angle EON. L

53 A street hoarding is rectangular in shape, measuring 3·6 m by 2·4 m, and is erected in a vertical plane with its longest side on horizontal ground and is supported at the rear by two straight struts of equal length. The struts are attached to the hoarding at its upper corners and the feet of the struts are placed symmetrically with respect to the hoarding 4·8 m apart and 2·4 m behind the line of the base of the hoarding.

Calculate the length of a strut and the angle which it makes with the horizontal. AEB

54

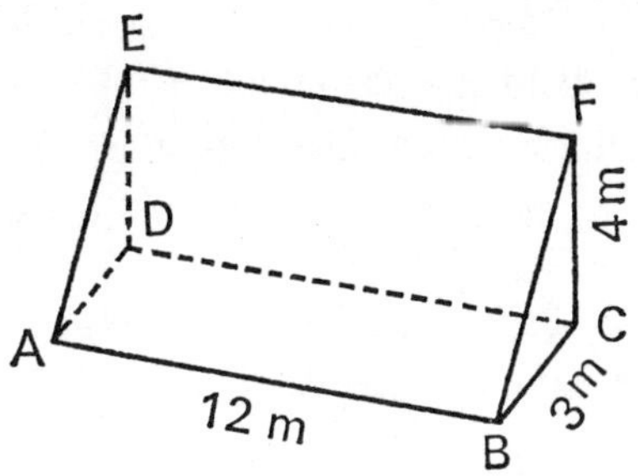

The diagram shows a section of a sea wall. The faces $ABCD$ and $CDEF$ are rectangular with $ABCD$ horizontal and $CDEF$ vertical. $AB = 12$ m, $BC = 3$ m and $CF = 4$ m.

Calculate:

(i) the angle of inclination of the face $ABFE$ to the horizontal;
(ii) the distance AF;
(iii) the angle of inclination of AF to the horizontal. NI

55 The diagram shows a regular octahedron $ABCDEF$. Which of the following statements are true, and which false?

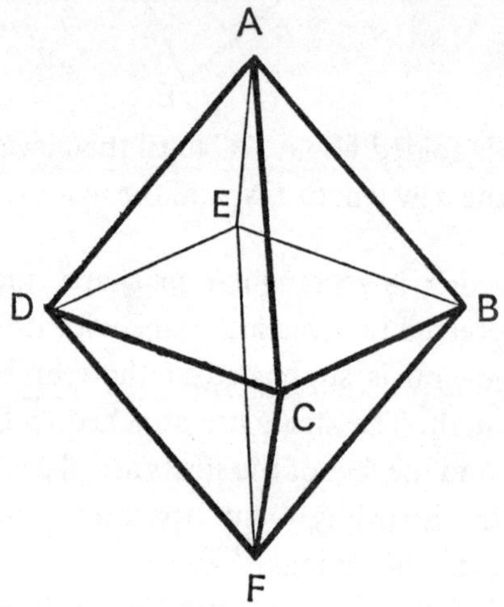

(*a*) The solid has exactly eight faces, six vertices and eight edges.
(*b*) The angle $ACE = 60°$.
(*c*) $EC = AF$.
(*d*) There are four distinct routes from A to B along the edges of the solid and passing through just two other vertices.

OC (SMP)

56 In the pyramid (Page 205) the triangle ABC is right-angled at B and lies in a horizontal plane. DB is vertical. State whether it is true or false that:

(*a*) the planes ADB, CDB are perpendicular to each other;
(*b*) the foot of the perpendicular from B to the plane ADC lies on DC;

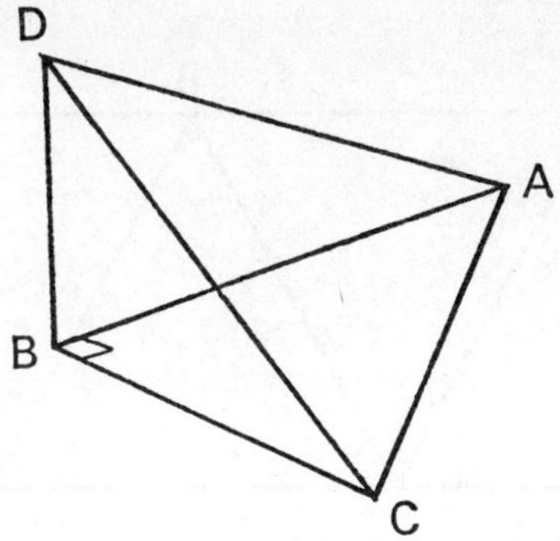

(*c*) if $BA = BC = BD$, then $\angle CDA = 60°$;

(*d*) the volume of the pyramid is $\frac{1}{6}AB \,.\, BC \,.\, BD$. OC (SMP)

57

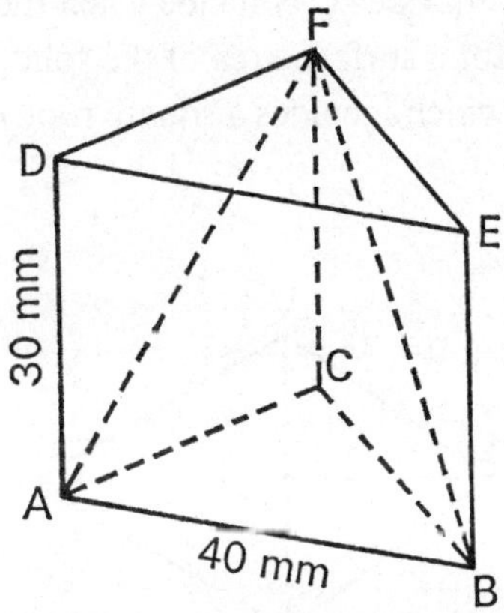

The diagram shows a right triangular prism of height 30 millimetres and with parallel ends, *ABC* and *DEF*, equilateral triangles of side 40 millimetres. Which of the following statements are true and which false?

(*a*) $AF = BF$.

(*b*) The prism has rotational symmetry about one and only one axis.

(*c*) Angle FAC = angle FAD.

(*d*) The angle between the planes *ABED* and *ACFD* is 60°.

(*e*) The volume of the triangular pyramid *ABCF* is one-third of the volume of the prism. SC

58

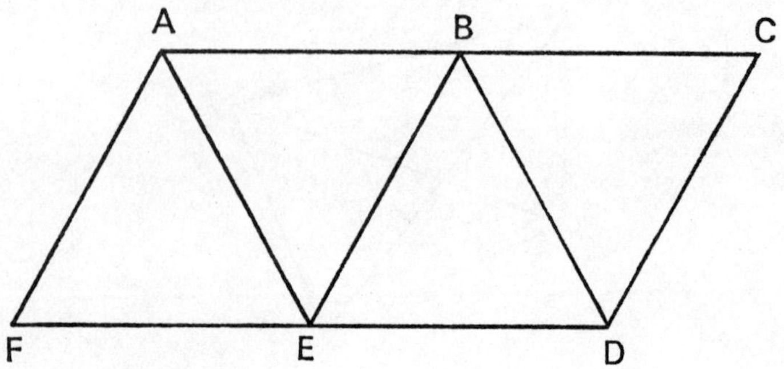

The triangles in the figure are all equilateral, and $AB = 50$ mm.

(i) Name the solid of which $ABCDEF$ is the net.

(ii) With which point does C coincide when the net is folded up?

(iii) Calculate the total surface area of the solid. (The answer may be given in a form which includes a square root.) OC (SMP)

59

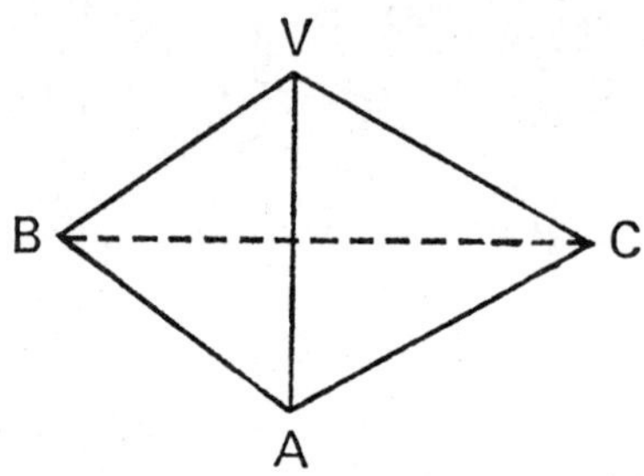

In the pyramid shown, the face VAB is equilateral with sides of 6 units; $CA = CB = 10$ units; $VC = 8$ units.

(i) State which angles formed by adjacent edges are right angles.

(ii) State the position of any plane of symmetry of the pyramid.

(iii) Adding extra lines if necessary to a copy of the diagram, mark angles which are:

(*a*) the angle between the planes VAB, CAB (mark this x);

(*b*) the angle between the planes VBC, VAC (mark this y).

OC (SMP)

60

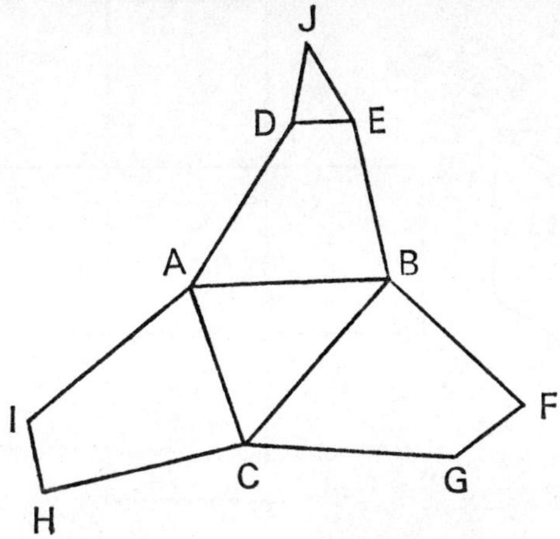

The figure shows the net of a tetrahedron (triangular pyramid, not necessarily regular) whose base is ABC and with its top sliced off. Which of the following statements are necessarily true and which are not necessarily true? (*The diagram is not drawn accurately.*)

(*a*) $AD = AI$.

(*b*) $\angle DAB = \angle IAC$.

(*c*) $JE = HI$.

(*d*) When folded to make the solid figure the points J, H and G all coincidc.

OC (SMP)

61 The two diagrams (Page 208) represent a cube of side unit length, and a net of the cube which could be folded to make a solid model of the unit cube.

Copy the net and complete the labelling of all its vertices.

Through a point Z on the edge BC passes a path from A to A' across the two faces $ABCD$ and $BCA'D'$. On your net, mark the shortest path AZA'. Also mark the shortest path AYA' if Y is a similar point on the edge DC for a path across the two faces $ABCD$ and $DCA'B'$.

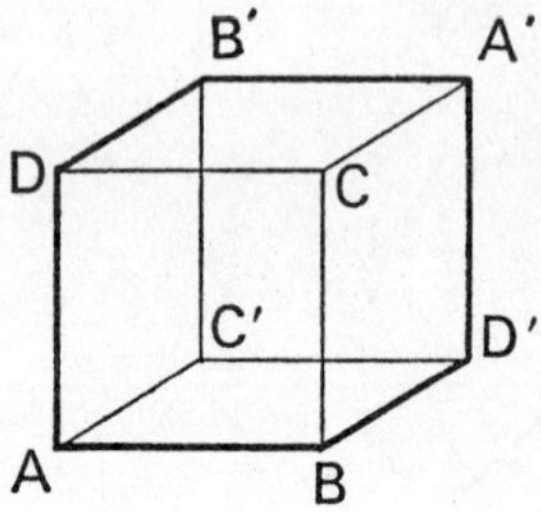

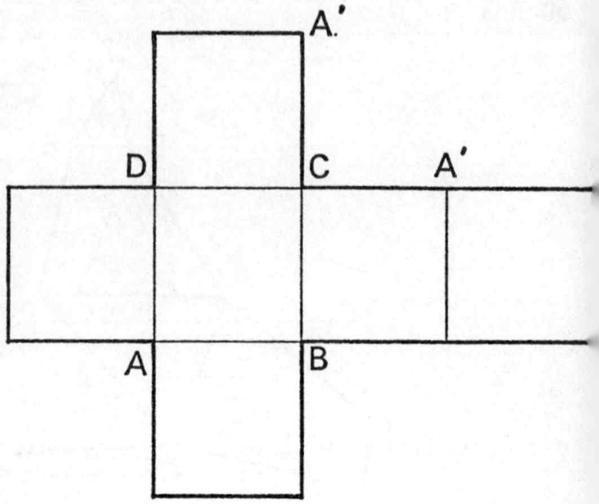

Calculate:

(*a*) the lengths of the paths AZA', AYA';
(*b*) the area of triangle ZAY;
(*c*) the angle ZAY.

If O is the midpoint of the diagonal AA' of the cube, show that triangle ZOY is equilateral and that ZY is one side of a regular hexagon through whose vertices pass six equally short paths from A to A' each across two faces and one edge of the cube. L

62 The diagram represents a closed rectangular box with

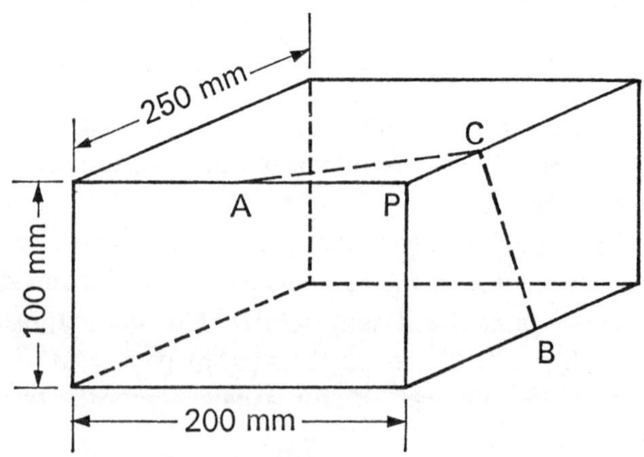

dimensions 200 mm, 250 mm, and 100 mm. A and B are the mid-points of their respective edges.

(i) Calculate the angle that the straight line AB would make with the base of the box.

(ii) A fly crawls from A to B on the outside of the box along a route such as ACB. By considering a net of the box calculate the length of the shortest possible route of this kind.

(iii) If Q is the point on this shortest route at which the fly is nearest to the corner P, calculate the distance PQ. OC (SMP)

Chapter Fifteen

Note: In this chapter the nautical mile used is the international nautical mile (1852 metres) and it may be presumed that this is the length of the arc of meridian which subtends an angle of 1 minute at the centre of the earth.

$$1 \text{ knot is } \frac{1852}{3600} \text{ m/s } (1{\cdot}852 \text{ km/h})$$

1 The shortest distance on the earth (assumed spherical) between (35°N, 15°W) and (35°N, 195°W) is

(*a*) across the North Pole;
(*b*) along the circle of latitude 35°N;
(*c*) not along either of the routes in (*a*) and (*b*). AEB

2 The shortest route from *A* (latitude 70°N, longitude 10°W) to *B* (latitude 70°N, longitude 175°E) is

(*a*) due east;
(*b*) due west;
(*c*) directly over the North Pole;
(*d*) none of these. OC (SMP)

3 The latitude and longitude of *P* and *Q* are *P*(75°N, 115°W) and *Q*(70°N, 65°E). Write down, in nautical miles, the length of the shortest route from *P* to *Q*. C

4 State the latitude and longitude of the place which is at the opposite end of a diameter of the earth from Cape Kennedy, the position of which is: latitude 28°N, longitude 80°40′W. OC (SMP)

5 Give the shorter of the two great circle distances in nautical miles from the point *A* on the earth, longitude 30°W, latitude 40°N to the point *B*, longitude 150°E, latitude 85°N.

OC (SMP)

6 State in nautical miles the shorter great circle distance between the points P (latitude 70°N, longitude 50°W) and Q (latitude 25°N, longitude 130°E) on the surface of the earth.

OC (SMP)

7 An aircraft starts from A (latitude 30°S, longitude 10°W) and flies due north to B, a distance equal to one-tenth of the world's circumference. State the latitude and longitude of B. OC (SMP)

8 On the equator a degree of longitude is approximately equivalent to 113 kilometres.

(i) Calculate the radius of the earth.

(ii) The southern tip of England has a latitude of 50°N. How far due North of the Equator is this?

(Assume that the earth is spherical and take π to be 3·142.) AEB

9 An aircraft flies due North from Norfolk (U.S.A.), 37°N 76°W, to Ottawa 45°N 76°W. Assuming the radius of the earth is 6370 kilometres and $\pi = 22/7$, calculate the distance flown. The aircraft then flies due East to Bordeaux 45°N 1°W. Calculate this distance. SU

10 Assuming the earth to be a sphere of radius 6400 kilometres, calculate the length of the circle of latitude 60°N.

(Take π to be 3·14, and give your answer to an appropriate degree of accuracy.) AEB

11 From Cape Finisterre, latitude 42°52′N, longitude 9°17′W, a ship sails due west for 1516 kilometres.

Calculate her longitude at the end of the journey.

(The earth may be taken as a sphere of radius 6370 kilometres. Take π to be 3·142.) AEB

12 Calculate the length of the parallel of latitude 39°N, assuming the radius of the earth to be 6400 km. Give your answer correct to two significant figures. A ship sails along latitude 39°N from longitude 5°W to longitude 65°W. Find how long it takes at an average speed of 18 knots. SU

13 Find the speed of an aircraft flying due west at latitude 30°N to the nearest knot if it is always at the same longitude as another aircraft flying due west at 500 knots at latitude 40°N. L

14 The point A on the earth's surface has latitude 30°N, longitude 20°W and B is the point with latitude 30°N, longitude 70°E. An aeroplane flies from A to B via the North Pole along the lines of longitude 20°W and 70°E at a steady speed of 800 km/h relative to the ground. Find the time taken for the journey. Find also the time taken if the aeroplane travels from A to B at the same speed along the circle of latitude 30°N. (Take the earth to be a sphere of radius 6370 km and π to be 3·142.) AEB

15 (i) U is the point latitude 57°N, longitude 20°W, V is the point latitude 57°N, longitude 160°E. Show that the shortest distance by air from U to V is about two-thirds of their distance apart along the common circle of latitude.
(ii) Aircraft A and B start off together to fly from U to V with equal speeds, A taking the shortest route while B flies due east along the circle of latitude. Find roughly the longitude of B when A arrives at V.

[If you need to use them, take the radius of the earth as 6400 km and π as 3·14.] OC (SMP)

16 An aeroplane is to fly from Tashkent (latitude 41°N, longitude 69°E) to Salt Lake City (latitude 41°N, longitude 111°W). The route is to be along the great circle or any small circle passing through the two places and is not to pass south of the parallel of latitude 41°N. Find in nautical miles the range of possible values for the length of the journey.

(One nautical mile at the equator subtends an angle of 1 minute at the centre of the earth.)

Find the locus of half-way points of all possible journeys under the given conditions.

Find also the longest possible journey if the last condition (not to pass south of latitude 41°N) does not apply. L

17 A certain type of radar equipment can detect aircraft within a range of x nautical miles. Two ships carrying this type of equipment are on the Equator in longitudes 10°W and 30°W. An aircraft flying along the Equator can be detected by both ships at the same time over a distance of 300 nautical miles. Show that $x = 750$.

A second aircraft flies along a parallel of latitude so that it just avoids detection by either ship. Calculate, in nautical miles, the distance it flies along this line of latitude from 10°W to 30°W. C

18

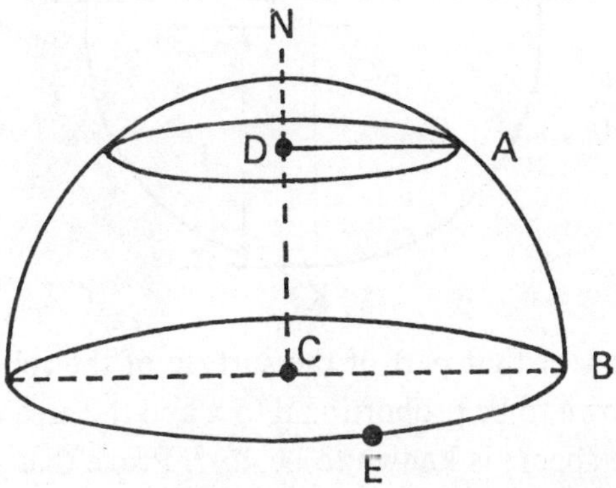

The diagram represents the Northern Hemisphere. N is the North Pole, and C the centre of the earth. B and E are points on the Equator. D is the centre of the circle of latitude 50°N. A is the point latitude 50°N, longitude 70°E.

State:

(i) the ratio of the arc NA to the arc AB;

(ii) the ratio of DA to CB;

(iii) the longitude of E if the distance of E west of B = the distance of A north of B (distances being measured along the earth's surface). OC (SMP)

19 If N is the North Pole, and A and B are points on the Equator with longitudes 10°W and 100°W, express the area of the earth's surface bounded by NA, NB and AB as a fraction of the earth's total surface. OC (SMP)

20 The figure shows a section of a sphere of radius r through a diameter HK. A plane λ cuts HK at right angles at a distance x below H. A second plane μ is parallel to λ at a distance h below it.

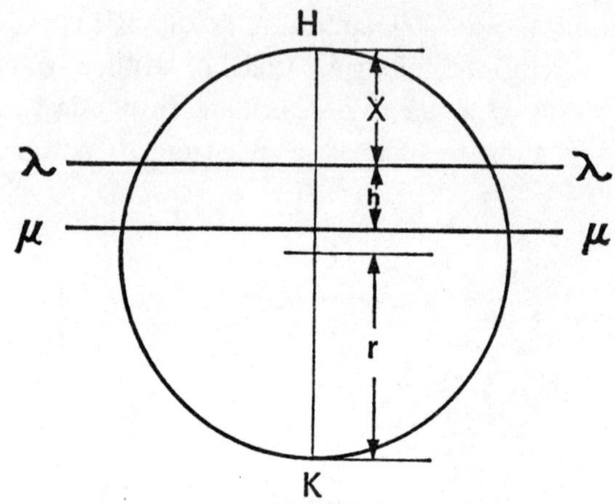

(i) The area y of that part of the surface of the sphere which is above λ is known to be proportional to x and the area of the whole surface of the sphere is known to be $4\pi r^2$. Prove that $y = 2\pi rx$.
(ii) Deduce from this result that the area of the part of the surface of the sphere cut off between λ and μ is $2\pi rh$.
(iii) Taking the earth to be a sphere of radius 6370 kilometres, calculate the area of the zone between latitudes 14°N and 32°N, giving your answer in millions of square kilometres.

OC (SMP)